MW00715464

In Search of
YESTERDAY

DAVID TURNER

PORTLAND•OREGON
INKWATERPRESS.COM

*Scan QR Code to learn
more about this title*

Publisher: Inkwater Press

Paperback
ISBN-13 978-1-59299-957-6 | ISBN-10 1-59299-957-3

Kindle
ISBN-13 978-1-59299-958-3 | ISBN-10 1-59299-958-1

All paper is acid free and meets all ANSI standards for archival quality paper.

1 3 5 7 9 10 8 6 4 2

This book is dedicated to the memory of my parents, whose valuable recollections provided not only the nucleus for my writings ... but the inspiration as well.

Contents

IN SEARCH OF YESTERDAY

Solomon and Martha

When one really stops to think about it ... it's nearly impossible in today's mechanized, computerized, high-tech world to comprehend the physical challenges our forefathers endured for the sake of owning their very own piece of land. As the 1800s wore on, European settlers by the thousands pushed their way into Ontario's virgin forests, following the Toronto-Sydenham road that ran diagonally from Ontario's capital directly into Grey County. With nothing but crop failures and overcrowding behind them, these settlers were coming to lay claim on the fifty-acre lots the Canadian government was advertising.

A "veritable garden of Eden" claimed the brochures. Hardly; Grey County was probably the most inhospitable region laid eyes upon in the late nineteenth century. In 1888, my great-grandfather Solomon Turner emigrated from Lincolnshire, England, and with his wife Martha, purchased 100 acres in the Beaver Valley just below the village of Eugenia. It was here they raised three sons and five daughters. A dozen years later, with the family outgrowing the valley farm, they bought 200 acres in Artemesia Township, two and a half miles east of Eugenia.

No buildings existed on this parcel and the land was only partially cleared, but except for a proliferation of stones, the soil seemed fertile and well drained. Realizing this was a long-term investment, my great-grandparents remained on the valley farm until the new one could begin producing and a house and barn built.

About ten more acres were cleared the first year, an overwhelming task with only the aid of oxen, horses and a family of strong backs. Pine was the preferred lumber for building; it was plentiful and fairly easy to work with, an important aspect when every tree was felled by axe and sawed by hand. The biggest challenge was the removal of the stumps left behind.

Although horse-drawn stump removers were available by this time, a great deal of hand labour was still required, digging around the structure to sever the roots. Sometimes these root systems were so complex even stump pullers failed and the stump had to be left as is.

Next was the seemingly never-ending chore of "picking stones." Most were of the size that could be lifted or thrown onto a "stone boat," a low, flat platform on skids. However there were always a percentage that had to be literally pried from the ground with steel bars, hooks, and shovels. Occasionally, boulders of gigantic proportions would be discovered, sometimes six or seven feet in diameter. These rocks, although huge, were often exaggerated like fish stories among the early settlers, each claiming to have unearthed the most spectacular sized specimen in their "back forty."

One can only imagine the disappointment encountered the following year, upon discovery of a brand new crop of stones sprouting through the ground so painstakingly cleared the previous season. Over the next few years the reality of the situation would finally register. It was almost like some geometric equation; for every rock removed, another takes its place. As the decades passed, four generations of Turners would engage in the annual ritual, and as each aching back bent to retrieve yet another stone, I'm certain his or her thoughts no doubt returned to "old Solomon" and his questionable homesteading decision.

As for buildings, a barn was the first and most important agenda. In 1900, a farmer's stature in the community was governed largely by simple barn dimensions; therefore Solomon chose a structure sixty by ninety feet, at least as large, if not larger than anything else in the neighbourhood. The first task in any building of course is a foundation and in that era that meant stones. But this was Grey County, so no problem there.

At the beginning of the twentieth century, monetarily a new barn cost very little. When "barn raisings" were the event of the day, only the foundation contractor and main framer counted as paid labour. The neighbourhood men of course charged nothing for their time, nor did the ladies who provided the food. Everybody simply helped everybody else. My great-grandfather had been part of numerous barn raisings himself and expected to be part of many more. All the structural lumber was harvested from your own woodlot, so only the milling costs to cut the logs into the desired dimensions were considered expenses. The only other "real" costs were miscellaneous items like nails, hinges and assorted hardware. Therefore the total figures for a new barn...about $300.00; or in perspective ... a year's wages in rural Ontario at the time.

Next project was a house, an even bigger undertaking. Like the barn, the timber was home grown, brick being the biggest expense at $5.00 per thousand, supplied by the Bowler Brick Yard in the neighbouring village of Markdale.

The house axis was positioned north and south to capitalize on sunlight, an important aspect in pre-hydro days. A large kitchen occupied the northern section of the house, while a living and dining room were situated off the kitchen on the west side. A parlour and bedroom on the east, four bedrooms upstairs, plus an additional double-sized bedroom above the kitchen, rounded out the living accommodations. Through this large bedroom ran the pipes from the kitchen cook stove, making this room the most popular in winter. The "bathroom" of course was outside, tucked discreetly away among the lilac bushes.

My great-grandparents were both active members of the community but very different in character. Solomon simply enjoyed people's company; his relaxed manner, wit and buoyant personality making him a favourite at any gathering. Meeting a person just once or twice in his life, Solomon took great pride in calling them by their first name. An enviable trait ... except he was often wrong.

Martha was much more serious in nature. She had little patience for laziness, idle chatter or gossip that in her mind was nothing more than a waste of a person's valuable time. Strong religious faith and sound work ethics were the answer to everything. If diplomacy was needed, that was Solomon's job; if someone needed "tuning in" ... well, that was her department. It was an extensive list, those individuals put in place at some point in time by Martha's sharp tongue.

By 1918, with both nearing their seventies, my great-grandparents purchased a home in Eugenia and transferred ownership of the farm to their youngest son, Oliver (my grandfather) Although he may have sold the farm, Solomon certainly wasn't through with agricultural interests, so when the fields were dry the following spring, he was ready to assist his son with the seeding. Work had progressed well and by May 19, the last field had been planted and Solomon was in the process of rolling it. Oliver's wife Janie was hanging clothes on the line outside the back door of the house when her attention was drawn to a cloud of dust just beyond the orchard that quickly materialized into a team of horses at full gallop heading towards the barn. Immediately sensing something wrong, she ran towards the scene in question.

At the same moment, Oliver, working in an adjacent field, *knew* something was wrong! He too saw the runaway horses heading towards the barn, the roller swinging crazily behind them and his father nowhere to be seen. Running back down the laneway, Oliver discovered his father lying unconscious upon the ground. A temporary stretcher was fashioned to carry him to the house while the doctor was summoned. No doubt something spooked the horses and in their fright they had begun running. Solomon, trying to stop them, had obviously lost his balance and was pitched forward off the seat and directly into the path of the heavy steel roller.

It was an agonizing wait for a doctor in rural Ontario in pre-automobile days ... and when he did arrive the report was grave. Definitely broken ribs; possibly a punctured lung; internal bleeding? He could only guess. Surgery, crude as it was, was undertaken at once and a ruptured bowel discovered. Consequently, blood poisoning developed. No penicillin or antibiotics in those days, so every night, with Oliver holding the coal oil lamp, the doctor opened and drained the infected organ, reclosing the wound when completed. This continued for a week but to no avail. On May 25, his seventieth birthday, Solomon lost the fight. He'd always been a valued and respected friend and neighbour in the community, and this fact was made clear two days later when the largest crowd to date gathered to pay their final respects at Salem cemetery.

Always independent, Martha became even more so following her husband's death. Refusing to completely sever her ties with agriculture just because she was "in town," Martha grew practically everything she needed to sustain herself and bartered for the rest. A few Rhode Island Red chickens were kept in the back yard, and in a paddock behind the house a lone Jersey cow grazed. A water trough beside the well handled the cow's drinking needs in summer, but during winter every pail had to be carried to the shed where she was housed. In fair weather, Martha's cow roamed relatively free, foraging on neighbourhood grass when its own pasture was depleted. A common sight in Eugenia was the old cow grazing on the baseball diamond across from Martha's house. Neighbours wryly noted that no "bases" were needed on the playing field when the cow was there and one could literally "slide" into home plate.

Martha lived next door to a Mrs. Wilson, and both being widows enjoyed each other's company, although a casual observer might have thought otherwise. "I had the fire going an hour before I saw smoke from Mrs. Wilson's chimney. She must have been getting her beauty sleep."

" ... I had my washing all hung before Mrs. Turner even started. In her old age she must have forgotten what day it is ... " This constant sparring continued as long as the two lived side by side, but those acquainted knew this was just their way of looking out for one another, and in truth each would have been lost without the other.

Martha generally kept to herself, "minding my own business" in her words ... but there was always a cup of hot tea and homemade baking for any family member or neighbour who dropped by. Martha made little effort to visit herself ... "that's what phones and letters are for." Her preference for an enjoyable evening would consist of reading the Bible or working on one of the many beautiful quilts she patterned for friends and relatives over the years. Another delight was nursing the numerous species of houseplants that brought such brightness to her home.

My mother as a youngster never fared particularly well with her grandmother during summer holiday visits. Although she liked children, Martha was a strong advocate of "they should only speak when spoken to" axiom. This was definitely against the nature of my mother, who was forever asking questions. "Why is the sky blue? What are clouds made out of? Where do the birds go in winter? Why do the leaves fall off the trees in the fall? How come the sun isn't hot in winter? How come you can't see the wind?" ... Martha preferred Mom's younger sister Jean. Jean didn't ask annoying questions. Jean hardly talked at all. Martha loved Jean. *her Mom*

It never took long for things to derail when my mother and Martha crossed paths. Like the time Martha had baked a cake for some special company and upon retrieving it from the pantry discovered "someone" had trailed five little fingers through the chocolate frosting for an obvious taste test ... or the occasion the United Church minister's wife was visiting and upon leaving was unable to find her outerwear. Martha discovered her granddaughter staging a fashion show in the living room for her sisters complete with her guest's coat, scarf, hat and gloves ... it really hit the fan the time "someone" got hold of a pair of scissors and practiced her cutting skills by snipping a neat slit up the front of one of Martha's dresses!

Even the most innocent of circumstances had a way of unravelling. My mother had been given a harmonica for her birthday. Leaving it on a chair, she went outdoors to play, but later noticed it in the kitchen window. Martha, attempting to gain some fresh air, had used the instrument to prop up the window. Regaining what was rightfully hers, my mother reached into the opening. Down came the heavy wooden frame on her wrist! Once discovered no serious injuries had been sustained, there would be little sympathy. "You shouldn't have had your hand in there!"

Heading down the back steps of the house that led to the cellar one day, my mother startled an unsuspecting chicken roosting above the doorway. The chicken flew from its perch, wings flapping wildly, and landed directly on Mom's head. The bawling and screaming was certainly enough to bring Martha running. Again, satisfying herself her grandchild had suffered only a few scratches, so ended any more compassion. "You can't blame the chicken, you know. It was minding its own business. You'd do well to do the same!"

Despite Martha Turner's continuous lessons on how children should conduct themselves ... that exercise would continue to be an elusive one for not just my mother, but all concerned.

Then came that June day in 1937 when the village of Eugenia lost its most elderly and best-known resident. Martha had been out to church just the previous Sunday.

In fact it had been a rare Sabbath, regardless of season, that Martha wasn't seen walking to church services, wearing the black bonnet no one had seen her without since Solomon's death eighteen years earlier.

But this June afternoon would be the final farewell as Martha Turner was laid to rest beside her husband. Reverend Bushell's message to the mourners assured that "the soul of the deceased has passed from a land of turmoil into one of peace and glory, and those who knew her best can be assured that she is ever with the Lord."

... Following the ceremony, someone was heard to remark that those departed souls already in Heaven would have to be on their best behaviour tonight with the arrival of their latest guest.

Independence Day

All his family were present that July morning in 1934 when Harold boarded the train at the Flesherton Junction railroad station. Mixed feelings abounded among those gathered. A few thought traipsing off to Business College in the midst of the greatest economic collapse anyone had ever seen ludicrous. Some envied him. Whatever the emotion, all wished him well. "Have you got some money?" someone hollered from the platform. "Have you got your lunch?" yelled someone else. "Don't forget to write," added another. The rest was drowned as the whistle announced its departure note.

It had been a long and often frustrating road leading to this day. My father had been filled with such optimism that September day seven long years ago when entering his initial year at Flesherton High School.

As the semesters passed, Harold envisioned the career choices waiting. Initially, his aim was high ... maybe veterinarian school. A school teacher was always near the top of the list as well. However, a factor that no one had foreseen back in 1927 ... a major economic upheaval forever to be known as "The Great Depression" had changed the program dramatically. Since that black day in October 1929, the pace had been one direction only. By graduation five years later, there couldn't have been a worse time to look for a job, let alone a career.

The only prospect to surface during this period was an invitation to enroll in a business course at Orangeville, a small town about forty miles north of Toronto. Their sales representative, Herbert Juene, did his best to convey to the student faculty that a future in the business world was the way to go. Harold wasn't convinced; he still hadn't ruled out teaching. Mr. Juene had obviously run up against this argument before, for in a somewhat frustrated tone, complained how so many young people were obsessed with the ideals of the "little red schoolhouse." It didn't matter anyway. With the family farm barely scratching out a living, there was no money available for business college, teachers college, veterinarian or any other kind of college.

With nothing on the horizon, Harold spent the next four years helping his parents on the farm. Except for a few dollars now and then, it was basically room and board. However by 1934, the invitation to attend Orangeville Business College once again presented itself. The biggest hurdle of course was still the money ... 180 Depression dollars. By now, my dad's sister was teaching, so she lent him the tuition fee, while his father maintained he could finance the board.

Even with the monetary question settled, Harold searched his mind for reasons not to go. He'd never been away from their Grey County farm overnight in his life. The unfamiliarities of a new way of life were unnerving. Deep down, he seriously wondered if he had what it took, or if he even wanted a career in the business world. It would be so much easier to simply stay home and farm with his dad ... and yet ... there was something that called out, something reminding him that perhaps there was more to life than staring at a horse's ass from behind a plow.

Throughout the fifty-mile train ride to Orangeville, Harold contemplated what lay ahead. Boarding arrangements had been established at an earlier date with a Mrs. McKinnon, who turned out to be one of those people who made you feel welcome and comfortable from the outset. For one room, laundry service and three meals a day, the cost was $5.00 a week. It took a while to fall asleep that first night. Cars and trucks passing by on Highway 10 were distracting, as were the streetlights that illuminated the main thoroughfare from end to end. What a difference from the silent blackness of his family's pre-hydro farm back home! Homesickness was prevalent those first few weeks as well. The simplest situation ... seeing a cow in a field ... would nearly bring my father to tears.

Orangeville Business College had been founded in 1907 and operated by various personnel throughout the years, the most recent, Caroline Martin. A general decline in enrolment had been evident lately, a condition brought to some degree by competition from larger and more advanced colleges, but the main reason was simply the Depression.

Harold arrived at the two-storied structure just west of Orangeville's main intersection Monday morning. The college shared quarters with Merlina's Fruit Market, which occupied the lower level. Climbing the stairs to the second floor, Harold discovered he was the first one there. Caroline Martin, a petite woman who my father guessed to be about forty, was seated behind a desk at the front of the room.

Four rows of student desks filled the width of the small room and on each desk sat a covered typewriter.

Teacher and student made small talk until nine o'clock, when she stated they may as well begin. Harold gazed around at the vacant desks and somewhat timidly suggested perhaps they should wait for the rest. Miss Martin smiled slightly and announced that he was "the rest." She explained to his rather bewildered expression it was an ongoing course without enrolment quotas or time agendas. "It'll pick up in the fall." There seemed more a note of hope than fact in her voice, Harold thought. But so it went ... just the two of them for the next three weeks.

As Caroline Martin suggested, with the arrival of autumn came new candidates. It certainly didn't qualify as a flood ... perhaps eight or ten, but it was still individual tutoring all the way. This system of private teaching governed your speed, and whether the course required ten, twelve or fifteen months to complete wasn't important. Included in these new recruits were a couple of girls from Orangeville, as well as Jay Graham from Harriston and Jack Arras from Corbetton ... whom everyone referred to as "Jack Arse." The class act, however, was "flapper" Ellen Hastings.

For younger readers ... "flappers" described a number of young women in the 1920s and '30s who rebelled against established female roles of conventional attitudes and conservatism. Hair cut short, plenty of make-up, tight dresses above the knee ... were all part of the protest campaign. They smoked ... in public ... and also swore on occasion.

Miss Martin had a salesman by the name of Herbert Juene, who when he wasn't out recruiting, often aided in teaching (the same gentleman who had come to Dad's school several years before). On this particular day Mr. Juene was dictating, pipe in mouth as usual. Twice during the exercise, Ellen asked to have a phrase repeated. "Have you trouble hearing, Miss Hastings?"

"No sir ... but maybe if you took that damn pipe out of your mouth I could understand what you were saying!" It certainly woke up the small crowd at OBC! The students from the "sticks" especially went into shock, unaccustomed to such language by a young lady ... and to a teacher!

Since day one, rumours had abounded about Ellen, pertaining in particular to her extracurricular activities and how she financed her tuition, but Ellen never worried too much about what people thought. Surmising Harold was an ideal candidate for the "all work no play" syndrome, she invited him up to her room one evening, enticing him with her best Mae West impersonation. "I have a radio," she cooed. "We could sit on my couch and listen to it ... or whatever." Morality triumphed and my father declined, explaining how his sister was putting him through college and his father was financing his board and how he had to study and ... well, that was fine ... there were plenty in line, so Dad never was offered a second chance and consequently never did get to "whatever."

Loneliness was never far away during those early weeks, so when the Turner family reunion was held near Toronto that autumn, Dad couldn't wait to attend. Although accommodations were hardly first class as my father joined fifteen or twenty others in the back of Frank Taylor's truck. Frank operated a livestock trucking business back home in Grey County, so merely cleaned out his truck and placed some benches in the back.

Pocket money was practically non-exis
point ... the occasional few dollars Harold's in.
spare being the extent of his income. From time to time,
Dad's cousin and best friend Lester Samson would visit,
provided he could get his father's car and enough gas to
drive the fifty miles. Sitting in the car watching people walk
up and down Orangeville's main street, or walking up and
down the main street watching cars drive up and down the
street, was the extent of the excitement.

The local event of the summer in Orangeville had been
the Merlina daughter's wedding. As the family store was
directly below the college, my father and fellow students
had witnessed this grand event first hand from the upstairs
window. Men in black suits, women in fine gowns and a
row of Packards that stretched an entire block made for a
fine spectacle.

But the Merlinas did everything in style. Sam Merlina's store was miles ahead of the competition. As well as
the usual oranges, lemons and grapefruit from Florida and
California, he sold grapes from Malaysia, endless varieties of nuts from across the globe, figs from the Mediterranean and chocolate from Belgium and Switzerland, and
purchased bulk virgin olive oil from Italy by the barrel.

With only a couple of trips home since July, it was with
anticipation Harold headed home for the Christmas break.
His mother had asked if he could purchase a tricycle for
his youngest brother and he found one for three dollars,
lugging it home on the train with him. My father had a
great fondness for train travel, especially on crisp, winter
days. There was something almost magical about steaming through the frosty snow-covered farmland, the whistle

echoing far off down the track and wisps of smoke drifting lazily past the coach window.

A strong proponent of the "practice makes perfect" theory, Harold wrote home often, utilizing the typewriters that were available day or night. By his own admission, he was a fast typist ... "I made a lot of mistakes, but I was fast!" Shorthand was his favourite however. Nearly sixty years later, Dad claimed he could still handle shorthand dictation if given the opportunity.

With the arrival of another summer came the news for which my Dad had been waiting. A clerical position had been secured at a candy factory in downtown Toronto ... $11.00 for a five-and-a-half-day week. That evening, Mrs. McKinnon congratulated him on his upcoming job, relating how she'd miss him. Harold had to admit the same. For a scared and lonely country boy, she'd been a godsend.

Although he'd looked forward to this day, the feelings of apprehension that had dogged him at the outset quickly returned. It had been an enjoyable twelve months, but how would he fare in the real world where profit and loss ledgers decided your future ... in a city where no one knew you or cared to? Mr. Juene had stressed just recently how Harold would have to get over his shyness if he was ever to make it in the city. "If you don't learn to look people in the eye," he said, "then your chances in Toronto are about the same as a snowball rolling towards Hell!"

Well ... I guess time would tell.

Working at the Candy Store

The city of Toronto, as most cities scattered throughout North America, was still struggling with the fallout of the world's greatest economic depression when Orangeville Business College's latest graduate hit town in July 1935. There had been improvement, but for many, conditions were still in the near desperate state. The construction industry, particularly, was still depressed, despite government work projects. The most notable was the four lane limited-access highway stretching from Toronto to the U.S. border at Fort Erie. Work was slow due to lack of capital, four years lapsing since the start, and another four before the road to be known as the Queen Elizabeth Way (QEW) would be completed.

Neighbouring cities like Oshawa that relied on the sale of big ticket items like automobiles still counted devastating numbers of unemployed. Newly elected Ontario Premier Mitch Hepburn promised how his Liberal government was embarking on a new course to get the province back on its feet. As a gesture of good faith, Hepburn set about firing hundreds of civil servants from "worthless jobs" and at Toronto's Varsity Stadium, in front of a crowd of over 8,000, auctioned off fifty government limousines.

Atlantic Avenue, home to the Dainty Confections Company, was a workingman's neighbourhood. The short avenue running between King Street and the Exhibition Grounds, as well as the area surrounding it, was blotted by a variety of factories manufacturing a variety of products. It was here in his new role as office clerk that Harold Turner would finally be able to utilize the knowledge he'd accumulated during his year at Business College.

Dainty Confections was a family-run operation begun in 1920 by two army buddies, Jack Simpson and Doug Farmer. The organization also featured Farmer's wife, his brother-in-law and Simpson's daughter. Office personnel shared a common room, each with his or her desk scattered about the floor space. Discovering he'd have his own desk was a definite high point for the new office clerk. Typing invoices, billing statements and order contracts, as well as the mailing of all paperwork would be how my father would earn his $11.00 per week pay.

Practically all of the little factory's output was of the hard candy variety, that product being a staple from the beginning. As for most manufacturing ventures, the 1920s had been kind with substantial profits. Most of their trade was through medium and large-scale stores like Woolworths and Kresge's, but a still important segment of smaller stores kept between sixty and seventy factory workers busy, as well as five salesmen on the road.

But as with most small businesses, the last few years had been tough to say the least. It didn't take a scholar to figure that nonessentials like sweets were the first to suffer in a collapsed economy. The latter part of 1934 and early 1935 had seen a resurgence, however, totally due to the Dionne phenomenon. With the arrival of the quintuplets, it didn't take long for manufacturers to discover ways to exploit the five little girls from Northern Ontario. Dainty Confections lost no time cashing in on this lucrative market with their "quintpop," which resembled a normal lollipop, only with five coloured candies protruding from its stick base.

It was a notable Friday two weeks later when Harold received his first paycheque. With the exception of a small allowance he received at home, this was the first "real" money my father had earned in his twenty-year life span. Weekends were a lonesome time in a strange city for a boy from the country, so to pass the time Harold took a streetcar out to visit his Uncle Will and Aunt Reba Carruthers. My father had been boarding at a house set up by the college, and whether he broached the subject or his aunt and uncle ... but someone sometime during that visit opened the discussion, with the final result being that Will and Reba acquired a boarder. This important family component was the answer indeed for the young man no doubt overwhelmed by the vastness of Toronto (he thought Orangeville with its population of 2,000 was big!)

So began the ritual of one junior clerk. By leaving the Carruthers' residence shortly after 7:30 and cutting through the Parkdale Railroad Station, my father discovered he could be at Dainty Confections within twenty minutes.

Once on the job, there were no coffee breaks. Everyone worked straight through the morning until noon, but a full hour was allotted for lunch. Harold purchased his meal each day from a delicatessen just down the street from the factory. The proprietor sold cold meats, cheeses, meat pies, fruit pies, ice cream, pop and juice.

From day one, Harold spent his lunch hour there, consistently ordering the same thing. A meat pie, a Coke and a dish of vanilla ice cream ... fifteen cents; every day the same meal, every meal the same place. It was strictly a take-out establishment, but the owner let his best customer use a chair and tiny table partly hidden behind a partition. From this vantage point, my father could eat his lunch in relative obscurity and still easily watch the coming and going of customers.

Every Friday at noon, the meat salesman made his rounds, taking orders for the upcoming week. The order was similar each week. Several pounds of wieners, a bit of sausage, lots of bologna, maybe a few pounds of head-cheese ... then he'd always end the list of goods ... "and I'd better have about twenty pounds of horsemeat." Harold never knew if horsemeat was actually being ordered or if it was merely a standing joke. During the Depression, it wasn't uncommon for a struggling butcher or restaurant owner etc. to throw in a little "something else" to make things go further. There was always someone around who could tell you that so-and-so utilized horsemeat or "other things." ... "Have you noticed the lack of cats around here lately?"

Whatever might have been digested, it was back to the candy factory for four more hours, then the walk home. The area immediately adjacent to the factory was a rather rough neighbourhood. On King Street, care was needed not to be sideswiped by over-inebriated personnel staggering out of an alley or to trip over one lying on the sidewalk.

As summer progressed into autumn, Will and Reba's oldest daughter, Evelyn, returned home from her summer job as a camp counsellor, resuming her regular job at the

Queen and Lisgar Library. From this period onward, Harold would meet his cousin, as it was on his way and they'd walk home together.

Through his letters, my father tried to convey to the folks back in Artemesia Township that he had a pretty good handle on Toronto. Truthfully, with the exception of walking to and from work, he had little idea where he was most of the time. A trip downtown, a day at the Canadian National Exhibition etc. ... he counted on Evelyn. Like a pup, he'd trail directly behind her while embarking and disembarking streetcars or entering department stores. Revolving doors were a special challenge, as he'd try to occupy the same section as his cousin for fear of being lost in the swell of the crowd approaching from behind. The sheer size of Ontario's capital really was overwhelming for a country boy. Walking along the canyon-like downtown streets with neck craned skyward, eyes bugged out and mouth agape ... simply confirmed it.

Business was slow at Dainty Confections in the winter of 1936. Harold perhaps noticed the decline in orders, but not with any great concern. He hadn't been there long enough to familiarize himself with the high and low cycles of business and besides he'd received a fifty cent per week raise at the beginning of the year, so things couldn't be too bad!

A more important indicator that perhaps things weren't on solid footing was how anytime an official looking person showed up at the factory, they were told the head of operations was "out," whether they were or not. And in ever increasing frequency, whoever didn't want to be disturbed could be seen lurking in the hall until the visitor departed ... definitely not the sign of a healthy organization. Still, it came as a shock when personnel arrived at the office that particular Monday morning to discover the doors locked. An announcement tacked to the door simply stated that Dainty Confections had "ceased operations."

Will Carruthers convinced his nephew to place a legal claim for the $23.00 two weeks' lost wages, but when the bankruptcy was settled nothing remained for junior clerks. So, on March 17th in the middle of a late winter snowstorm and with no new prospects on the horizon, my father boarded the train at Union Station and headed back home, leaving Toronto pretty much as he'd arrived. With the exception of a $22 Tip Top Tailor suit and some clerical experience … it was as if he'd never been there at all.

In the Good and Not So Good Old Days

On April 10, 1912, the largest and most elaborately equipped vessel to ever sail the seas left on her maiden voyage from Southampton Harbour in England and headed westward to New York. Four days later just before midnight, the RMS *Titanic* struck an iceberg 300 miles off the coast of Newfoundland, and despite its grandiose claim of being "unsinkable" did just that a couple of hours later, taking over 1500 of the 2300 on board to their watery graves.

The sinking of the world's biggest ship was certainly the news story for 1912 as newspapers printed seemingly endless articles discussing every minute detail of the doomed ship's last hours and running background stories of prominent personnel who perished.

Not much wonder "everyday" happenings got hopelessly lost in this myriad of ink … like this one … "On May 25, 1912, to William and Rebecca Carruthers of Beaconsville Ave. Toronto, a daughter, Evelyn Patricia."

Later that same day, Thomas Carruthers retrieved a partially filled bottle of fine Scotch from the kitchen cabinet stashed for medicinal and special occasions only, poured a shot for himself and his son, and together toasted their new granddaughter and daughter ... and my mother.

Now, one hundred years to the day, May 25, 2012, I sit at my office keyboard and try to get some semblance of what life was like a century ago when my mother entered this world.

One of her earliest memories and a graphic one was when Spanish influenza invaded North America. Not since the European "Black Death" of the mid-1300s had a virus of such proportions been seen. Beginning in the dying weeks of 1918 and running unabated until the summer of 1919 when it mysteriously disappeared, it claimed nearly 65,000 Canadian lives ... more even then the recently concluded war!

Everyone naturally panicked. People refused to shake hands or even kiss. Schools were closed. Streetcars were disinfected nightly. To curb the spread of the virus, an assortment of home remedies were tried. Onions, garlic, pepper and mustard were consumed in large quantities. Some inhaled fumes of hot water and turpentine, while others favoured poultices of raw onions worn around the neck. Barbers in Toronto wore surgical masks when cutting hair but nothing really helped. Only six years old, Mom however remembers vividly the endless procession of funerals that passed their street during that winter and spring.

The Carruthers family moved to a small duplex on Hickson Street that same year and although her two younger sisters failed to comprehend the significance, Mom made an amazing discovery the day they moved in. This house had something grown-ups called "electricity" and she was absolutely mesmerized by the little switches that mysteriously illuminated each room.

Shirley Street Public School, where my mother received most of her primary education was just a block from home. Evelyn liked school and any subject that called for extensive reading was a favourite. Like all city schools, teachers taught one class only until grade eight was achieved, where all subjects were taught by the principal and vice-principal alone.

Schools were highly regimented in the 1920s. At the sound of the bell, students lined up military fashion in front of the building, boys in one line, girls the other. They even entered by separate doors. Only after everyone was queued to the satisfaction of the principal ... arms by your side, backs straight, no talking ... were the students allowed entry. The playgrounds were segregated too; junior and senior boys and junior and senior girls.

As my mother was the oldest of five girls, responsibility was learned at a tender age. Whether it was to school or a trip to the corner store, she was the one expected to make sure her sisters arrived and returned safely. Business responsibilities such as delivering payments for gas, water, hydro and other general accounts, grocery shopping, even department store shopping were hers as well, helping her to grasp early the value of a dollar. It wasn't uncommon for my mother to check out a price at Eaton's department store, cross the street to Simpson's only to find the article two cents more, only to return to Eaton's for the purchase.

My grandmother spent most of her time at home. With five children over a span of eleven years, little time was available for outside interests. Life was an endless routine of cooking, cleaning, scrubbing, sewing, baking, mending, making lunches, making beds and just making do. Each autumn the workload increased as jams, relishes and fruit preserves were "put up." The Carruthers had little room for a garden but purchased some fruits and vegetables, plus any time they visited rural relatives a store of produce would return with them. After one of these excursions the air would be saturated with the smell of preserves simmering on the stove.

And on the subject of odours, one could be counted on with monthly regularity throughout the year. A Saturday morning awakening would be met with a pungent aroma filling the air. "Oh no ... not senna tea! Do we have to drink that stuff?" ... "Yes you do" was always their mother's answer. "It's good for you." That was debatable. Senna tea was derived from some species of tree native to South East Asia and the pods were supposedly filled with a pulp that provided a laxative to "clean out the system."

Other remedies equally distasteful served a similar purpose; the best known ... castor oil. It was vile medicine and parents had to be imaginative in persuading their kids to drink it. Mixing it with orange juice was a common disguise or hiding it within a bowl of oatmeal, but nothing really covered up that bitter taste. If a cough was heard, a hot mustard plaster placed on the chest was the answer. Another alternative for a stubborn cough was a woollen sock soaked with hot goose grease.

There were several diseases floating around in the 1920s that no remedy, home or scientific, could cure ... the worst being diphtheria, a highly contagious virus that formed a membrane-like coating over the breathing passages. In this era it was a rare family that escaped this deadly disease. My grandmother's brother had died while in his twenties, just two months into marriage. The initial signs of diphtheria were fever and sore throat, and if a household was even suspected, health officers would post a quarantine sign on the front door and only the breadwinner could enter or leave. The quarantine would remain in effect up until three weeks after the last active case had been diagnosed.

But life wasn't all doom and gloom. A popular attraction that was always part of a Toronto summer was the city's "Poor man's Riviera" better known as Sunnyside. The amusement park, opened in 1922 on what was then Toronto's western outskirts, had become the city's most enjoyed summer haven. Whether it was the rides, restaurants, hot dogs, games of chance, dance halls or its marvellous stretch of white sandy beach, Sunnyside Park afforded its guests a welcome respite.

And no talk of summer was complete without mentioning the Canadian National Exhibition … CNE for short, but fondly referred to by locals as simply "the Ex." During those two weeks in late August the exhibition transformed Toronto into a world within a world. The numerous buildings that sat mysteriously idle all year overnight turned into gala pavilions modelling culture from the four corners of the earth.

When Mom was in her teens it wasn't uncommon to attend the Ex a half dozen times over its two-week duration. Once your twenty-five cent admission was paid, little else was needed. Especially food; the Food Building could satisfy any appetite with its endless array of delicacies from the world's kitchens … free of charge.

Because of its close proximity to the CNE, 8 Hickson Street became a popular stop for those visiting the show. My grandmother probably lost count of the times friends and relatives phoned to announce they were "dropping in," causing her to silently wonder how many were coming, for how long and was there enough food available?

Just regular daily routine had its entertaining qualities, for example the merchants plying Toronto's streets in the 1920s and '30s. There was the iceman with his tarpaulin-covered wagon loaded with fifty-pound blocks of ice. A trail of water marked his route throughout the city in the summer. There was the baker with his assortment of cookies, cakes, bread and buns, all carried in a large wicker basket; a man who just sold vegetables, another bananas and still another who sold tea and coffee, offered in one-pound paper bags.

Coal delivery had to be one of the toughest and dirtiest jobs in the city. If you lived on a ground floor the coal was shovelled down a steel chute into your basement, if not it was bagged and carried in 100-pound bags up the fire escape.

The milkman was a regular visitor. If one awoke early enough you could hear the glass bottles clinking all the way down the block. His horse never had to be directed on where to stop, knowing every customer on the route by memory. During winter it was important to retrieve your milk from the porch quickly or the contents would freeze, sending a frozen column of milk out the top of the bottle ... an attraction for the neighbourhood cat population.

An especially interesting character was the junkman. During summer when windows were open, one could hear his refrain from the street. "Bottles ... bones ... bags and rags ... bottles ... bones ... bags and rags ... " One's attention was immediately drawn to an elderly man with the most dilapidated looking horse you ever saw. As such, one usually made an extra effort to find something to donate, although popular consensus dictated he wasn't nearly as poverty stricken as he appeared, figuring this antiquated horse was only an avenue to monetary gain. There seems to have been some merit to this theory as more than one person had witnessed the junkman's daughter riding the streetcar complete with furs and silk stockings!

This seemingly endless procession of personnel included the mailman. The one who served the Hickson Street/Brock Avenue area was a grouchy old bugger who suffered chronically from sore feet. He often employed the help of neighbourhood children to deliver the mail, saving him the agony of climbing the steps to individual houses. It was always amusing at Christmas time however when his aches and pains miraculously disappeared and he'd come right up the steps and ring the doorbell. "Hello Mr. Carruthers ... Merry Christmas!" Although he fooled no one, my grandfather would usually give him a fifty-cent bonus. "Oh ... thank you ... I didn't expect this!" It would be all the household could do to control their laughter at this character transformation each Yule season.

Childhood diseases are certainly nothing new. Despite strides in medicine, kids still fall victim to mumps, measles and chickenpox but for my mother it didn't stop there. When she was nine, what began as flu symptoms soon transformed into a red rash covering most of her body ... the diagnosis an infectious case of scarlet fever, a disease entertaining many side effects including heart and kidney problems, meningitis and pneumonia. Six long weeks of quarantine followed, spent in bed. Once the rash disappeared, skin peeling at an alarming pace was the next stage. The final stage was hair loss by the handful. Mom seemingly survived without any long-term effect, except when her hair grew back it was curly ... a condition that remained for life.

Before elementary school was finished Mom was stricken with appendicitis and by the time it was diagnosed the appendix burst. Even today a ruptured appendix is serious but in 1924 before the discovery of penicillin, events quickly escalated to grim and grave as peritonitis developed. Without the aid of drugs to neutralize the poison, the best medical technology could muster was the insertion of a series of tubes in the abdomen in hopes the poison would drain. A slow recovery began followed by six weeks in hospital plus another month's recuperation at home.

For my grandfather it was the beginning of huge medical bills. No health insurance at that time of course, but doctor's bills had to be paid, plus surgeon and anaesthetist fees, weeks of hospitalization and a nurse for most of that period. Mother recalled many months later delivering the final payment of eighty dollars and how her mother stressed the importance of such a large sum of money. Eighty dollars was substantial when one considers my grandfather was earning about $15 a week.

My grandfather had figured one way to save money during periods of budget restraint and that was to cut his five daughters' hair (definitely not their choice). Will Carruthers employed just one cutting style, shearing each girl's locks halfway down their ears. Mom would forever protest, stating her hair was curly and for her father to cut accordingly, but her plea always went unheeded. Noticeably shorter than her sisters' when dry, with ears protruding from the side of her head like some sprouting vegetable, my mother was embarrassed to be seen in school for at least a week following each haircut.

In 1927 Evelyn Carruthers began her freshman year at Parkdale Collegiate. Similar to public school, boys and girls were totally segregated, each with their own entrance and no mixed classes. Even outside, boys and girls were forbidden to walk on the same side of the street. These regulations were the norm in the 1920s and accepted without argument or even a second thought.

Mom still enjoyed any subject that involved reading and sports as well … particularly basketball. As captain, my mother led her team to championship status in the 1929–30 school semester. In those days, entertainment was what you made it. In fair weather the game of choice was "street softball." On little travelled Hickson Street, a team could play for most of the evening with few traffic interruptions.

Will Carruthers worked for Massey-Harris and coached and managed their baseball team and whether by choice or obligation, Mom attended regularly. If it was to provide moral support, her father couldn't have fared better as she would get boiling mad at any negative remarks directed towards her father from disgruntled fans. I guess this was sort of a role reversal of the "sports mom" scenario so prevalent today.

Like so many young women of that era, my mother's dream upon completing high school was that of a school teacher. However by the time of graduation four years later, the worst economic catastrophe in world history, forever known as the "Great Depression," would dash, or at the very least … change many career plans. The following decade would be more challenging than anyone could have possibly foreseen and it would take every ounce of stamina, hope and courage to survive what lay ahead.

A Race to the Bottom

For the first few years following World War One, Canada's economy in general had stagnated as business tried to adjust to peace time practices, but as the decade developed the economy steadily increased its pace. Unions had helped boost wages and workers were earning and spending more. A greater number were buying automobiles and telephones were practically a regular feature in every household. Hydro ... at least in the cities ... was just as popular. Modern appliances were freeing women from the drudgery of domestic chores and farm equipment companies were in frantic competition with one another to provide the utmost in labour-saving machinery. Installment purchasing was the new wave. Put a few dollars down and take it away.

On the western prairies, farmers had enjoyed several successive wheat crops of record yields. In July 1929, wheat hit a record $1.60 a bushel on the commodities market. Wheat ruled the stock market of that era as oil and minerals do today and speculators were investing at the Winnipeg Grain Exchange by the millions, assured the price would climb even higher. Other commodities were soon riding the crest of this gigantic wave and some investors were becoming millionaires in a matter of weeks. It was a euphoric state that prevailed the last year of the decade.

A similar story had been developing across the United States border until October 1929 ... when after three or four sharp dips, the New York Exchange suffered its worst decline yet. Shaken by this huge weakening, wheat on the Winnipeg Exchange dropped sharply and investors began to pull out. Just this one day's avalanche of selling wiped out thousands of large and small shareholders.

This scenario started investors quickly cashing in stocks from other commodities. As word spread of the massive selling market, more and more speculators followed suit until Tuesday, October 29, when sheer panic exploded into utter pandemonium. On that "black Tuesday" as it would be forever known, desperate stockholders sold more than 16,000,000 shares. Crowds of panic-stricken people besieged the New York Stock Exchange hoping to unload whatever stock they owned before the bottom fell completely out. Most discovered it had already happened.

It was the same story in Toronto where nervous investors clogged the city's Bay Street Exchange. Although a huge number of investors ... both Canadian and American ... lost everything they had in that one week, the Great Depression, as it's referred to, took two or three years to really hit bottom. As the months progressed, governments, banks and industry stopped investing, stopped lending and stopped expanding. The process simply multiplied until finally, nearly total stagnation was the result.

As the economic pace continued to slow, both Canadian Prime Minister Richard Bennett and American President Herbert Hoover hastened to assure a shaken populace that the worst was over, neither leader imagining economic conditions would drop to the level they did. A joint effort to study methods to improve business conditions by adjusting tariffs with other Commonwealth countries thereby encouraging trade was the best they could come up with. Reality stated this Depression was already too well entrenched to be reversed by conferences, meetings and studies.

Most analysts and historians agree that 1933 was the year the Great Depression sank to its lowest point. By then, one out of three of Toronto's workforce was unemployed. Many were forced to accept the welfare relief the government provided, a hand-out available only to persons with a family to support. For a family of five, the relief worked out to about $1.20 a day. The charity was usually in the way of food and it was easy to spot the recipients returning from the welfare depots each week with their white cotton bags.

Toronto, as most cities in Canada, was made up of a proud workforce who believed a job was the most important thing in life, and to have to go begging with their "pogey bags" was more embarrassing and degrading than many could stand. Some only took the offering if their family was literally starving. Any morning one could count hundreds walking along Queen Street towards the unemployment office. All knew before they left home the journey was fruitless, but followed the formality nevertheless, at least satisfying themselves they still had a spark of pride and hope.

The greatest victims of the Depression were the single, homeless men. They could be seen standing on street corners in any city you can name, asking passers-by if there was an odd job available for a few cents' change or a meal. You'd see them walking along the railroad tracks, scavenging for chunks of coal dropped from passing trains, enough perhaps to provide a little warmth for the coming night.

There was one other option for this unfortunate group ... the government relief camps. These camps were scattered across the country, and anywhere a road needed building or help was needed for some defence project, these single men would be hauled in. In truth they were nothing but slave camps with slave wages. Most of the Royal Canadian Air Force base at Trenton, Ontario, was built on twenty-cent-a-day labour.

The Great Depression by now was so ingrained it mattered little if you lived in Toronto or Tulsa, Winnipeg or Wichita ... the scenario was the same ... no jobs. Nobody seemed to understand what had really happened or how to cure it. Every day for the unemployed was a battle for existence, and as always the poorest took the main impact and fought hard to protect each other. Large groups would gather trying to scrape together enough change to pay someone's rent, and if that failed, vigilante committees would be formed to prevent bailiffs from evicting neighbours.

A man who watched this economic and social decay with increasing anxiety was Maurice Zeidman, a Toronto Presbyterian minister. A Polish immigrant, Zeidman knew all about hard times, and as the Depression deepened, he witnessed equally difficult times right in his own city. It moved him to open a section of his residence for a few hours each day, offering any needy person a hot bowl of soup and a sandwich.

This charitable venture needed volunteers so my mother joined Zeidman's team. She had lots of time available as the only work she had been able to find upon graduating from secondary school was a few hours a week at the local library at twenty-five cents an hour. The Depression had left everyone with such a feeling of helplessness any contribution was a personal and spiritual lift. A year later Zeidman opened a permanent location on Spadina Avenue, known as the Scott Street Mission. The mission still operates as of this writing, providing hundreds of meals each day.

Through all this upheaval my grandfather Will Carruthers was still clinging to his job at Massey-Harris ... just two days a week. Only his twenty-five-year seniority helped him to hold on at all. As did all farm machinery manufacturers, Massey-Harris had suffered greatly. Their loss column would have alarmed even the most optimistic lending institution ... nearly $20,000,000 in the period of 1930-36 ... a lot of money in 1930s Depression dollars.

But for those still working, the Depression was actually providing a break as commodity prices had fallen with everything else. However it was still a challenge to provide for a family of seven and no matter how bad things got there were two items my grandfather would not eat ... beans and rice. He claimed that during the war he had one or the other every day for four years.

As always, my grandmother budgeted for the household. Grandpa Will received enough for his cigarettes and once-a-week bowling game. One concession to hard times was rolling his own instead of buying "store bought." Need breeds creativity and the hard times certainly provided opportunity to stretch the few dollars available. Hydro, water and gas were used as sparingly as possible. If you could save a nickel streetcar fare by walking, you did. A few extra shaves from each blade would save the dime for a new package. My grandfather became a fairly accomplished cobbler, fabricating new leather to old shoes, replacing soles, relining inner soles with cardboard ... anything to get maximum mileage from a shoe.

Employment was wherever one could find it.

One Easter Sunday, Mom typed letters for Woods Sanitation Company, the job lasting a full day. However, she received $5.00 … a fortune! A less lucrative endeavour involved needlework on bedspreads for a Georgia company that had a factory in downtown Toronto. A good day was needed to complete one of these spreads, as all had to be specially handled to give the blanket the proper "fluff" pattern the company demanded. For eight hours of sore fingers and scissor blisters, Mom received seventy-five cents.

Meanwhile "down on the farm" on the other side of the family tree, the Turners and their rural neighbours were also groping their way through the Depression. Along the gravel roads of the township, news of the October "crash" had been read with interest, but little else. Farming had failed to capitalize in the so called "good years" of the 1920s, so the steady slide towards stagnation that had so devastated the cities was less apparent. The rural area certainly suffered, but simply didn't have as far to go to reach bottom.

By 1933, with economic conditions at their lowest level, Canadian and American voters had sent their leaders packing. Both had enough of the philosophy that "prosperity was just around the corner" and were replaced by Mackenzie King and Franklin Roosevelt respectively.

The worst conditions of this era were in the western prairies of both Canada and the U.S., where severely depressed wheat prices were a factor certainly, but the main culprit was Mother Nature. Over the years, several mild winters featuring little snow covering in conjunction with dry springs, along with poor farming practices, had turned the rich fertile prairie soil into rolling dust storms. Whether it was Manitoba, Saskatchewan, Oklahoma or Kansas, dust was everywhere. Filling irrigation ditches, piling in snow-like drifts around buildings, sifting under doors, around windows, into cupboards, into food, into clothing ... nothing escaped.

As depicted in John Steinbeck's *The Grapes of Wrath,* American dustbowl victims headed to California while their Canadian counterparts headed to British Columbia or Ontario. They like so many others had no choice. How heartbreaking was it to stand helplessly season after season as crops withered and died and the once rich topsoil drifted away in the wind? How devastating to watch livestock starve to death and have no crops to feed them? Even if feed were available, there was no money with which to buy it. A decade had transformed the prairie wheatlands from breadbasket to dustbowl. Another decade would pass before the land would again even approach its potential, and then only after more intelligent cropping practices were adopted.

Things weren't that bad in Ontario. At least they had crops even if they were worth next to nothing. Similarly with livestock prices; market hogs went as low as $3.00 each. A couple would be saved for the "pork barrel" and the rest were often killed at birth, as feed costs would far exceed what the hogs would ever be worth. Beef cattle sold for about three cents a pound. Even a milk cow could be bought for $25.00. Like most, the Turner family rode out the Depression on the graces of their livestock, gardens and orchards.

One unique method of making sure everyone had an adequate supply of meat year round was the "beef ring." Each farmer who chose to belong was expected to donate one good steer throughout the summer to the local abattoir.

To keep track of everything, a large diagram of a side of beef hung on the wall, showing the various cuts, each bearing a number. Another chart listed each customer's name and what cuts they received. This way, every week each family received at least one choice cut along with poorer ones. The meat was placed in numbered bags and the farmers took turns delivering. With no means of refrigeration in rural areas, the beef ring proved a good system, as no other way existed to have fresh beef available throughout the year.

One time a steer on its way to market went berserk and gave everyone quite a chase before it was rounded up. The experience somehow affected the meat, for in my father's words, the meat that week "really stunk" when cooked. But the system worked well for the most part, keeping stomachs full even if pockets were empty.

After bottoming out in 1933, the economic pendulum slowly began a recovery, each year in succession a little better than the previous. Then came another sharp recession in 1938, severe enough that some analysts predicted another Depression was on the way. This "economic dip," although frightening at the time, proved relatively short-lived.

At the time ... 1938-39 ... if any economic forecaster had predicted that two or three years down the road, factories all across the country would be operating twenty-four hours a day churning out a dizzying array of product, and a labour force that once staggered under 30% unemployment would be reduced to zero ... it would simply have been written off as "pie in the sky" mentality. However, that would be exactly the case.

But it wouldn't be sound economic structures or studies or conferences or new monetary policies or fewer tariff restrictions or any of a number of trial balloons politicians introduced to cause this astounding turnaround. (What would inevitably winch Canada and the U.S. from this decade-long economic struggle would be something no one considered ... another world war.

During these next few years in Canada alone, over 800,000 men and women home and abroad would find employment in one of the three armed forces services ... army, navy or air force. Talk about job creation!

By 1945, the greatest economic upheaval known to mankind would be history ... but so too would be the lives of 42,000 Canadians.

War on the Home Front

In 1934, at the age of twenty, Harold Turner had left the family farm in Grey County with his sights set on Ontario's capital. Still well embedded in the world's greatest economic depression, Toronto was a tough place to find a job. When a clerical position at a candy factory ended abruptly in bankruptcy two years later and with nothing new on the horizon, my father headed home to regroup.

He couldn't have picked a hotter summer than 1936 to return to the labour-intensive vocation of agriculture. July had witnessed unrelenting high temperatures. Great for curing hay but hard on humans and animals. For them, conditions these past few weeks had cycled between uncomfortable and unbearable. And career-wise my father was no further ahead than two years ago. Back working the family farm, once again sweating through another haying and harvest.

Hard labour never bothered Harold, but working with nothing to show for it certainly did. While in Toronto he'd become accustomed to having a little cash in his pocket. And although a full year had passed, there were still aspects of the big city he missed. Obvious ones like a regular paycheque and a world of choice on which to spend it. Less obvious perhaps ... he missed Evelyn Carruthers. On foot or by streetcar, covering the length and breadth of the city, Evelyn had educated her "country boy" on Toronto's high interest points.

Evelyn also educated him on her first love ... books. And she saw no reason to cease this worthy habit just because he was no longer in the city, so instigated a "books by mail" system. For a dime, two or three books could be packaged and sent on the morning train from Toronto, arriving at the Flesherton Station by noon. Due to financial restrictions, visits remained few and far between, so correspondence was by mail. Harold would compose long flowery letters, often resurrecting poetic passages recalled from school days to make his true feelings known.

In addition to letter writing, listening to the radio helped pass the time, especially during those long dark evenings of winter. Amos n' Andy; Ma Perkins; Jack Benny and Lux Radio Theatre were some of their favourites. Harold could imagine Evelyn sitting close to her radio as he was to his, listening to the same programs.

Unlike her admirer, few of Evelyn's evenings were spent alone. Between her part-time library job, church functions and visiting friends and relatives, little "home time" remained. And much to Harold's dismay, some of these social occasions she attended with other suitors. One in particular, Norman Brown, in an effort to gain her favour, escorted Evelyn to performances at some of the greatest theatres that flourished throughout Toronto. As well, they were frequent visitors at such highly esteemed concert centres as Massey Hall, the premium venue for classical orchestrated music in that era.

Harold of course stood no chance against such odds, but in a calculated gamble stated that Evelyn would have to make a choice ... now! Nellie Day, a friend of Evelyn's since childhood, declared Harold had no right to issue such an ultimatum. "It's not like you're engaged, you know!" Her position was ... "let him sweat." In the end though, Harold held a trump card ... country living. Realizing and understanding Evelyn's passion for rural lifestyle, he felt confident with his ultimatum, so perhaps it was her other suitors that never stood a chance.

In the interim, both families awaited the outcome of the drama, some silently, some not. The question of Harold and Evelyn being first cousins after all, had been the elephant in the room from the outset. When Mamie Turner, Evelyn's future mother-in law broached the subject, Evelyn explained that nowhere in the *Presbyterian Book of Marriage Ethics* did it forbid cousins to marry. And, in a shot aimed directly at Mamie, claimed that some churches, Anglican for instance, forbade marrying your wife's sister.

For the sake of clarification, several years after his wife's passing, my grandfather Oliver Turner had married her sister Mamie. (It just keeps getting more intriguing, doesn't it!)

Evelyn was right about the Presbyterian point of cousins marrying ... sort of. But only recently had that thorny issue been addressed, and the law reversal had sparked a sharp division among some ministers of the church, who in direct defiance refused to recognize the change.

It's interesting that some of the fuss had nothing to do with being cousins. A greater concern from Harold's family, at least, stemmed from the fact that he was marrying a "city girl." In their opinion, this was the gravest mistake a farmer could make. Although being a Carruthers didn't help either.

Many of the Turners were convinced the Carruthers connection thought themselves just a little better than everyone else. Harold's father could usually see a broader picture, but also worried that a "city girl" would make a poor choice for a wife. As far as being cousins ... he kept that concern to himself.

There was no need to guess on what side of the fence they were stationed when it came to Evelyn's family ... opinion rang loud and clear! Her mother blamed herself for the entire situation, recalling that day two or three years earlier when she offered her nephew room and board while he was employed at the candy factory. To Reba Carruthers, how you presented yourself and moreover how people judged you ... were paramount. The "stigma" attached to this marriage would have far-reaching effects in her mind. The greatest squabbles however were between Evelyn and her father ... but they'd scrapped their entire lives, arguments erupting quickly and frequently, but like a summer thunderstorm usually dissipating just as fast, although their differences had never declared a clear winner.

Personally, Will Carruthers liked Harold, "but he's your first cousin," he pleaded with his daughter ... "Harold's father and your mother are brother and sister! ... just think about that!" But Evelyn had heard this recording once too often, explaining to her father as she had for countless others what the Presbyterian Doctrine stated, also what she'd read in books. "I don't give a damn what the church says nor do I give a damn about something you read in your dream world of books, Evelyn ... this is reality!"

"Did you know that Franklin and Eleanor Roosevelt are cousins?" queried Evelyn, as if she'd never heard a word. "And did you know Canadian Prime Minister Mackenzie King married his aunt?" At this point Will Carruthers would usually return to reading his newspaper, knowing further discussion was fruitless.

Over the past two decades, an enormous amount of research has been performed on the hereditary aspect of "unconventional" marriages. Research has concluded that the rise of any such birth aberration from a first cousin union is in their words "infinitesimal" ... but this is now and that was then. A first cousin marriage today would still provide plenty of fodder for conversation, so imagine seventy-five years ago!

Both Will and Reba Carruthers were convinced this "gene pool" would produce nothing but a crop of dysfunctional misfits, and questioned whether Evelyn was mindful of the kind of risks such a marriage could pose. My mother was a voracious reader, so there's little doubt of her awareness that the medical thinking of that era stressed how certain hereditary traits had to be scrutinized, as a genetic weakness could show up in children ... but as she solidly believed ... so could exceptional genes.

As far as Mom's sisters, they were caught in the middle. They wanted to support their big sister, but doing so alienated their parents. Jean and Alma liked things to run smoothly ... "don't rock the boat" was their philosophy. Lois, on the other hand was more strong-willed; the two always being close, she therefore made it clear she was beside her sister all the way ... and that meant standing next to her on her wedding day despite any resistance or resentment the rest of the family might harbour!

And so the soap opera continued ... as family members took sides, providing more than a deserved share of gossip, accusations and general ill-feeling. Time is a great healer, however, and eventually most realized there were more important things in the world to keep their minds occupied. For the uproar they had generated, Dad and Mom must have felt somewhat like King Edward VIII and Wallis Simpson. But despite the turmoil, in the end ... like them ... Harold and Evelyn chose "the one they loved."

As in all towns and cities across Canada some seven decades ago, Saturday night was "open night" in Owen Sound, Ontario. This particular spring evening in 1938, Harold and Evelyn were interested in only one store. Tonight at Buzza Bros. Jewellers, they would choose the diamond Evelyn would wear for life. Protocol dictated no price limit should be set, but was usually considered to be equivalent to a month's pay. From the glittering assortment, choice wasn't easy, but finally a $25.00 engagement ring was chosen. For another ten dollars they chose a matching wedding band, but being short on cash laid it away until the actual wedding day.

With all that had transpired over the past year, feelings of mixed emotion must have certainly accompanied the couple as they stepped out into the warm air of that May evening so long ago. However, despite all the discord, I'm certain at that moment they felt they were the luckiest two people in all of Owen Sound ... maybe even in the whole country!

But this was 1938 and events were taking shape that would change not only the face of the country, but the world besides. The seeds for this scenario had been planted back in 1920 when a German soldier, still bitter over Germany's defeat in 1918, recruited a small group of members into what he called the National Socialist German Workers

Party. Later this force became better known as the Nazi Party as did their leader ... Adolf Hitler.

In April of 1938 Austria had been absorbed, and in August Czechoslovakia was being studied for occupation. Only the most optimistic person could see a way to rationalize with Hitler and divert global war. Enter Neville Chamberlain, Britain's Prime Minister, who signed an agreement in Munich drawn up by Adolf Hitler forcing Czechoslovakia to secede nearly a quarter of its territory to Germany. This "agreement" encompassed 800,000 Czechs and practically all of the country's industry. When Chamberlain returned to London, he declared the Munich Agreement had brought "peace in our time."

Feelings were mixed around the world following Chamberlain's return. First elation ... then skepticism and suspicion; at 8 Hickson Street in Toronto, Will Carruthers read the newspaper report. To no one in particular he announced, "They've sold Czechoslovakia down the river ... that agreement will never last." Unfortunately that was the consensus among many; more unfortunate was the fact they were right.

But despite world events, life goes on as life does and Harold and Evelyn counted down the months, then weeks to their wedding. In the interim they made the most of what a Depression courtship would allow. If in Toronto they'd sometimes attend a movie ... eighteen cents at "The Brock." "The College" cost twenty-five cents but offered plush cushions and a bigger screen. "The Brock" had "china night" however. Each Tuesday, management gave away one piece of china with every ticket sold. This would be a set pattern so through time, one could collect a full set of dishes.

In Eugenia, gas and money were just as scarce so often the couple would simply park on the main street and watch the world go by. In winter, courting slowed even more. No one drove cars as the back concessions weren't plowed, so the first big snowfall you wheeled the car into the garage, drained the radiator, let the air out of the tires, jacked up the wheels, removed the battery, then waited for spring. Meanwhile, courtship was via horse and sleigh. Snuggled under a thick fur robe on a crisp evening with a string of bells bouncing off the horses' back, courting couldn't have been more romantic! The robe was basically to cover your knees but was of sufficient size to completely disappear under if one chose. Bells added a certain charm to winter sleighing but were actually required by law for night driving. A set of bells safely signalled the approach of an otherwise silent horse and sleigh.

As the big day grew near, Evelyn continued to add to her hope chest, describing her purchases in detail through letters to Harold, who sent two or three dollars or whatever he could afford from time to time. Mom's most prized possession was a set of dishes, including silverware and crystal, 101 pieces in all, from Simpsons for $17.95, financing it over a period of ten months at $1.90 a month.

Three days before the wedding, Toronto was honoured with a visit from King George VI and Queen Elizabeth. In an obvious attempt to gain support for the Monarchy, which they knew they would soon need because of developments in Europe, the King and Queen undertook an extensive goodwill tour of Canada and parts of the USA.

On May 22, the Royal couple's specially built silver and blue train arrived in the city. My father, a true monarchist if there ever was one, wouldn't have missed this event for the world. After all wasn't he the one who, when King George V died three years earlier, thought he and Evelyn should cancel the plans they had made for that evening? The two had planned to go skating but Dad thought it poor taste to be enjoying themselves on such a solemn occasion.

Dad drove down from Eugenia and he and my mother followed the Royal motorcade wherever it went throughout Toronto. Across the Dominion it was the same. Huge crowds waited everywhere. In the prairies, where endless miles separated towns and villages, people lined the sides of the tracks for a glimpse of the Royal couple.

Despite the excitement and glitter of the Royal visit, after departure my parents confessed at being left with a strange feeling of emptiness and despair, as probably most Canadians did. With war clouds threatening England, no one could be sure what lay ahead for the King and Queen, their country, or the world for that matter.

"As Long As We Both Shall Live"

Dad

At two o'clock Thursday afternoon, May 25, 1939, Evelyn Carruthers and her sister Lois stood before Reverend Gilbert Little inside Chalmers Presbyterian Church in Toronto. My mother worked at her job at the library until noon, then after giving a final and tearful goodbye to her co-workers and friends of so many years, rushed home to dress and get to the church.

A rough and tumultuous ride to say the least had brought my mother to this day. As promised, Lois was by her side, but as far as other family members ... what you see is what you get. No parents ... no other sisters. "It would have meant so much to Evelyn if we had been there that day," her sister Alma confessed decades later. "I'm certain she knew we were on her side, but showing up at the church would have sent a much stronger message. We should have gone, regardless of how our parents felt ... I regret that decision to this day."

So the battle lines were drawn and the players took their positions ... Mom's sisters had wrestled with their conscience but buckled when faced with their parents' opposition, who made it clear from the outset they wouldn't be

50

there. Oliver (father-in-law) no doubt would have attended but didn't want to upset his sister Reba. Mamie (mother-in-law) and her sister Ila would be definite "no shows" but no loss there as far as my mother was concerned. There was no doubt about Harold's sister and her husband's support, probably the only ones truly understanding the difficulties my parents had endured these past two or three years. But with so many opposing factions, Mom and Dad figured it was easier to just "go it alone."

All these conflicting thoughts raced through Evelyn's mind as she stood at the altar. And there was even greater concern at the moment; where was the male half of this impending and important ceremony? The two PM deadline had passed, and as the minutes ticked by, my mother began to harbour the thoughts that have haunted brides for centuries. With all that had occurred over the last while, maybe she wouldn't have blamed Harold for heading for the hills!

The groom hadn't changed his mind, however; he was just temporarily sidetracked. It was the same route he'd always taken into Toronto when visiting Evelyn, down Weston Road to Keele Street, then to Dundas. Where Dundas Street sweeps southeast just below Bloor, Dad's "best man" and best friend Lester Samson who was in the lead car, instead of taking Dundas, simply drove straight down Roncesvalles Avenue. Harold just followed merrily along, not realizing his mistake until the waterfront was reached.

At least Reverend Little had come through for the bride and groom, rising above the controversy unlike some of his colleagues. He believed simply if those in authority had made an informed and educational decision on marriage law and ethics in the church ... then it was his duty to fulfil that commitment. End of discussion.

And he was also getting anxious as the minutes passed ... as he had a funeral to conduct immediately following this wedding ceremony! Finally our two wandering souls found their way back to the church and with no more time to waste, the formalities began.

"Dearly beloved, we are gathered here to today in the presence of God ... " Frequently his words were drowned out by workmen unloading coal into the church basement. Every minute or so another bag would be opened and its contents spilled down the steel chute. With each interruption, Reverend Little would raise his voice to compensate. He didn't have to include the ceremonial question ... "If any person has reason for this couple not to be joined in holy matrimony ... " as there was no one there. When the minister pronounced them an official couple and informed the groom that he could now "kiss the bride," for some reason, my father answered, "I guess I'll wait until later."

As was customary at the time when my parents married, following the ceremony the wedding party plus family and friends would normally return to the bride's parents' house to open gifts and cut the cake. Of course "normal" and "customary" never came within miles of this wedding day as Will and Reba had steadfastly refused to host any such gathering.

Evelyn's long-time friend Nellie Day intervened at this point. Sympathetic to her friend's frustration and disappointment, her family graciously opened their house to the wedding party. And Nellie's mother, in an attempt to salvage some resemblance to a "normal" wedding day, baked and decorated a cake in their honour. Someone in Nellie's family ... no one seems to remember who ... snapped the few pictures taken on that memorable afternoon.

Both Mom and Dad had enjoyed the ruggedness of Northern Ontario the previous year when they visited Dad's sister and brother-in-law in Sudbury, so decided to combine their honeymoon with another visit. They spent their wedding night in a cozy two-dollar cottage in Huntsville. Dad always claimed it was the best two dollars he ever spent.

Back on Eugenia's "eighth line" following the honeymoon, the newlyweds set up housekeeping in Oliver and Mamie's house, which had been divided into separate living quarters. As for working arrangements, my father was promised $35.00 a month from April through November and $15.00 for the four winter months. All milk, cream, eggs and meat were included and my parents had full use of the family Chevrolet. There was no hydro although it was coming closer. Three neighbours had signed, the minimum required by Ontario Hydro to install full service up the eighth line so at least it was within reach once they could afford it. Water was retrieved from the pump outside the back steps, wood was carried from the woodshed, water for cooking and washing was heated on the woodstove and the "bathroom" was hidden outside amongst the lilacs.

This wasn't the original "two holer" that Oliver's father Solomon had built at the turn of the century when the house was built. That one burnt down. Oliver had a habit of placing ashes from the stove down the hole, which acted both as a disinfectant and a means of disposal. One day I guess the ashes were too hot when he made his delivery on route to the barn. When he returned an hour later, the outhouse had been levelled.

Like most newlyweds of that period, savings were non-existent. A minimum amount of furniture was bought on the "time payment" plan and my mother had (surprisingly) received fifty dollars as a wedding gift from her parents, allowing her to purchase a mattress plus numerous odds and ends. A thrifty person could buy quite a bit for fifty dollars. A year earlier, Dad had given her ten, allowing her to buy a camera, housecoat and an alarm clock. The "eighth line" neighbours sponsored a shower, adding a set of table and chairs plus some cash to their modest collection.

As well as his farm wages, Dad supplemented his income raising mink, having about seventy at this point. Prepared mink feed was expensive, so groundhogs played an important role in complementing the ration. Groundhog burrows flourished throughout the pasture fields from spring to fall and anyone with a good rifle and accurate eye could have all they wanted.

Even romantic strolls back through the fields were never undertaken without gun in hand, always returning with at least a couple of dead groundhogs. If the departed rodents weren't needed immediately they were stored in the cellar, the natural stone floor providing an ideal cooler. It was when the remains were needed that Mom's services were called upon. After Dad skinned the carcass, it was her job to process it through a regular meat grinder ... flesh, bones and all. During pelting season, the mink skins were stretched and tacked on boards and left to cure for several days. A room immediately adjacent to their bedroom served this purpose.

Years earlier when my father was writing those embellished love letters to Mom, offering "country living" as an enticement to marriage ... I wonder if she ever thought it would extend this far! Some days, Toronto and all that it offered must have seemed far, far away.

Loneliness and isolation were key factors no doubt that first winter, but two other couples who had married about the same time helped pass the long winter evenings. My parents didn't dance so seldom went to house parties, but occasionally would attend a movie in Owen Sound, thirty miles away. This was despite Oliver's suggestion to his son that now being married, such things were pure extravagance.

Often an evening of euchre would be the entertainment, although having Dad for a partner frustrated Mom to no end. She liked to play freely and quickly while Dad preferred to visit and was forever losing track of the game. Around the table the hands would be played ... zip ... zip ... zip. Then it would be Dad's turn. "Let's see now ... what's trump?" Around again ... zip ... zip ... zip. "So ... hearts are trump ... well I'd better not play that ... let's see now ... what did you lead, Evelyn?"

Often in the spring of the year when Dad was working in the fields, Mother would pack a basket with bread and butter and a beverage and after picking some wild leeks, make sandwiches for the two of them to enjoy in a make-shift picnic beneath a shady tree. Mamie, her mother-in-law, of course thought such excursions not only ridiculous, but just plain stupid ... something that could only be manufactured by a "city girl."

The only thing that could interrupt this tranquil setting might be a groundhog sighting, although Harold was pretty careful following that incident a couple of years back.

He'd been sowing grain with the brand-new Massey-Harris seed drill just bought that spring. He stopped to rout a groundhog from under a stone fence, leaving the three-horse team unattended. The rodent gave a whistle, spooking the team, which took off for the barn. Charging up the back lane at full gallop they somehow missed both gateposts as they entered the barnyard. Oliver heard the stampede coming and managed to slow the frightened horses, but not before the seed drill smacked into the corner of the barn's stone wall, severely denting one steel wheel.

Oliver never directed any anger towards his son for the mishap. Perhaps he was just grateful Harold wasn't hurt. After all, it was from this very field he'd witnessed a similar stampede many years before ... the one that took the life of his father!

Mom never did adjust ... and that's putting it kindly ... to the "two-family" arrangement. Constant squabbles were seemingly part and parcel of each day. By the summer of 1941 with no sign of improvement, my parents were ready to move on. Another altercation with Mamie had brought things into even clearer perspective. Disagreeing on some decision she had made concerning the farm, Dad reminded his stepmother how things would operate when *he* owned the farm. Mamie answered evenly that nowhere was it written he would even get the chance. And just to make sure he got the point, added, "You'll never come ahead of *my* boys!" (Two sons born to her and Oliver were now thirteen and seven respectively.)

Just at that time, Dad's friend Lester discovered a farm near the town of Brampton, just north of Toronto, that was looking for help, so long story short, next thing he was on the payroll. Just one little problem ... there was no room for my mother yet. Building construction was being curtailed by the war that was now raging, so it would be several months before their new home would be ready. So for the time being Evelyn would remain exiled with her in-laws.

Because of labour shortages, Dad only received every fifth weekend off so correspondence was once again by mail. He embarked on another letter-writing campaign that rivaled his courting days. Letters that numbered two or three a week, discussing his new job, his undying love and always his wife's health and the baby she carried. Was she getting enough rest? The right food? She wasn't doing anything foolish to endanger their unborn child was she?

For the latter concern, Mamie joined forces with my mother at least for this occasion. One day Mom was looking out the kitchen window, watching Oliver's big, black Berkshire boar rooting about the orchard. Mamie grabbed Mom's arm, giving her a stern lecture of the dangers of staring at something so ugly during pregnancy. According to time-honoured superstition, such an act could cause the baby to inherit some of the pig's characteristics!

My mother had the option to return to Toronto and await the arrival, but chose instead to have the baby at the Flesherton Maternity Home, operated by long-time resident Elizabeth Nuhn. During her twenty-year career, Nuhn had helped more than a thousand babies into the world. To my mother, this homey atmosphere was much preferred to "some huge, cold hospital in Toronto."

When Mom would be reading her stash of letters from Dad, Mamie's sister Ila, who resided at Mamie's much of the time, would be dying to know what could possibly fill all those pages. "So, how is Harold?" ... "Fine" ... "How's he getting along?" ... "Fine" ... "How does he like his new job?" ... "Fine" ... "What else does he say?" ... "Oh, not much." Ila would be completely frustrated by now. "A person doesn't write nine or ten pages just to say he's fine!"

Then arrived Tuesday, October 28; ever since he'd received the message "It's a girl!" my father could think of nothing else. Because of his work schedule, he couldn't get to see his wife and new daughter until Saturday night. "I'll be there by eight," he promised. Eight o'clock came and went. So did nine, then ten. Mom was imagining all sorts of terrible scenarios by now.

Unknown to her, Harold and Lester had been stumbling around in the darkness on Highway 10 south of Orangeville trying to retrieve a wheel from Lester's car. Since he'd left home, Dad had no car, so was hitching a ride in Lester's Ford when the right front wheel disassociated itself from the axle and disappeared into the blackness of an October night. They had been late getting away as is, and without aid of flashlight had thrashed around in swamp and ditch for over an hour before someone finally tripped over it.

Out at the farm the next morning, Mamie inquired, "Did you see the baby last night?" "Just for a few minutes ... she was asleep." "I think she looks like you Harold!" ... "I guess all babies look the same at that stage," Harold answered. "Do you think she'll have brown eyes like you?" ... "I have no idea." "Have you a name?" "Vivien." (My parents had gone to see *Gone with the Wind* that summer and had been impressed not only by Vivien Leigh's acting abilities but obviously her name as well.)

Later Dad stopped in to see mother and baby on his way back to Brampton. Vivien was wide awake this time and while marvelling at the little pink-wrapped bundle, Dad mentioned his conversation about eye colour with Mamie. "Babies' eyes are always blue," Mom commented, then added, "I guess Mamie's afraid the baby will look like me." Dad left instructions with Mom to let him know as soon as she and the baby were ready to travel and he would take her and Vivien to Toronto until their new home was completed.

Family relations on Mother's side of the fence had warmed considerably since the wedding two and a half years earlier. Not that my parents had been banned from visiting ... far from it. Time was simply needed to relinquish some pride and forgive and forget words spoken in heated moments. Because the fact remained ... as a person, both Will and Reba liked Harold. He was everything one could wish for in a son-in-law; kindness, consideration, generosity and respect were all traits to which he subscribed.

But most importantly ... and they both realized this from day one despite everything that had transpired ... Harold loved their daughter. When he promised to "love and honour 'til death do us part" he wasn't merely repeating some well-worn phrase. He meant it with all his heart and would until the end nearly sixty years later. The crowning touch seemingly was that cute, cuddly, beautiful ... and normal ... little baby girl that melted any lingering feelings from the past.

The general mood on the opposite side of the pasture fence ... although improving ... hadn't quite reached that warm fuzzy stage. While Mom waited to return to Toronto, both Ila and Mamie kept a close watch on the infant. Mamie constantly assured my mother that Vivien was looking more and more like Harold with each passing day. Ila nodded in agreement, adding, "I guess there's always hope."

War and Milk

Looking at Brampton, Ontario, today, submersed in the midst of the sprawling suburbia known as Mississauga, it may be difficult to visualize it was ever a quiet little town. Situated in the valley of the Etobicoke River, Brampton had become the centre for a rich farming community. An Englishman, John Elliot had seen the potential of this area in the 1820s when he purchased and cleared a portion of his property into lots, naming the new neighbourhood after his hometown of Brampton, England. The arrival of the Grand Trunk Railway in 1858 provided distant markets for Brampton's two largest industries, Haggard Foundry, manufacturer of farm machinery and stoves, and Dale Nurseries, soon to be famous for its hybrid roses and orchids. As the years passed, other nurseries arrived, earning Brampton the title of "Flower City." These industries in conjunction with its agricultural base made Brampton a community to be envied when my parents settled into their new home in January 1942.

Five months earlier, a close friend had landed a job helping with the harvest at B.H. Bull's Ltd., a large dairy operation on the edge of Brampton. Following harvest, he got a job in one of the dairy barns, but in the interim went home and told anyone who would listen about the great place he'd discovered .

With his interest piqued, Dad drove down to Brampton from his home in Eugenia Falls and introduced himself to the farm manager. If interested, Dad learned he'd receive a new house by the end of the year, free board in the meantime, $65.00 a month ... plus all the milk he could drink. "When could I start?" asked my father. "Right now!" was the answer. "We're short of help. What size rubber boots do you wear?"

Nothing could have prepared my father for an operation this size. From a dozen-cow herd of Shorthorns back home in Eugenia Falls milked entirely by hand, to four barns consisting of eighty registered Jerseys each, was like day and night. He learned one cow in the herd held the record as top milk-producing Jersey in the world. At home where all work was still being handled by horses, it's no wonder when heading to the barn that first morning, Dad stood in awe as no less than four McCormick-Deering tractors passed by on their way to the fields.

Each barn employed four men plus a herdsman. Bob Flood, an amiable chap, was the herdsman in the barn in which my father worked, handling all feeding and veterinary chores. Milking took place three times a day ... four AM, seven AM and four PM. Four hours of "free" time between the second and third milking was as good as it got. In the house for supper at seven PM, read the paper, then early to bed as it started all over again at four.

The war in Europe had now been raging for over two years and was beginning to have an effect on the routine supply of normal services, so Mom and Dad were fortunate to be able to move into their new home early in 1942. Before another year would pass, private home construction would practically be at a standstill, as the war monopolized not only material but the labour market as well. One of the few positive aspects of the war lay in the fact that after nearly a decade of unemployment, men were almost immediately swept from the streets. The young went to Europe, the older into the factories at home, as did thousands of women as well.

While the European battle continued, another country was showing its might ... the Empire of Japan. Alarmed and suspicious of Japan's aggressive tactics during the last year, the United States had initiated a trade embargo, as they had been the country's largest trading partner. No problem ... Japan simply turned to Germany and Italy for raw materials. Relationships between the U.S. and Japan continued south ... then came Sunday, December 7.

My father and the rest of the milking crew were just beginning the afternoon shift when Bob Flood entered the barn. Bob was obviously excited. "I just heard on the radio that the Japs have bombed Pearl Harbour!" Everyone knew Pearl Harbour was the giant U.S. naval base in Hawaii. With some satisfaction, Bob added. "That'll finally get the Yanks into the (European) war!"

Meanwhile across the fields from B.H. Bull's, the Victory Aircraft Co. at Malton was building towards a workforce of 9,500. Lancaster bombers were being assembled at the site and during peak production, Victory would turn out one of the giant aircraft every single day. Because of their proximity to Malton Airport (now Toronto International), B.H. Bull's witnessed plenty of activity as Scandinavian and Polish pilots trained in Canadian skies around Malton.

One evening just at sunset, a large Norwegian plane landed in a pasture field on Bull's' property. Despite an abundance of speculation as to what or whom the plane might be transporting, it was never learned what it was all about, as no one was allowed anywhere near. Air force personnel guarded the suspicious aircraft throughout the night, and at first light it lifted off with the secret nature of its visit intact.

By the summer of 1942, rationing was becoming commonplace in Brampton as elsewhere. Imported food-stuffs were the first to be rationed, namely sugar, while gasoline soon followed. After Pearl Harbour, Washington in an effort to save precious metals decreed all vehicles must contain no stainless steel or chrome. Auto manufacturing soon ground to a halt. It was the same story in Canada, with Chrysler Motors in Windsor being the last to shut down. More than three and a half years would pass before they'd build another car. In the interim, like all manufac-turers, they would be churning out war-related materials twenty-four hours a day.

Throughout the following year the Lancaster bomber plant continued at full force. To protect the military produc-ing factory from sabotage, a brilliant searchlight operated each night. This light was a great aid for retrieving cows for milking in the early morning darkness, its revolving beam lighting up the pasture field like full daylight. Dad was often accompanied by Bob Flood, whose favourite pastime was singing. Bob's repertoire was varied. Hymns, popular songs of the day, World War One standards ... My father was one of Bob's greatest fans, never forgetting that rich voice drifting across the fields in the pre-dawn light.

Bob was one of B.H. Bull's' best employees and because each herdsman was responsible for his own barn, a healthy competition evolved. Bob was upset when highly prized twin calves born in his barn were transferred into the main barn where they'd receive that "extra touch" of loving care that Bob supposedly couldn't provide. Both calves died.

The large number of cattle in Bull's' operation meant of course an equally large volume of milk to be shipped each day. All milk was sent to Silverwood's Dairies on Dupont Street in downtown Toronto. This job was handled by the Moore's, a father-and-son trucking operation under contract to Bull's. They also handled all the livestock hauling.

Versatility was their game as they also moved Mom and Dad's belongings from Eugenia Falls to Brampton. Everything Mom had set out had been packed in the truck when Mr. Moore noticed another box. "What about that one?" Dad looked at the box. "Evelyn must be planning on sending that one by car." "We've plenty of room," continued Moore. "Well then," agreed my father, "I guess we might as well throw it in." It turned out to be all of Mother's crystal. When the box was opened at Brampton, it contained nothing but shards of broken glass.

As the war dragged on, rationing increased, now encompassing tea, coffee, butter, meat and ammunition. "Ration books" were the word of the day. Issued by the federal government for every man, woman and child, they were valid for several months and you went nowhere without them. Theoretically you weren't supposed to trade but who was to know, so trading went on regularly. After all, what good were tea and coffee coupons to young children? Trading for extra milk or meat made more sense. Bacon was severely rationed so a new breakfast companion was discovered ... fried bologna.

Sugar was still at the top of the list as well as associated products like jams and jellies. If you were a loyal customer, often your local grocer would drop a little something extra in your bag while packing, providing he had it as there was much scarcity. You paid for it of course, but the absence of a coupon was overlooked. One had to be careful though, as the War Prices Trade Board watched closely and fines were stiff.

Rubber was another scarce commodity of the war years, brought on by the numerous Japanese conquests in the rubber producing regions of the Far East. Thus, tires were strictly rationed. With the tight gasoline restrictions, the average person couldn't travel any distance anyway. Every vehicle was required to display a gas rationing sticker. Different letters signified different needs. An "A" was the lowest, issued for most "regular" driving. Taxis, salesmen, couriers, truckers etc. ... were allowed increased amounts in varying degrees depending on their needs.

Although B. H. Bull's operated their farm on a grand scale with a large workforce, they provided no manual labour themselves. Their family descended directly from the aristocratic society of England, where life consisted of parties, expensive food, booze and beautiful women. Barn tours were conducted frequently, the brothers complete in suits, caps and canes, demonstrating to their lady friends attired in satin gowns the workings of their enterprise. It mattered little that most of these ladies could scarcely recognize a cow. Any activity that might raise dust, such as sweeping floors, feeding hay or spreading straw was strictly forbidden during these tours. A cane in the air was the signal for the men to stop work and could only resume when the entourage had cleared the building.

Bull's even had the convenience of their own tavern near the farm where friends and employees alike were welcome for refreshment. The family enjoyed their lives to the hilt and their three fine homes on the edge of Brampton informed all of their success ... although conditions hadn't always been so rosy. At the close of the Depression their enterprise was near bankruptcy. During that period, workers literally ran to the bank when receiving their cheques as there was seldom enough for everyone. With the war came higher commodity prices, and along with improved management, the enterprise was debt-free by war's end.

However by his time, a change was in the wind. Dad had been reading the "want ads" and a prospect that caught his eye originated from a farmer from Bond Head, a place Dad had to refer to a map to find. A herdsman was needed for a moderately sized dairy operation, offering $100 a month plus a free house. So the next afternoon during his break, Dad headed off for Bond Head, a crossroads village on Highway 27, forty miles northeast of Brampton.

From the proprietor of the corner grocery store, Dad was given directions to C. J. Cerswell at Bond Haven Farms. Down the side road just west of the village, a laneway branched off to the left at the base of a steep incline. Nestled into the side of a series of snow-covered hills sat a barn and a red brick house. A striking brunette answered his knock, and establishing the woman as Mrs. Cerswell, Dad relayed his intentions. No, they hadn't hired anyone yet, he was informed. "It's very hard to find help these days."

Mrs. Cerswell noted the name and promised to pass it on to her husband. "If you want to look around the barn, go ahead." Dad didn't want to appear too nosy so just made a quick inspection. Facing each other in stanchioned stalls stood two rows of obviously well cared for Holsteins. Dad asked a worker a couple of general questions concerning the operation, but the man wasn't very talkative. Later, my father discovered for whatever reason, it was this man's job for which he was applying. I guess that explained the cool reception!

Nothing was heard for a couple weeks, when one afternoon a Buick pulled up at my parents' home. A man in his early thirties introduced himself as Charlie Cerswell. The job requirements, some history on the pedigreed Holstein herd Charlie was building and my father's experience with cattle were discussed at length.

Before Charlie showed up, Dad had mentioned the possibility of the new job to Bob Flood. Bob, who'd remained a true friend, stated that somehow if it wasn't to his liking, he could have his old job back anytime. "As long as I'm here, you have a job waiting." With that assurance, my parents now with two young children joined Bond Haven Farms, an association that would eventually span a decade and provide memories for a lifetime.

Portal to the Promised Land

Nestled at the base of a steep incline on No. 27 highway between the Simcoe County towns of Cookstown and Schomberg rests the village of Bond Head. One mile west of this village is a property owned by the Cerswell family since the 1830s. Today it's known as *Club Bond Head*, a 200-acre, eighteen-hole golf resort. Until recently, these rolling hills were the domain of one of the most respected and well-known Holstein herds in Canada ... *Bond Haven Farms*.

Although progress and modern philosophies may have changed the face of the land, as for the heart of the Cerswell property ... it's as if time has simply been too weary to continue. A tree-lined laneway leads to a fine brick house, still owned and occupied by the Cerswell family. A short distance west of the house, although its paint has faded over the years, a dairy barn stands as solidly as when built 150 years ago. Perched high on a hill at the extreme northern end of the long circular driveway sits a tiny white-framed wooden house that hasn't changed much in appearance since my parents and their two children moved into it in April 1943.

The previous October had seen an addition to our family. Vivien, now eighteen months, had a brother ... William ... or "Billy" as he would be known for years. Charlie and Phyllis Cerswell had two daughters, Joan and Anne, whose ages corresponded to Billy and Vivien. Throughout the next decade, this quartet would become almost inseparable.

In certain ways the Bond Haven set-up was similar to the B.H. Bull's dairy operation at Brampton where Dad had been employed the previous two years. Three times a day milking, but here the last shift began at nine instead of seven PM. However, personnel working the late stint got a reprieve from the four AM shift. An improvement in "days off" was also recognized. As herdsman, Dad now received every third weekend free.

Dad soon learned he'd be much more in tune with the actual daily operation. Shortly he could recite from memory the pedigree of any cow in the stable. There was always plenty of practice as owners and managers of other Holstein herds paid frequent visits, often by the busload.

Although Charlie Cerswell hadn't been long in the dairy business, he was already gaining notoriety in Holstein circles. At their first meeting, Charlie with some pride had told my father he had recently purchased a half interest in "Marksman." Dad hadn't a clue to what Charlie was referring, but later learned Marksman was a bull calf ... but not just any bull calf. Charlie had seen potential in this highly pedigreed calf and paid the unheard of price of $650 for a fifty percent share. His partner was another rising Holstein enterprise, Glenafton Farms at Alliston. That bull calf helped put both in the top category of Holstein herds in Canada.

After finishing high school, Charlie Cerswell attended Guelph Agriculture College but before he could graduate his father died suddenly, forcing him to return to take over the farm. He'd been at Guelph long enough however, to study the potential of pedigreed farming, whereby utilizing selected characteristics, one could supposedly build a premium quality herd.

It was during Dad's first year at Bond Haven that he received his draft notice, demanding his appearance at the Draft Review Board in Barrie. Charlie accompanied his new herdsman, vouching he was an integral part of his operation. In the 1940s, agriculture packed considerable clout, and anyone directly involved in food production was considered essential and exempt from military duty.

Rationing increased as the years passed. Rubber especially was a scarce commodity. Dad needed two new tires for his recently purchased '37 Dodge, but only vehicles for "essential farm service" qualified, so Charlie came up with the idea the old Dodge was needed to transport bovine semen between Bond Haven and Glenafton Farms at Alliston, some ten miles away. Charlie enjoyed that scenario … imagining some secretary at Toronto's W.P.T.B. office trying to explain and justify the request to her superior.

The big news from the warfront was of course June 6, 1944 … D-Day. Plenty had been learned from the Dieppe debacle two years earlier. More than 2,000 men had been killed or wounded and as many taken prisoner on that particular August day. This time, although still suffering high casualties, the Allied forces after landing in Normandy made steady progress inland during the next several months through France, Luxembourg, Netherlands and finally Germany, joining up with tens of thousands of soldiers who'd been making their way up the Italian peninsula. The German Empire, which at its height stretched from Norway to Africa and from the Atlantic coast to western Russia just two years earlier ... was now reduced to simply Germany.

By April 1945, with bombs descending on Berlin from above and armies advancing from east and west, Adolf Hitler took his own life. On May 7, Germany signed an unconditional surrender. Hitler's Third Reich, to last "one thousand years" in his words ... had lasted but twelve.

The next day, May 8, was celebrated as V-E Day (victory in Europe) in cities and towns throughout the British Empire. On Hickson Street in Toronto, my grandfather blew out the candles on his cake, noting no better way to celebrate his sixtieth birthday.

Down in the United States, the celebration was somewhat subdued. President Roosevelt, who'd led the country since 1932, had passed away the previous month, plus there was one gigantic problem unresolved ... the Empire of Japan; tens of thousands of lives had already been lost trying to regain control of the dozens of Pacific islands Japan had captured earlier in the war.

By the spring of 1945, plans for an invasion of the Japanese mainland were halted, while Roosevelt's successor Harry Truman, Britain's Prime Minister Winston Churchill and Russian Premier Josef Stalin deliberated on other means to end the war. The estimation figured another year of fighting and a million more lives lost. The U.S. had the means ... but should they use it? There was a sizable faction who wanted nothing better than to "get even" for Pearl Harbour. On July 26, 1945, an ultimatum for total surrender sent to Tokyo went unanswered. Eleven days later, warfare changed forever.

In the early hours of August 6, 1945, a lone bomber appeared on the radar screens entering Japanese airspace. No one paid much attention ... just one plane ... probably reconnaissance. At eight o'clock sharp over the city of Hiroshima from an altitude of six miles, a single bomb was released. Just above the downtown area, it exploded. The river that crosses the downtown area of the city literally boiled. Granite buildings within a thousand-yard radius melted. Pedestrians in the target area simply evaporated. Seventy-eight thousand Japanese civilians died instantly. Horrible burns claimed thousands more in the days that followed. For two more generations at least, radiation exposure would continue to seek out victims ... The world had just witnessed the destruction of the first atomic bomb.

A repeat performance was staged over Nagasaki three days later with another 40,000 meeting instant annihilation. Finally on August 14, a message was received from Tokyo accepting the terms of surrender ... For the time being at least, the world knew peace.

... In the aftermath of history's costliest war, it was difficult to know where to begin. One element of the devastating effects this war had inflicted would be the people themselves. As early as 1944, it was realized once hostilities ceased, a tremendous number of displaced people would be on the move following the destruction of their homelands. Newspapers and magazines periodically circulated questionnaires on the subject. What immigration restrictions if any, would you want to see imposed? Apart from British, what races would you welcome?

Canada held a dismal record in acceptance of immigrants. When Austrian Jews were fleeing their homeland to escape Nazi persecution in the late 1930s, Canada steadfastly refused to make any allowance on their immigration policy.

But then "Jew haters" weren't confined to Canada's capital of Ottawa. Every city and town had its Jewish backlash. The reasons weren't always clear, but Toronto especially seemed ill at ease and jealous of Jewish competition. My grandfather, Will Carruthers, never hid his dislike. "We should just send them out into the lake in a boat with a zipper on the bottom."

It's always disconcerting ... actually shocking ... to stumble upon such an unpalatable remark, particularly when it pertains to your own family. Such statements recall a phrase I read or heard somewhere ... "the search for truth is not for the faint-hearted" ... I guess my grandfather's prejudices were just a tiny part of a condition that has swelled to encompass a seemingly worldwide range of race, colour and religious intolerance.

As the years passed, Canada gradually relaxed its immigration barriers ... first with the Dutch. Special bonds seemed attached to the people of the Netherlands. Canadians had been the chief liberators of Holland and acted quickly when a request from that country asked for the admission of 15,000 members of farm families whose property had been flooded and bombed.

Charlie Cerswell felt this was a program in which he could help, and at the same time aid his chronic labour shortage, so he offered to sponsor a Dutch couple. Accommodation was a factor, so "no children" was specified on the immigration form. Months passed while government bureaucracy ran its course, but finally in May 1948 he received a notice of acceptance.

All he had the day he went to Union Station in Toronto was a picture and their names, Hendrick and Pietje Heimstra. A majority of the passengers were European immigrants, easily revealed by their bewildered expressions. Somehow, Charlie put two faces in the crowd with the photograph and introduced himself. Conversation was non-existent on the return trip as the Heimstras neither spoke nor understood a word of English. The Cerswell garage had to suffice as their first home in Canada, but uncontrolled tears gave silent expression in any language that the garage would do fine.

They'd come from a part of the world where just the slightest indifference to Nazi occupation spelt instant death. Later "Henk," as he became known, would tell how he was forced to hide for hours at a time in grain and hay stooks on his family's farm, while German military police conducting frequent searches for their labour camps probed with pitchforks from without. Not much wonder the Cerswell garage looked good!

By the time autumn arrived, the Heimstras were able to move into Mom and Dad's house, as they had a brand new one directly across the driveway from the barn. Both my parents and Charlie and Phyllis Cerswell tried their best to make the Heimstras feel at home. Phyllis and my Mom spent countless hours aiding Pietje with her English, while Dad did the same for Henk. If at times Henk seemed especially confused, Dad's solution was to talk louder, an approach Henk found amusing. Where hollering failed, pantomime generally succeeded. One day by using this universal language, Henk was sent for a shovel and proudly returned with a wheelbarrow.

When learning a new language there's always the possibility of picking up a few words or phrases not found in the English dictionary. Like the Verbeeks ... another Dutch family that Charlie sponsored. Mrs. Verbeek, readying the ground for her first garden in this new land, was in need of some of nature's fertilizer. Her husband had forgotten the request the last time so making sure it didn't happen again, she sent her five-year-old daughter to the barn where her father was working. "Papa", she hollered. "Mama says don't forget to bring a pail of shit when you come for dinner!"

When my parents moved into their first house at Cerswells, it had been a step backwards compared to the Brampton house, with no bathroom or running water. The new "herdsman's" house had both features but still no telephone. As before, all phone calls were sent or received at Charlie's house, as was the mail.

As with the first house, Mom was expected to keep two boarders, as housing was always in short supply. She received five dollars per week per man, paid by Charlie. Charlie offered an additional fifteen cents a day for laundry service, supposedly to help defray hydro costs. He recouped some of that as my parents had an electric "hotplate" for which Charlie charged an extra dollar a month. Items like the $1.00 a month hydro charge made Charlie appear kind of cheap, yet in other instances he was the opposite, for instance the $500 bonus he gave Mom and Dad the previous Christmas.

With the location of this new house, Dad was handy to the barn ... very handy. Anytime someone came to visit the Bond Haven herd, even if it was his day off, Dad felt inclined to show the guests around, explain the operation, detail the pedigrees and so on. He became quite an expert at showing off the headliners and bypassing the disappointments, talking of what he knew best and making up the rest. He obviously formed a good impression, for more than a few visitors were heard to remark over the years how they never met a man who took such an interest in another's man's cattle as Harold Turner.

While Charlie kept a close watch on all facets of his herd, he had plenty else to look after. Unlike B.H. Bull's, which operated with both inside and outside managers, Charlie handled all aspects. He coordinated haying, harvesting and planting, oversaw crop and pasture rotation, building and renovation, plus a large amount of the repair work on machinery. More often than not, it was Charlie sprawled beneath a broken-down machine while the rest of the crew would be leaning various parts of their anatomy against a wheel or some other convenient resting place until the fix was completed. Add to the above all the planning and decisions involved to keep his herd in the top echelon of the Holstein world, it's easy to see Charlie Cerswell definitely had his finger on the pulse of what made Bond Haven tick.

The arrival of the Heimstra family in 1948 was only the first of scores of immigrants Charlie Cerswell would welcome in the years ahead. From nearly every European country they'd eventually come, most with nothing more than their survival skills and a strong work ethic. All were searching for that new beginning, a fresh start ... that second chance to enjoy unrestricted freedom in this great new environment of opportunity. For countless families, Bond Haven's welcoming sign and open door would prove to be that opportunity.

RIDING THE CREST

As 1946 was dwindling down to its last dreary days, the Turner family was strengthened by an additional member ... Richard. A couple days before Christmas, Dad had taken Vivien and Billy to Toronto to be babysat at their grandparents until after the delivery. This arrangement hadn't sat particularly well with Billy, who was afraid he'd be missed by Santa Claus. How was Santa supposed to know he was at 8 Hickson? Well ... Santa's a smart guy, presents were delivered, the baby was delivered and the world moved on.

Charlie and Phyllis Cerswell had their third child that year as well, a daughter Linda, thus keeping alive the tradition of matching each other in the population race.

"Old timers" still talk today of the winter of 1947 as one remembered for its unrelenting snowstorms. This was certainly true in Tecumseth Township. In late February a new series of storms developed and by early March, drifts were twelve to fifteen feet high on the 7th line overlooking Bond Head. Taxed to the extreme, plows were losing ground by the hour, snow filling in as fast as it could be burrowed out. When the township snow plow broke it was game over.

In no time, the "tunnels" levelled in and vehicular traffic barely moving as it was … ceased completely.

The most serious and pressing problem for Bond Haven Farms of course was the delivery of milk. Charlie still had a team of horses he utilized for removing manure from the barnyard during winter, so cans of milk on a horse-drawn sleigh became the rule of transportation for the next three weeks, as continuous blizzards assaulted the area. The team and sleigh also became a lifeline for groceries, stove oil, mail, veterinary supplies, medicine or anything else that employees and their families might need.

When it seemed civilization as they knew it would never be seen again, the storms finally blew themselves out and the highways were opened. The 7th line was one of the last, but with help from a bulldozer and neighbouring township plows, it was reopened as well.

Charlie Cerswell's notoriety in the Holstein world maintained its climb throughout the last half of the 1940s. Breeders of other Holstein herds continued to make Bond Haven a regular stop. From all over the north and north-east states, the Midwest, Québec and the Maritimes they journeyed. Likewise, Dad and Charlie travelled to Chicago and Vermont to visit other fine herds and dined with Prince Edward Island Premier Walter Jones, a cattle breeder himself.

Even the regular "twilight" meetings where Holstein personnel got together were grandiose affairs when hosted by Bond Haven, often hiring a "live" band for the occasion.

"Non-Holstein" people were taking note of Bond Haven as well. A lady in Bond Head opened a retirement home and titled the building "Bond Haven Nursing Home." Charlie took a lot of kidding over that one. "Is that where you send your old cows, Charlie?" Although he'd say little, it was plain Charlie didn't think much of the idea. Nowadays, someone would no doubt sue for title infringement or something.

For the first few years Dad was at Bond Haven, the main "working" truck for hauling feed and cattle was a 1937 Chevrolet. It had seen better days, but with the war restrictions new vehicles were impossible and good used trucks scarce. The old Chevy had several shortcomings, the most serious being braking deficiencies. More than once, Dad had pushed the pedal only to feel it go to the floor. It was therefore a special day in the spring of 1947 when the new Chevrolet ordered so long ago arrived in Charlie's yard.

A big event each November which pushed the truck, new or old, into action was the Royal Winter Fair in Toronto. Whatever your farm might produce, "the Royal" was the place to showcase it. Horses, cattle, swine, sheep, poultry, grain crops, forage crops, plus a bewildering assortment of garden vegetables all competed for attention.

Charlie always transported a couple loads of his finest Holsteins and had received his share of awards as well. "Marksman" had captured the All-Canadian and World Champion bull three years out of the last four and another Bond Haven sire, "Rowsdale Sovereign," had taken home the Junior Champion ribbon.

Dad performed a large portion of the actual showing, except when it came to Rowsdale. Due to the bull's size and potential for disaster, Charlie shared duties with his herdsman. But there was the time Charlie was recovering from a car accident and Dad ran the show alone. The bull wasn't happy about conditions that particular day and was letting everyone know by continuous bellowing and roaring. The official in charge of the judging was terrified the bull was going to go berserk, probably having visions of the 2500-pound animal jumping into the stands, so demanded Dad get him away from the crowd and back to the stable ... quickly.

Dad liked the change of scenery looking after the cattle at the Royal even if it was the same routine. They had to be fed, milked and cleaned just as home ... as far as the cleaning department even more. Someone had to be on duty twenty-four hours a day so when a cow pooped the result was removed immediately. Hours were spent washing, rinsing, clipping and brushing. No bunkhouse existed for the workers; your bed was a bale of hay or straw in the alleyway in front of the cows. All hay and grain was hauled from home as well as straw for bedding. Charlie preferred wheat straw, as its bright colour enhanced the appearance of the cows in his opinion.

All sorts of little tricks were employed to make your particular animal just a little more attractive than its competitor. For instance milking; so your best cow's udder is a trifle slack? Simply don't milk her completely. You had to be careful not to leave too much, causing the teats to leak, thus tipping off the judge. Clipping was another area one could earn extra points. By deftly operating the clippers, low and high spots on an animal's framework could be governed accordingly. These actions weren't restricted to Bond Haven of course as it was an industry-wide trade.

In one instance, a herdsman got the bright idea to place a hose down a cow's throat in an effort to pump a little extra water into her stomach, thinking the cow a trifle gaunt for proper showing. The owner raised hell at such a suggestion to such a valuable animal as he'd been offered $6000 for her the previous day. The herdsman disregarded the warning and the hose instead of going into the stomach went to the lung and the cow drowned. Legend has it, the owner was charged with manslaughter when in an act of revenge he implemented the same method on his "ex-employee" with the same result.

Shadiness wasn't confined to the Royal. Registering newborn calves sometimes mandated a slight "alteration." According to guidelines set forth by the Holstein-Friesian Association, all calves in order to qualify for registration had to have a full white marking where each leg contacted the hoof. It didn't matter if it was half an inch, as long as it circled the leg completely. The tail likewise had guidelines, requiring a minimum of six inches of white at the tip.

A variety of methods were tried to test this ruling. One enterprising dairyman tied a piece of white gauze to the tail and in the photograph it looked like the real thing. Except, whatever x-ray technology the association used at the time spotted the "fake tail."

Charlie encountered a similar situation and opted for a chemical dye to transform the tail. It passed inspection without a hint of trouble ... except a couple weeks later the calf's tail dropped off! To explain the missing tail, Charlie invented a story about another calf chewing it off. Charlie was never at a loss for spinning a good yarn. Unfortunately he often forgot who he'd told. Next time he recounted the story ... the calf had gotten its tail caught in the latching mechanism of a gate. It was such incidents that prompted an employee to remark ... "Charlie has too poor a memory to be a good liar."

Although it amassed just two lines in the January 1949 births section of the local newspaper, on a dreary cold Friday morning complete with freezing rain, a fourth child was born in Newmarket hospital to Harold and Evelyn Turner. That baby boy was me.

Richard, just a couple weeks past his second birthday, matured quickly that week. Richard had long curly blond hair which Mom adored, but since she was away Dad decided it was time he became a "boy." A trip to the barber's and goodbye to the curls; he definitely looked different, so much so when Mom came home from the hospital and set eyes upon him she burst into tears. A week's dishes piled high in the sink, a stack of dirty laundry and toys scattered everywhere didn't help the mood either.

By the way ... not to be outdone, the Cerswell's fourth child, a son Jimmy, arrived that summer.

Bond Haven of course was noted for its cattle but was also home to one horse ... Nancy. During winter Nancy boarded next door in one of Charlie's secondary barns, but in fair weather she had the run of the Bond Haven orchard. This proved to be her undoing as she died one summer from an over-indulgence of unripe apples.

The horse actually belonged to Phyllis Cerswell. On warm evenings she'd saddle up and often disappear for an hour or two. On still nights one could hear the hoof beats of the chestnut mare a concession away. Riding was one activity where Phyllis could distance herself from the sometimes tiresome role of playing "Mrs. Charlie Cerswell." Phyllis was ten years younger than Charlie and her social life wasn't exactly what she wished. She much would have preferred a dance or house party compared to the endless Holstein banquets she was compelled to attend. However, if she was expected to attend, Phyllis made the most of it, dressed so no one would forget she was there. The men certainly noticed ... as did their wives.

Because Charlie did spend a great deal of time associated with "cattle events", Phyllis would often visit Mom or ask her to come down, especially if Dad was working or away. "I'll keep you company," was her excuse. Mom would've preferred to spend many of these evenings reading, a pastime that now seemed all too infrequent. Phyllis however had taken Mom into her confidence from the beginning so Mom never turned her down when she needed someone to talk to.

In May 1951, once again Mom and Dad's wish for another daughter and Vivien's for a baby sister failed when Brian joined the family. This time Charlie and Phyllis didn't respond to the challenge and conceded the title to my parents ... Mom vowed this would be her last as well, concluding five kids in ten years more than sufficient.

Charlie Cerswell's place in the Holstein world would continue to soar during the next decade and beyond. In 1961, Bond Haven's pride and joy of the milking herd, "Signet Sally" captured both a "Senior Champion" and "All Canadian" title at the Toronto Royal Winter Fair. And the celebration wouldn't be confined to 1961 as the special cow would win the same honour the following two years! At the close of the twentieth century that record still stood.

Charlie Cerswell was one of a few selected cattle breeders to be sent by the Canadian government on a trade mission to Japan to promote Canadian Holsteins during the 1960s. He was also instrumental during that same era in exporting Holsteins to South America, Cuba and Europe.

The shy young man from the tiny crossroads community of Bond Head, Ontario, had proven a lot of people wrong as to his vision as a renowned cattle breeder, for instance the Ontario Agricultural College professor, who after Charlie finished poorly in his first semester advised he quit, "because you'll never amount to anything anyway."

ACRES OF MEMORIES

Ever since my father's "business career" folded during the Great Depression and he'd returned to what he knew best ... agriculture ... it had been his wish to have a farm of his own. Recurring spells of arthritis, induced by years of confinement in poorly ventilated barns, had gradually taken its effect. Both B.H. Bull's and Cerswell's dairy operations were modern for their time, but humidity reduction through proper ventilation was still a few years away. Some days it was a challenge for Dad to merely get out of bed, often beginning by first rolling out onto the floor then painfully making his way to his feet. Medical wisdom at the time recommended that a more varied atmosphere would go a long way in addressing the situation.

Another reason for change was the way our family was growing. By the fall of 1952, Vivien was eleven, Billy ten, Richard six, I was four and even "baby" Brian was no longer that. Dad, nearing that magical age of forty, realized it was now or never. A psychological factor was at play also ... he missed that "feel of the soil" syndrome so important to one who has grown up with the land. Charlie understood all his herdsman's reasons for change and desire for independence, but nevertheless tried to persuade him otherwise, promising higher wages, more days off, fewer weekends, longer holidays ... whatever it might take.

But my parents had made their decision and following several Sunday afternoon drives that autumn, located a sixty-five-acre plot that seemed to fit both their financial and spiritual needs in the neighbouring township of West Gwillimbury, about four miles from Bond Haven. They'd saved enough for a $1500 down payment and the new proprietor would handle a mortgage for the $9000 balance with occupancy in the spring. Many hours would be spent that upcoming winter planning our future as landowners ... but more than a few would be spent looking back.

So many memories ... so many friendships begun; some of the more memorable would include the Heimstras who became friends the day they arrived from Holland and would continue so for another fifty years.

Another lasting friendship whose seeds were sown at Bond Haven was Linton Fraser. He boarded with Mom and Dad and his personality made him a favourite. As well as helping Henk Heimstra with his English, Lint was a great aid to my brother Richard, who proved slow when it came to talking. Richard was three before he said anything that made sense. A couple of his first phrases thanks to Lint were "Mickey Mouse" and "Ford tractor."

There was Frank Foran ... Frank was an incessant talker and Dad always found it difficult to get anything done when around him. He'd lean on his manure fork talking about anything and everything. For some reason Frank left his wife the second night of their honeymoon. The details weren't clear, but a few of his friends apparently tracked him down and "persuaded" him to return.

Clarence Webb was Bond Haven's unofficial mechanic and outside manager. Manure hauling was a large part of Clarence's vocation. When he first arrived at Bond Haven, manure was hauled by horses but following the war Charlie purchased a four-wheel-drive surplus army truck. Clarence was a good worker but reckless. Everything had to progress at full speed. So frequent were the repairs during one period, Charlie warned Clarence from that point onward, all repair costs due to carelessness would be shared equally. It wasn't long after, Clarence rolled the army truck over in the manure pile. Fortunately for him ... and his wallet ... the landing was soft and little harm was done.

Harold Benson ... He volunteered to help fashion quilting frames for Mom one day. The one-inch by four-inch planks needed holes drilled every four inches throughout their length and Harold had just the drill for the job. In no time he had all the holes drilled, including several through Mom's linoleum floor.

Harold had got married at Eugenia in Grey County and the newlyweds drove all the way to Bond Head, a distance of fifty miles, with the streamers and tin cans still dangling from the bumper of their old Plymouth. They spent their wedding night at Mom and Dad's and although it was very late in the evening when they arrived, Marie, his new wife, was still decked out in her wedding dress, complete with white gloves and big floppy hat. It was all Mom and Dad could do to contain their laughter when she also wore it to breakfast the next morning. She'd seemingly waited most of her life for her wedding day and was taking full advantage of it.

Mom took Marie shopping on one occasion and wound up in Eaton's Annex, the bargain centre of all bargain centres in Toronto at the time. Marie began trying on aprons as though they were evening gowns. "Do you think this becomes me?" Mom just wanted to die.

There was a Dutch lad, John Roos, who drove a Prefect ... a little English car. It was a tough car. His girlfriend upset it and since she had no licence and he no insurance, fixing it was out of the question. With the help of a couple of friends the car was rolled back onto its wheels. Except for a dent in the roof necessitating that John scrunch his head down a bit, the car was fine.

Ted Edmunds had a job with the British government in Malaysia during the war and when it ended, so did the job. Both Ted and his wife had enjoyed a high life complete with servants, therefore were severely out of place in this farming atmosphere. Whereas other wives would be wearing cotton dresses, Mrs. Edmunds could be seen anytime throughout the day attired in satin gown and high heels, no doubt trying to hang onto a scrap of the "old life." Things took a turn for the better in the early 1950s when Ted was hired on with Avro Aeronautics, the former Victory Aircraft Company at Malton.

I myself have only the briefest recollections of Bond Haven, but I do recall delivering the day-old *Barrie Examiner* to the Edmunds' house on occasion. They lived in the house Mom and Dad first occupied when they came to Bond Haven. For delivering the newspaper, Mrs. Edmunds often gave me an oatmeal cookie.

Another Englishman was Bob Smithurst ... he was full of stories of his escapades as a pilot with the Royal Air Force. Bob loved nothing better than a gullible audience. A wife of one of the Bond Haven workers was an especially easy candidate. Bob recounted what a hard-to-handle little devil Princess Margaret (daughter of the British King) was. "Why else would they not allow her out without a guard!"

Wray Smith was recalled with a note of sadness ... he wished to go to Barrie one weekend and asked if he could buy a couple of gallons of gas. This was during the war when fuel was heavily rationed, but Charlie said okay, so Dad helped him fill up the two jugs. Next day on the way home he was involved in a car accident and his wife was killed.

There was Carl Lind from Copenhagen, who had an incredible memory storage for pedigrees, milk production records, etc. Carl was probably one of Bond Haven's best employees, except no one could work with him very long. Carl was one of those people who know absolutely everything and could be seldom convinced otherwise. His somewhat arrogant matter never endeared him to my mother either ... in fact she couldn't stand him! Nevertheless, Carl was one who continued to stay in regular touch through the years.

An interesting couple were the Muys. George the husband, pronounced his name "Mize." His wife preferred "Mews." To everyone at Bond Haven they were "Mr. Mize and Mrs. Mews." Mrs. Muys (Mews) had developed some sort of allergic reaction to Mr. Muys (Mize). Ever since he'd returned from the war she'd break out in a rash when he came near. Divorce was inevitable, but settled amicably. Mr. Muys (Mize) took the youngest child, Mrs. Muys (Mews) the oldest. This suited her fine as she'd often stated she never liked the youngest one anyway.

There was Clarence Gilroy who always had some gadget to sell. He offered to sell my parents a beautiful new top-of-the-line RCA Victor phonograph for $100 but Dad always thought it a little "mysterious" how and where Clarence acquired his merchandise, so passed. At the time he didn't really have the hundred to spare anyway. Clarence then sold it to Charlie and Phyllis.

Andy Davis had the hots for Phyllis Cerswell. Anytime she happened to be out in the garden or sunning herself in the backyard, one would find Andy staring longingly in her direction. He admitted to Dad one day: "Boy, I could really go for her!" With all the time Charlie spent away from home and Phyllis noted for a "wandering eye," I guess it's just as well she wasn't aware of her admirer.

Nat was a Dutch Catholic who refused to work Sundays ... which didn't always sit well with the rest of the crew, who worked the Sabbath on a rotational basis. Nat always wore wooden shoes while he worked and left them in the barn. Each time before leaving the stable he would remove the wooden shoes, then wash his feet and walk to the house barefoot.

Another Dutch lad, John Van de Boer, purchased the 1930 Chevrolet that had seemingly been in the Turner family forever. My grandfather Oliver Turner had bought it back in the mid-1930s and kept it until 1950. Whether he wasn't used to driving or what ... but John upset it the very first day he owned it.

There was Jim and Bill Murray ... a father and son team who worked at Bond Haven. Bill, the son, was a real good hockey player by all accounts. He played for the Beeton team, who were consistently at the top of their league. Nobody disagreed Bill wasn't a good player, but there were a few who complained he spent too much time practising his fancy stick handling and would be better off to "just shoot the damn puck!"

Over the years, Charlie hired help from many European countries. He even considered hiring a German, realizing their country needed as much, if not more help than the Allied countries. Charlie reconsidered when a Dutch employee made it plain "a German just might find himself dead some morning!" For the generation who lived through World War Two occupation and suffered the atrocities that accompanied it … I guess most could never find forgiveness.

The fondest and most lasting memories of Bond Haven however would be reserved for Charlie and Phyllis themselves, who from the beginning treated my parents more like partners than employees. Despite my dad's arriving in that spring of 1943 with little experience of what a herdsman's duties entailed, Charlie had taught, coached, discussed and debated his goals with him and together they'd enjoyed their successes and graciously accepted the defeats. During the ten years he'd worked at Charlie's side, Dad could honestly admit never a cross word had been directed between them. Countless incidents of patience and understanding when he was still "learning the ropes" would earn Charlie high respect in Dad's eyes … a respect that would continue to grow in the years to come; "Without a doubt … the best ten years of my life!"

WORKING AT THE MASSEY

Every summer I plan to attend at least a couple of agricultural "steam shows," and one this past summer in our area featured Massey-Harris. As I ambled up and down the rows of red and yellow paint, I was reminded of the deep connection our family holds with this venerable old company ... way back to 1887, when my great-grandfather Thomas Carruthers, newly arrived immigrant to Toronto from Scotland, secured a job with the Massey Manufacturing Company.

Just eight years earlier in 1879, Massey had moved its entire operation from Newcastle, Ontario, and built a large factory on a six-acre lot bordering Toronto's waterfront. The then state-of-the-art structure had no equal in this city of 150,000, containing such novelties as steam-powered elevators, sprinkler systems and telephones. Beneath one roof was all the floor space needed to manufacture all the machinery of the Massey line. Adjacent to the main building stood smaller units, housing foundries, blacksmith, engine and boiler rooms.

My great-grandfather laboured at a variety of jobs for the first two or three years, but eventually settled in a permanent position in the painting department, spending forty years in all with "The Massey" as he called it. In 1891, Massey merged with lifelong competitor A. Harris and Son of Brantford, Ontario, to become Massey-Harris. This merger made no difference whatsoever to Thomas. For as long as he worked there ... he never referred to his company in any other way but "The Massey."

In 1910, his son William, my grandfather, followed his father's path, and with the exception of a four-year interruption during World War One training recruits for overseas duty, began a forty-year career of his own with the company.

It's doubtful who was most proud that summer Monday morning more than 100 years ago when the two struck off toward the Massey-Harris plant. Start-up time was 7:30, but you had to be there ten minutes earlier or your pay was docked. No problem with these two! Since day one, Tom had set a precedent by arriving at least a half hour in advance. If he wasn't the first through the company's swinging steel gate each morning, he considered himself late. This "always early" characteristic would be paramount through his entire working profession and fanatically maintained by his son through his own career as well.

My grandfather Will Carruthers began his apprenticeship in the cream separator department of Massey-Harris. Their separators were strong sellers and the division a major financial asset for the company. Will worked in every facet of this department from painting to assembly, to set-up, to final inspection.

Early in the 1920s he was offered a job as service advisor for southwestern Ontario. Thus began a decade of "riding the rails," setting up new separators at farms or troubleshooting problems with units already in operation. Generally the culprit in most of these farm service calls would be an imbalance in the multiple discs that were the heart of any cream separator. My grandfather was well known to the numerous dealers that serviced southwestern Ontario, and they were always somewhat amused how "the man from Massey," as he was referred to, could operate on a machine in his signature white shirt, tie and fedora with no sign of grease or grime when the job was completed.

As time passed, Will became quite familiar with the southwestern Ontario towns, dealers and customers. Before each trip, Massey-Harris would furnish him with sufficient funds to cover meals, and lodging if the venture called for overnight accommodation. More often than not, the customer himself would provide at least one meal. Although the telephone took care of local news, distant happenings required outside contact and what better way for a farmer to catch up on the news and exchange gossip than at the dinner table with someone from head office!

In a short span of time, my grandfather had discovered the best eating-places in each area and made a point of being there at mealtime. The area Massey dealers were of considerable help in this regard, pointing out whose wife made mouth-watering rhubarb pie, or the "best biscuits in the township." My grandfather claimed the years spent in this capacity were his favourite. Instead of merely building, supervising and inspecting separators for unknown dealers and farmers, he was now meeting these people and becoming part of their lives, and at the same time enjoying the ever-changing scenes of rural Ontario.

It was tough times for everyone in the 1930s ... Massey lost more than fifteen million Depression dollars between

1931 and 1935 ... but through seniority ... although on reduced hours ... my grandfather managed to keep reasonably busy doing a variety of jobs in various departments of the company. The days of "road trips" to area dealers were a thing of the past though, as belt-tightening curbed such extras as train tickets and expensive lodging.

To help ends meet and ease the burden of the Depression, Will earned a few extra dollars doing "extra-curricular" work for the T. Eaton Company, a task with which he was well acquainted ... balancing cream separator bowls. Since Eaton's were in direct competition with Massey-Harris, the exercise was kept low profile. Once a week, a man from Eaton's would deliver two or three bowls, discreetly wrapped in canvas. My grandfather had a balancing machine (probably Massey-Harris property) in his basement and received $3.00 for each balanced bowl.

During the war years, while a large portion of Massey's plant was producing 40 millimetre anti-aircraft shells, my grandfather was involved in many aspects of the Clipper combine program.

Will Carruthers reached mandatory retirement in 1950. From assembler of cream separators, to inspector, to area trouble-shooter, to service advisor and finally working with binders and combines, my grandfather gained a vast knowledge with Massey-Harris. It had been an enjoyable career. The Massey-Harris picnics each summer were the event of the year for employees and their families, as well as the annual Christmas party when every child of every employee received a gift.

Massey-Harris also had a well-respected baseball team that for many years my grandfather managed. They played several industrial teams throughout the city and a couple of times a year would cross the border to compete with their Massey counterparts in Batavia, New York. Will Carruthers managed the team to two pennants, one in 1922, another in 1924. The company bestowed cuff links and key chain medallions upon him in appreciation of the two championships.

By 1950, Massey-Harris had evolved from a family-run company to an organization now operated by business consortiums, lawyers, accountants and politicians. To my grandfather, it must have seemed a world away from the company he began his career with forty years earlier. Although it was a company steeped in tradition ... it was also a company deep in transition. With Harry Ferguson's exclusive hydraulic system and their almost complete domination of the combine market, the company ... soon to be known as Massey Ferguson, would be the agricultural leader for the next quarter century.

During the first week of September 1950, a letter displaying Massey-Harris letterhead and signed by president James Duncan was delivered to my grandfather's mailbox.

Dear Mr. Carruthers

In accordance with the company's regulations, you have been granted a pension of $83.33 per month, commencing September 1st, 1950; such pension to continue until such time during your lifetime as it may be changed or discontinued by the Board of Directors.

The Board derives great pleasure in recognizing your long association with the company and the faithful service you have given in this way. They hope that in the period of retirement upon which you are to enter you will find enjoyment and rest from your arduous duties which you have heretofore been performing and sincerely trust that you will be spared for a generous period of years in which to have satisfaction and pleasure in the greater time at your leisure.

With good wishes on behalf of the Board for happiness and long life, believe me to remain,

Yours very truly
James S. Duncan

The letter's last sentence proved chillingly foreboding when on a wintry afternoon just a few months later, an urgent call from Toronto informed my mother that her father had suffered a serious heart attack and to prepare for the worst. Critical days passed, then slow improvement. But very slowly; all his life a man of slight stature, Will Carruthers was reduced to mere skin and bones. With the aid of regular medication and a cane, however, he made a remarkable recovery, living a fairly active life until the age of seventy-nine.

When my grandfather died, I was barely into my teens. I wish now I could have sat down with him in his later years, asking about the people and projects he worked with and worked on, while at Massey, especially near the end of his career when associated with the Clipper combine program that I always found fascinating. Like most at that age, any interest in family history was a long way down the road … if at all. That indifference in my case would certainly change as the years passed … but it would be too late … On an August morning in 1964, while the city of

Toronto was preoccupied with the opening day festivities of the 85th Canadian National Exhibition, "the man from Massey" passed from this world.

Great-grandparents Solomon and Martha Turner ... 1870

Jean and Evelyn Carruthers (my mother) ... 1915

Evelyn ... 1920

Harold and Evelyn, wedding day, May 25, 1939

My parents' honeymoon hotel at Huntsville, Ontario

My father and sister Vivien ... Brampton, Ontario, 1942

*Bond Haven Farms. House in foreground is where
my parents lived from 1946 to 1953*

"Billy" showing off one of Bond Haven's fine Holsteins ... 1952

My grandfather William Carruthers at Massey-
Harris plant, Toronto, 1938

ON OUR OWN

On March 17, 1953, Billy Turner sat on the steps of the schoolhouse just east of the village of Beeton, his eyes focused toward the road. This was Ritchie Canning's farm auction sale today ... the farm that would be legally ours in another few days, and my brother was filled with anticipation.

Twelve-thirty was the appointed pickup time and at 12:45 he was still sitting there. When the school bell sounded fifteen minutes later, his teacher inquired if he was indeed sure his father was coming. Billy was experiencing a few twinges of doubt himself but answered optimistically, "He'll be here any minute." Finally when he'd lost nearly all hope, the Pontiac rolled into view.

It was an unusually warm day for the middle of March. Rivulets of water rushed anywhere there was sufficient grade to carry them as the late winter sun fought to dismiss the remnants of the season past. Countless rubber boots had transformed the sale site slush into thick gooey mud ... mud we'd come to know well in the seasons ahead.

Being we'd never farmed on our own meant buying everything from machinery to tools. Because finances were limited, it was our father's intention at least at the outset to farm "the old way" with horses. He even purchased a complete set of harness. This despite the fact that the progressive people at Department of Agriculture had been certain the end of the war would also signal the end of the draft horse. However Dad wasn't so sure. There were plenty of jobs even on a 1950s farm where a team of horses could be more valuable than a tractor. Hauling manure, picking stones and loading hay all could be better served by a horse in his opinion. "Oats are cheaper than gasoline."

However by sale day, the "horse" idea had been relegated to the back burner, with Dad at least considering a tractor. Ritchie Canning had a nice McCormick W-4 but Dad thought the $1200 price tag a little high for a used tractor. Canning's hay equipment all fell into the relic category and sold accordingly, so Dad bought the mower, dump rake and hay loader. By this time balers had doomed the hay loader to near extinction so we got it for next to nothing. With any of these implements, either animal or mechanical horsepower would suffice.

Ritchie Canning had purchased his farm in 1936. Ten years later, plans for a new multi-lane highway joining Toronto and Barrie were proposed, the resultant right-of-way slicing the farm in two. This severance generated two properties. Ours was the eastern half with the newly named "400" serving as the western boundary.

At the entranceway to our farm in 1953, one might have made the following observations. Two six-foot-high cement and stone pillars stood vigil either side of the gateway. (My seven-year-old brother Richard informed us they were monuments and Indians were buried beneath.)

A couple hundred feet up a slight grade, the laneway dropped away sharply to reveal a yellow brick house, two barns, a couple of small outbuildings, a windmill, a wooden silo and orchard. On the eastern perimeter a mixture of wild trees and plant growth abounded along a combination rail and wire fence that stretched the length of the property. The western side as stated was completely contained by Highway 400.

Charlie Cerswell, Dad's former employer, gave us a huge boost with his "lend a cow" program. We received ten cows free of charge. Charlie got the first heifer calf, we got any subsequent heifers, plus any bull calves. In the interim we received the milk.

The 25th of March witnessed Charlie's Chevrolet "Maple Leaf" truck backed up to the doorway, while inside the truck our modest furnishings awaited transfer to their new home. Dad's brother Eldon donated his pickup the entire week for the movement of smaller items, taking our Pontiac in exchange. Sometime that week the pickup's entire spare wheel and tire assembly disappeared into a ditch somewhere never to be recovered. I don't know if Dad ever compensated Eldon for that or not. With all the help available, which included Dad's father, brother-in-law, uncle and cousins, moving went relatively smoothly. The most challenging task was lifting the huge kitchen stove in and out of the truck. Those old cast iron ranges didn't move anywhere fast.

I was only four years old, but what I remember most about moving day was running up and down the two sets of stairs of our new house with my brother Richard. One stairway exited from the kitchen, the other, complete with beautiful wooden bannister, ascended from the hallway off the dining room. A large kitchen, dining room, living room and bedroom occupied the lower level, while four bedrooms, including a double-sized room directly above the kitchen, filled the upper floor. I also remember running past this wooden box attached to the kitchen wall just as it sounded its bells. Never having a telephone in our former house, I remember being startled by the ringing. Our ... I long ... 4 short ... number, in conjunction with the rest of the party line, meant we'd be hearing those bells more than enough as time went on.

Our barn wasn't ready to accept cattle at the outset, compelling Dad and Billy to spend many hours of clean-up and repair to the stable before Charlie brought the cows over a week or so later. Dad purchased a DeLaval milk cooler, installing the machine in the implement shed as we hadn't an "official" milk house. To transport the cans from the barn to the milk house, a local machinist was commissioned to build a "milk cart." Pushed by hand on two large steel wheels, the combination steel and wooden cart had capacity for three eight-gallon cans.

Milking machines also from the DeLaval company were purchased. It seemed to cost so much to just get off the ground, with machinery requiring the biggest chunk of capital. Dad had now convinced himself that a new tractor was the way to go. There were a multitude of choices in 1953 including McCormick, John Deere, Case, Allis-Chalmers, Massey-Harris, Fordson, Minneapolis-Moline, Ford, Ferguson, Oliver and Cockshutt. Duncan McArthur, the Allis-Chalmers dealer in Bond Head, won the sale ... a brand new CA model, $1400 plus $7.00 more for a foam-filled seat. Dad also complemented the tractor with a two-furrow plow and cultivator.

The day the tractor and implements arrived was a memorable one. Everyone in the family had to have a ride on the shiny new orange machine. My Aunt Alma was visiting from Toronto that weekend and we even persuaded her to mount the seat for one of the many photos we snapped that special day.

A sidebar to the new tractor story occurred later that summer when Dad was driving through Bond Head with Grandpa Carruthers in the passenger seat. As they passed the corner on which the small dealership sat, Grandpa Will said. "I used to know a Dunc McArthur. He was a pitcher on the Massey-Harris baseball team … the team we won two championships back in the 1920s." It turned out to be the same "Dunc" McArthur alright. Next day Dad took his father-in-law over to Bond Head and he and Duncan spent a couple of hours reminiscing about their teammates and team and just old times in general. Small world!

Second only to the excitement caused by our new tractor was the day our herd finally arrived and filed into the stable for the first milking. To me they looked as fine as anything that graced the pages of *Hoard's Dairyman* or *Holstein Journal*. There was Abbey, Beauty, Belle, Betty, Calamity, Diana Segus, Dixie, Dunbarton, Juliette, Mina, Sovereign Sally and Sylvia Chief … no mundane bovine names like Spot, Bossy or Blossom in this lot!

Our first milk cheque wasn't received until May 20, so naturally it was an exciting day when it arrived in the mailbox. Just having our own mailbox was a major accomplishment. Grandpa Carruthers painted HAROLD TURNER in big block letters on both sides of the metal box and there wasn't a doubt in our minds that it was the best looking mailbox on the 9th line.

An item that arrived in the mail that spring with Dad's name printed boldly on the envelope stated that on May 23, 1953, Harold Turner of Bradford Ont. had been admitted membership in the Holstein-Friesian Association of Canada.

Another certificate from the HFA that spring informed us our prefix "HARLYN" had been accepted and now could be used to register any new calves born to our herd. Dad and Mom had deliberated and debated on a wide variation of titles and names, but finally settled on a simple coupling of Harold and Evelyn as their first choice. The official letters accompanying both certificates were short and to the point ... but to all of us, said so much.

Breaking up the heavy soil in preparation for our first crop proved to be a challenge for our new Allis-Chalmers. Following a heavy rain, that West Gwillimbury clay would pack like cement. Factor in a dry year like 1953 and fissures sometimes an inch wide appeared. (Richard informed us these were "snake holes." "They're shaped like that so the snake can roll right in.")

Despite the dry summer, our farm was appearing quite productive. The oats were in full head, and the wheat planted the previous autumn was beginning to show a hint of the deep golden hue to come. Haying was progressing steadily despite the archaic machinery with which we had to work. Mom drove the hay loader and Dad and Billy built the loads. Mom didn't mind tractor driving if the fields were relatively level, but was terror stricken negotiating the hilly slopes that were a feature of our farm.

As it had been for generations of farms, we utilized the "hayfork" method to unload hay once it reached the barn. However instead of "real" horsepower to operate the fork, we used "Pontiac" power. With the rope hitched to its axle, our '47 Pontiac was driven down the gangway pulling the rope, thus lifting the hay fork upwards complete with a jag of loose hay. Following the release of each bundle, the car was reversed and the procedure repeated until the wagon was empty. As inventive as the hay loader and fork were, their time had passed. The baler was fast taking its place and by next year we too would follow that route.

We relied heavily on our neighbours in those early days of farming. Oats were planted by Orville Hughes and harvested by Herb Hounsome. Wheat was handled through the expertise of Wilfred Faris. "If you want your wheat combined properly Wilfred is the man to do it" was the word up and down the concessions. Quality and quantity, not number of acres threshed in a day, was Wilfred's priority. As well as his John Deere combine, Wilfred provided his Studebaker truck to haul the crop to the elevator in Cookstown. If the elevator operator knew Wilfred combined the crop he wouldn't even bother checking the moisture, such was his reputation.

The personalities of our new neighbours were as diverse as the tasks they performed. Herb Hounsome and his three sons went at everything at full speed ... whether working in the field or eating at the dinner table. Getting back to work in the least possible time was paramount. The slow and steady nature of Wilfred Faris contrasted sharply with the Hounsomes and he seemed to get just as much accomplished. Wilfred never stopped to eat ... "just bring me a beer and a sandwich" which he'd consume while driving the combine.

Orville Hughes on the other hand liked nothing better than a home-cooked meal and good conversation ... mostly his own ... and the longer spent at the kitchen table the better. I'm reminded of the time he was seasoning his plate as he chatted and became so involved with his story he failed to notice the pepper shaker lid had dislodged, blanketing his meal with the black spice. His first inkling of anything wrong was a sneezing session.

Although we'd been blessed with good crops that first year and our milking herd was providing a regular income ... it wasn't enough. Gas, feed supplements, fencing supplies, hardware, tools, tractor and machinery payments and of course the mortgage all had to come from the milk cheque. Plus there were seven of us to feed and clothe. The "baby bonus" helped, but budgets can only be stretched so far and Dad realized he'd have to find some off-farm income.

Through all those years he dreamed of owning his own farm, I don't imagine this scenario had ever crossed his mind. But dreams are one thing, reality another. Subsequently Dad managed to find a job at the local Ralston-Purina dealer in Bradford.

As well as selling livestock feed, Bradford Farm Supply raised chickens. Dad's job consisted of selling feed and mineral supplies, gathering eggs, also grading and candling. A less glamorous task was cleaning the cages, a job made more miserable due to the lack of straw. The main reason for the scarcity according to Dad was the company was "too cheap." However it was steady work, providing nearly full days during winter. In busier seasons, Dad could pick and choose his hours, often going in for two or three hours in the afternoon.

This second job definitely stole valuable time from the farm, so the rest of the family had to pitch in. Feeding hay and silage and watering the cattle were time-consuming tasks. Following milking and just during the winter season, the cows were housed in our second barn. Inside this building was a huge cement trough. The windmill would pump the trough full in short order if Mother Nature cooperated, but otherwise it had to be done manually, as Dad figured he couldn't afford a "back-up" electric pump at the time.

If oats were to be chopped, Dad and Billy would fill the required number of bags after Dad got home from work. Next morning our faithful Pontiac would be transformed to pickup truck status. A half dozen bags in the back seat, another three or four in the trunk, plus one on each front fender. It sounds comical now and must have looked so even then, but we were far from alone in this mode of hauling as few farms of that era had both a car and truck.

During summer many of the more time-consuming jobs were eliminated but new problems arose, mainly fencing, as our wire and rail boundaries were often less than satisfactory. Our Holstein herd did suffer one casualty that first summer, but nothing to do with poor fences. While putting the cows in for milking one evening, we noticed Belle wasn't among them. A quick search discovered her lying on the pathway leading from the creek to the barn. She'd evidently suffered a heart attack en route and dropped in her tracks.

From as far back as I can recall I beheld this misty picture in my mind of a dead cow lying in the hot summer sun, while flies buzzed around the carcass. I never knew what it meant until some forty years later while Dad was reminiscing and he happened to mention the incident about old Belle. Finally after all that time I discovered the vision's source.

Whereas 1953 was dry, the 1954 season was just the opposite. Haying was spread over a lengthy period as we tried to dodge the frequent showers. We parked the hay loader that year and the Hounsome organization baled our crop with their John Deere baler, doing their best to provide a hay crop of decent quality ... not an easy task in a season of challenging weather patterns. It was the same story for the wheat and oat harvest as prolonged wet weather slowed their respective seasons as well.

The corn crop was also harvested in muddy conditions, but was finally packed safely in our wooden silo. As in the previous year, Dalton Jackson handled the corn silage. Dalton worked at a leisurely pace during the best of times so muddy field conditions dictated about three days for him to finish our six-acre crop.

The soggy conditions had made our second season of farming a challenge indeed, but as that old adage proclaims ... we hadn't seen nuthin' yet!

A NIGHT IN OCTOBER

Buried deep within the pages of our daily newspaper, an item on Friday, October 8, 1954, reported that a tropical storm off the coast of South America near the island of Grenada had been officially updated to hurricane status, making it the seventh recorded that season. More importantly in our household that day was observing my brother Bill extinguish twelve candles on his birthday cake. Birthdays at our house meant ginger ale, ice cream, and of course cake, a flavour of the celebrator's choosing.

The following day, Bill's birthday was but a memory, but this hurricane which had been given the name Hazel was gaining momentum, although seemingly without direction. First it veered north, then northwest, then northeast, slamming into Haiti on October 12, its 200 kph (120 mph) winds practically blowing the island apart.

By now Hazel was receiving some real press as it headed towards Florida, then changed direction again, opting instead for the South Carolina coast. Throughout Thursday the 14th, the hurricane ravaged the Atlantic seaboard northward all the way to Virginia, before turning slightly inland and attacking Maryland and Delaware. Roofless barns, uprooted trees, downed power lines, flooded streets, roads and homes were all left in its wake.

Most people in southern Ontario were aware of Hazel by now, but few gave it much thought as a threat. Walking to and from school the previous week, it seemed as if it had rained nearly every day, so "that hurricane in the States" was simply the most convenient to blame.

It was raining Friday morning so Dad drove my sister, two brothers and myself to school, went home and finished the farm chores before leaving for his part-time job at Bradford Farm Supply. The rain continued throughout the morning, necessitating yet another "indoor" noon hour for Miss Brown's pupils. Somewhere between two and three o'clock, a knock sounded at the door and in the entranceway stood Mr. Wilson, a member of the local school board. After a short conversation, Miss Brown informed us ... "that hurricane in the States seems to be affecting our weather more than we thought and Mr. Wilson has informed me that some of the lower roads are already flooding and suggests I dismiss the entire class early." A roar of approval arose from the class. What better way to start a weekend!

The rain was falling in sheets as we left the schoolhouse and we were soaked before we'd travelled a hundred feet. Raincoats were no match for this deluge. Water rushed by on either side of the road as we descended the grade towards our farm, spilling into the swelling creek at the bottom. Underneath the "400" highway bridge, the water was already several inches deep, providing great splashing opportunities.

Upon our arrival at home, Mom immediately ordered us stripped while she scrounged for dry clothes. Even our underwear was wet enough to literally wring water. It was probably nearing four o'clock by this time and I recall how abnormally dark it was, as if someone had enveloped our house with a huge grey blanket. It was kind of cozy though, with the rain splashing against the window panes, while inside we were warm and comfortable.

Less comfortable was our mother. Apprehensive of the weather, she'd phoned Bradford Farm Supply to suggest Dad not wait until five o'clock to come home. The owner informed Mom he'd been concerned as well and had sent him home. "How long ago was that?" ... "Over an hour ago" she was told. Now she was really worried as it was just a ten-minute drive from Bradford. "Where could he be?" I overheard Mom ask my sister when 5:30 ticked by with no sign. The wind had strengthened considerably with sustained winds well over 100 kph (60 mph) and higher gusts were blowing sheets of water against the windows. We took turns pressing our faces to the glass, straining our eyes for a glimpse of headlights. Six o'clock came and still no Dad. As I recall that scene, Mother must have been on the verge of hysterics.

Suddenly the kitchen door opened and there was our father. Mom could say nothing for a few seconds as the first wave of relief swept over her. "Where have you been?" she finally blurted out. Dad seemed a little surprised at her emotion, but answered easily. "Choring." ... "Choring!" Mom echoed. "I phoned over at four o'clock and they said you left nearly an hour before!" Dad began to remove his wet clothes. "Well, I went and got a haircut and then went over to Charlie's and then" ... "You went to Charlie's!" Mom yelled. The anguish of waiting, the thankfulness of seeing him and then this stupid story about getting a haircut and going for a visit in the middle of a hurricane was just too much.

"You mean you've been at Charlie's all this time?" Mom pressed ... "No, I told you I was doing the chores. When I got home it was so nasty I thought the power might go off, so I hit straight for the barn" ... "Well," answered Mom, "Would it have been too much trouble to tell the rest of us you were home!" She was having difficulty grasping the fact her husband had been not 200 feet away the past two hours. "I blew the horn as I passed the house," Dad answered defensively. "How in the heck were we supposed to hear a car horn in all this wind and rain?" My father could only offer that he was sorry, for he had no idea what his wife had endured. At least we were all together now and it was just a matter of waiting out the storm.

Hurricanes by their very nature tend to ease as they come inland, and as predicted, Hazel weakened considerably crossing the Allegheny Mountains and by 7 PM had passed through Buffalo and Rochester, heading out over Lake Ontario. The Weather Bureau reiterated an earlier statement that the weakening storm would pass east of Toronto sometime before midnight and the rainfall would cease shortly thereafter.

However Hazel continued to be unpredictable and out over the middle of Lake Ontario collided with a blast of cold air moving easterly across Canada. The combination of warm tropical and cold western air put the hurricane back in force, hitting Toronto with 130 kph (70 mph) winds and torrential rain, recording six inches in the space of twelve hours. With such proportions of rainfall, evacuation centres had to be set up in low-lying areas as Friday evening wore on.

Our house was feeling the effects of Hazel now. The volume of rain combined with the wind velocity was driving water in everywhere and Mom was continually stuffing towels under doorways and windows to curb the flow. Next, the ceilings began to leak; first one room, then another, slowly at first, then faster as the rain fell unabated. Anything that would hold water was drawn into service ... pots, pans, pails, basins and bowls. It proved to be a steady job, dumping and replacing containers. Added to this gloomy scenario, the hydro gave out as Dad predicted, necessitating all work be done by candlelight.

Sometime later that evening, conditions improved remarkably, everyone heaving a sigh of relief. But it was only temporary. The "eye" of Hazel had passed just east of us and this brief interlude was only the calm before the wind changed directions and we were subjected to another round of Hazel's wrath. More wind, more heavy rain.

It was very difficult to go to sleep that night. The howling wind and driving rain outside, while inside, the sound of water dripping into an assortment of receptacles scattered about the house only added to our anxieties. Dad, who never had a problem sleeping regardless of conditions, went to bed, while Mom elected to stay up awhile as someone still had to still dump the water from the multitude of containers scattered around the house.

At first she thought it was just the wind, but near midnight a knock sounded at the door and upon investigation Mom discovered a man in his early twenties standing in the entranceway. Needless to say he was nearly drowned. Over a cup of coffee heated on the wood stove, the unfortunate chap explained how he'd been trying to get home to his parents' place, a couple of concessions north. The road was completely washed out and he'd been forced to abandon his car. Somehow through the wind, rain and darkness, he'd stumbled upon our gateway.

The stranger's worst anxieties centred upon the worry he must be causing his parents, and Mom could do nothing to help in this regard as our phone had been inoperative for hours. Not a single article of dry clothing for the young man could Mom find; it seemed every towel, sheet, blanket, even shirts and coats had been utilized to sop up the water. Finally after a thorough search, Mom did find an old coat hidden away in a closet and offered it to the stranger, along with an invitation to spend the remainder of the night on our kitchen couch. The storm seemed to be slackening somewhat, so Mom retired as well ... It had been a long evening.

When Dad awoke the next morning everything was strangely quiet. No wind. No sound of falling rain, no hydro and no phone service. Mom got up at the same time, bringing Dad up to date on events after he'd gone to bed. The stranger in the night was gone and only the damp coat spread over the arm of the sofa remained. When the storm passed, he'd obviously struck out for home on foot.

As far as the house itself, it appeared about the same as a few hours ago. Perhaps a little worse; maybe it was the way the first rays of dawn filtered through the mud-spattered and rain-streaked glass that added that extra touch of gloom. Every room looked like an obstacle course, with containers strewn about holding various levels of water. Mom sighed as she observed the numerous sections of wallpaper still soaked to the touch and already beginning to peel.

Meanwhile, Dad went outside. Surprisingly things didn't appear too bad. Several house roof shingles were missing and a varied assortment of branches and debris littered the ground all the way from the house to the barn. It wasn't difficult to trace the course of rushing water from the previous evening, as a vast network of gullies and ravines was visible throughout the yard. The greatest change due to the hurricane concerned the creek that flowed through our farm. It had completely re-routed in the night and gouged out an entirely new section of field.

As for the barn, a few loose sheets of steel on the roof appeared to be the only casualty on the outside. In the stable itself, the gutters were level with water and the walk-way flooded, but for the most part, the rushing water had merely entered one side of the barn and departed the other. This was especially true in the pig pen, through which a virtual river had flowed, taking manure, straw and anything else in its path. The pigs on the "high side" of the pen were sleeping soundly in their dry bedding, oblivious to the torrent that had passed just a few feet away. Our cattle herd was safe and dry in the adjoining barn.

My oldest brother Bill was up by this time and went about helping with the chores. It would be a much longer milking this morning due to the absence of hydro.

When we younger ones arose, the sun was shining brightly and warmly, making it hard to comprehend the difference of just a few hours. Mom was hard at work washing and putting away the "flood" containers and my sister was hanging soggy towels and blankets on the clothesline. By now, Mom realized where a great deal of the water that had battered our house had ended up ... in the basement. The water level reached at least the third step, and everywhere Mom's carefully stored jars of preserves floated mysteriously about. Due to the depth of water it was difficult to tell, but mainly it appeared as if the majority of the glass sealers had passed the night "on the water" without incident.

We still had no idea at this point the magnitude of destruction Hazel had wrought as we were still without power for radio. What really had us mystified was the complete absence of traffic on the "400." Well ... we'd find out soon enough. Meanwhile, a monumental bailing job was in store to empty the cellar. Mom bailed, handing the pails through the cellar window to Vivien, Bill and Richard to carry and dispose of. A couple of neighbour kids showed up later, excitedly telling us about the road conditions beneath the 400 overpass. Upon inspection we discovered what our night visitor had meant, as beneath the bridge the road was completely blocked. It looked as though a giant jackhammer had gone berserk. The entire paved section preceding the bridge was a mass of asphalt and gravel heaved in every direction imaginable.

We later learned more than a dozen bridges in our township had been washed out. It wasn't until hydro was restored later that afternoon did we begin to absorb what all had transpired the previous evening.

We didn't have far to look ... Bradford, just three miles away. The town of Bradford is perched on the rim of a thirty-square-mile patch of fertile black earth known as the Holland River Marsh. In 1954 it was capable of producing more than five million bushels of carrots and onions each year. Early on Saturday, October 16, all that appeared was a vast lake, and the only visible sign of a building was the steeple of the Springdale Christian Reform church, thrusting skyward from the flood below. Three thousand residents of the marsh had been evacuated to Bradford when flood waters rose more than fifteen feet, flowing clear over the "400" highway. (This explained the absence of traffic.)

As most of the marsh houses were built without foundations, some floated all night, drifting as much as thousands of feet from their point of origin. One house floated through the darkness with the family grouped in the attic. The fertile marsh of the previous week was now filled with debris, wrecked houses, machinery, vehicles and of course vegetables. Even from our place three miles away, over the next couple of weeks a southerly breeze would usher in the distinct odour of rotting onions. When the water receded from the "400," the asphalt was layered with them. Property loss so soon after the hurricane was incalculable. The worst kind ... human loss, was more readily accountable.

On the Beeton Road, there's a small creek that every morning for several years Vivien and Bill crossed over on their way to school. Except for a few days each spring, this creek meanders unhurriedly through the Tecumseth Township hills. On that particular Friday night, Irwin Joyce was making his way towards his home in Beeton. Mr. Joyce was the Sunday School superintendent at the Presbyterian church our family attended.

As he approached the creek, Joyce noticed the bridge had been completely washed out and a river of water was tearing across the road in front of his car. He managed to get stopped, but then noticed a car approaching from the opposite direction. He tried to warn the other driver by wading into the water and signalling, but was completely unaware of the extreme depth and power of the torrent and was swept away in the tide. The other car then plunged into the river, coming to rest upright in mid-stream.

Jackson Glassford, through whose farm the creek ran, witnessed the car go into the water and with his son Allan desperately tried to rescue the four occupants, who had managed to get out of their car and were clinging to the roof. The river by now was six feet deep and nearly 50 feet wide. Cables, ropes and chains of varying lengths were utilized without success in an attempt to pull the stranded motorists ashore. Finally, a rowboat was manoeuvred into position in the raging torrent and the four succeeded in climbing in. Just as they were being readied to be hoisted ashore, a huge wave overturned the craft, spilling all four into the churning water. Next afternoon in varying distances downstream, five bodies were retrieved from the creek that by now was regaining more normal flow rates.

As the weekend wore on and report upon report was heard of mass property damage and human suffering and death, comparisons such as flooded basements and wet wallpaper quickly paled. In the town of Southampton on the Lake Huron shoreline, the inbound train from Palmerston derailed where the tracks had disappeared in a washout. Engineer Gordon McCallum of Palmerston and fireman Stewart Nicholson of Southampton were scalded to death when the boiler burst as they lay trapped inside the locomotive's cabin.

Just outside the village of Breslau, the site of that year's International Plowing Match and Machinery Show was a shambles, as gale force winds blew down every tent standing. The site had been a "mudfest" all week due to the wet conditions. Hazel simply put it out of its misery.

Hazel expended a great deal of her wrath on the city of Toronto's lowlands. By late Friday evening, everything in the Humber River floodplain was under water to some degree. Emergency crews worked all night rescuing victims from cars and rooftops. Five local firemen were drowned when their truck was swept into the raging Humber River.

The worst tragedy was on Raymore Drive, a residential street alongside the Humber River between Scarlett Road and Lawrence Avenue. As the street lay completely in the floodplain, some residents, at the urging of officials, evacuated, but many chose to stay, figuring they'd seen floods before.

The first hint of danger was when one of the bridges that crossed Scarlett Road gave way on one side. The opposite side held, as did the supports for the bridge's platform. All the flood debris churning down the river immediately built up against these support cables still connected on either side. With the normal flow stopped, the river quickly changed direction ... right across Raymore Drive. The tidal wave smashed houses from their foundations and threw them into the maelstrom that seconds earlier had been the street. Thirty-six died in just a few minutes. One man alone lost his son, a daughter, a daughter-in-law and all six of his grandchildren.

During a visit to Toronto in the 1970s, my cousin who lived in the vicinity gave me a tour of the area that was once Raymore Drive. The street was never rebuilt following the hurricane and in the interim had become part of the Humber Valley Conservation Authority. A memorial plaque among the trees and well-trimmed grass was the sole reminder to passers-by of what had taken place that October night two decades earlier.

VEHICLE VIGNETTES

When I resurrect memories of our family's past ... often, it's automobiles that ignite a recollection and hence another story.

Dad drove a car for sixty-five years, owning nearly two dozen in the process. His first set of wheels was his father's Model T Ford bought new in 1927. A year later Dad got his license, and as his father was never comfortable with the transition from horses to automobiles, his son became its designated driver for the ten years it was owned. It had never been my grandfather's intent to keep the Ford that long, but then the Great Depression of the 1930s changed a lot of plans.

In the autumn of 1937, father and son went car shopping and wound up at the local General Motors dealer in the village of Flesherton. The best they could find within their limited budget was a 1930 Chevrolet. Although just three years newer than the Ford, the Chevrolet could boast some distinct advantages ... mainly six cylinders versus four, four wheel brakes instead of two, disc wheels as opposed to spokes and a more traditional floor-positioned gear shift instead of the Ford's pedal-operated transmission.

Overall the Chevrolet appeared in good condition and sensing their interest, owner-operator George MacTavish offered the car for the weekend. After a promise to address a leaking valve cover gasket, squealing brakes and a front end shimmy, a deal was signed. This Chevrolet had enjoyed some local notoriety, as it was originally owned by then current Grey County Member of Parliament Agnes MacPhail. As our family were strong supporters of MacPhail and her political policies, for this reason alone the Chevrolet always remained a little bit special.

Dad's first vehicle with his name on the ownership was a 1937 Dodge purchased in 1943. At the time the car was sorely in need of a valve job, so much so it barely had the power to propel itself up moderate inclines. A $10.00 "valve grind" restored its vigour. In conjunction with poor quality fuel during the war and the inherent characteristics of low octane gas in general, grinding the valves ... which called for removal of carbon build-up on the valves ... was almost routine maintenance of that era.

The last family trip for the Dodge had been some three years later, Christmas Eve 1946. Mom had been admitted to Newmarket hospital early that morning to await arrival of her third child, so Dad took Vivien and Billy to Toronto to their grandparents. Neither child was very receptive to the idea of being away from home Christmas Eve, but were assured that Santa always knew where to find good little boys and girls.

This explanation failed to convince either, but what really caused things to hit the fan was the realization that while they were preoccupied with jig-saw puzzles and colouring books in their grandparents' basement ... Dad left for home without them!

Although their father certainly wasn't forgiven for abandonment, next morning, learning of the arrival of a baby brother followed by a new tricycle and carriage which had been hidden in the trunk on the trip down ... at least helped.

When Dad finally returned a few days later a surprise was in store, as he was driving a different car ... a 1939 DeSoto. Being it was a "coupe" meant it had no regular back seat, merely two "jump seats" that could be folded when not in use to provide additional luggage space. The DeSoto brand was a medium-priced car of its day, designed to fill the price gap between Chrysler and Dodge.

All the way from Bond Head to Toronto, some forty miles, it had snowed, so Dad was anxious to return in case conditions worsened. By the city's northern outskirts his apprehension had been realized. It was a slow drive up Highway 27 with frequent white-outs, but the DeSoto laboured along until just north of Schomberg, about ten miles from home, where it stopped. No warning splutter, no hesitation ... it just expired. Barely was there time to pull onto the shoulder before rolling to a stop. A couple of tries of the starter proved futile.

Sitting in the cold, blustery darkness, Dad pondered his next move. Occasionally through the drifting snow a farmhouse light was visible and Dad discussed the idea of walking for help, or at the very least to use their phone. My sister and brother would have no part of such a plan. They'd been ditched once this week and wouldn't fall for that again ... either they all went or nobody went! Despite Dad's best efforts to convince them they'd be better off in the car rather than outside in the bitter cold, his argument went nowhere.

Twenty minutes passed without sight of another vehicle. The car's interior was becoming colder by the minute. Whether he bundled the kids in blankets or left them in the car, he had no choice but to go for aid of some sort. One last time the starter was given a whirl; it started! Not questioning the wherefore or why, Dad put the car in gear and started once again into the wintry night. The stormy conditions showed no signs of improvement but the DeSoto also gave no hint of resistance the remainder of the trip.

For three years' ownership, the DeSoto's mysterious stalling would surface upon occasion. Wait a few minutes and the problem would rectify itself. A tiny pinhole somewhere in the fuel system was the most educated deduction at the time. Dad never figured the problem serious enough to warrant an in-depth study and merely looked upon it as a quirk.

A few months after the DeSoto was purchased, an official letter from the War Time Prices Board arrived, pertaining to the sale of the '37 Dodge. Because of material shortages, the WTPB was launched during the war to prevent price gouging and uncontrolled inflation, especially when returning soldiers were involved. The letter advised the selling price of $800.00 was in excess of their guideline of $650.00. This difference, Dad was informed, must be returned to the buyer.

With no option but to comply, Dad got in touch with the soldier who'd bought it. Apparently he wasn't too keen on "government interference" either, for when he was shown the document he replied he was perfectly happy with the agreed price. To honour the request, Dad gave the soldier a cheque for $150.00 for which he was issued a receipt. The

Dodge owner gave Dad a cheque for same, everyone was satisfied and the WTPB was none the wiser.

By 1949, the DeSoto had simply run out of seating capacity when a fourth child (me) joined our family. It was also the year my parents decided they were finally in a financial position to purchase something for which they'd never come close ... a brand new car. But what make of car? Variety abounded in 1949. In the low to medium price range was Chevrolet, Pontiac, Ford, Meteor, Monarch, Plymouth, Dodge, DeSoto, Studebaker, Hudson, Kaiser and Frazer.

As well as a proliferation of North American models, a growing segment of European cars were beginning to arrive on Canadian shores. Practically all were of the British variety, the Vauxhall and Austin being the most popular. The Canadian government and of course that of the British Isles continually stressed the importance of "buying British." Their auto plants had been decimated for the most part during the war and were just now staggering to their feet; huge amounts of capital had been invested in the re-building process and consumers from both sides of the Atlantic were urged to help the cause.

Dad looked at a number of different makes, including the English variety, but found the latter just too cramped for our growing family. A great many people agreed with this conclusion; however, many imports found their way to Canadian driveways, establishing a sort of "big little" camp. The "made in North America" consortium had all sorts of fun ridiculing the curious little cars from across the ocean, going as far as concocting limericks to suit the occasion.

There was a young man from Boston
Who drove a baby Austin
There was just room for his ass
And a gallon of gas
And his balls hung out and he lost 'em.

So much for Motherland patriotism ... After several circuits of car dealers, Dad settled on a Meteor. A Meteor was a regular Ford body but with slightly different grille and taillights, more resembling a Mercury, and was exclusive to the Canadian market. It was still a seller's market in 1949 so the wait would be lengthy.

In the interim, Dad was struck with health problems. A dull abdominal pain one morning gradually worsened to the point of agony. Newmarket doctors after some consultation agreed it must be appendicitis, although it seldom caused such constant sharp pain to their knowledge. A go-ahead however was given, with my father actually prepped for the operation, when the pain suddenly and mysteriously disappeared.

Now the medical staff was really confused. Dad was wheeled back to his room and monitored closely throughout the night but the pain didn't return. When the doctor in charge relayed to Mom what had taken place I guess he thought she would be relieved; instead she was left with a feeling of uneasiness. She well remembered her appendicitis ordeal twenty-five years earlier. When the pain subsided she figured everything was fine; instead it was merely a signal the appendix had ruptured. This didn't prove to be the case with Dad as he improved quickly, doctors concluding that'd he'd passed a gallstone.

However the very morning Dad was lying in Newmarket hospital while surgeons deliberated his case, the Ford dealer in Schomberg phoned that our new car had arrived. The call couldn't have come at a more inopportune time. Mother, unclear at that point what actually was wrong with her husband ... would he be off work for a short duration or extended period? With no health insurance to cushion an uncertain period of recuperation, Mom was forced to make a decision. It mattered little to the dealer; he had a waiting list a yard long ... but he had to know now! The choice was to pass. It had all boiled down to timing. A week later ... perhaps even a day later would've been a different story. I guess a new car for our family just wasn't meant to be.

Instead the joining the long new car line-ups again, Dad opted for a used unit. Ted Hipwell, who operated the grocery store in Bond Head, had purchased a new Pontiac and offered his '47 model with just 16,000 miles for $1100.

The Pontiac's first major trip was to Collingwood for our annual family reunion, held the last Sunday in June 1949. With Mom and Dad and Billy in the front seat and Mom's parents, Vivien and Richard in the back and I on Mom's lap, off we went ... but not far. The tell-tale signs of a flat tire soon were made evident and the Pontiac limped ingloriously to the side of the road. It seemed to take forever to unload the picnic supplies for seven and a half people from the trunk, plus my carriage folded in the bottom.

When the spare was finally wrestled from its mounting, it was found to be little better than the flat one. Dad hadn't paid a lot of attention to the spare until this point, a most exasperating fact as a brand new tire sat comfortably back home in the garage. Ted Hipwell had included it in the transaction, but with all that needed to be packed for a family picnic that morning, space was at a premium and consequently the tire was left behind. The only solution was a new one except Dad didn't have enough cash to cover the $20.00 price, so embarrassingly had to ask his mother-in-law to make up the difference.

The trip to our family reunion five years later was equally memorable. A severe thunderstorm had chased us out of Collingwood and by the time we reached Alliston, its main street more resembled a fast flowing river. The Pontiac slowly waded through the water that reached halfway up its wheels, but even at this cautious rate the car's wiring soon became waterlogged and the engine died. Someone behind us in a big Oldsmobile or Buick offered a push and although several attempts were made, the car wouldn't start.

At that point I recall Mom yelling: At the main intersection, two cars were approaching from opposite directions on the green light. Dad hit the brake pedal, but between the water-filled street, equally soaked brakes and momentum of the pushing car, the operation proved useless. Dad laid on the horn, either to warn the approaching cars or the one behind of impending doom. Because of the sheet of water being splashed up from our car, the guy behind us obviously couldn't see the red signal and simply kept pushing.

Exactly what happened we're not sure, perhaps at the last moment the two cars slowed slightly or we were just lucky, but we somehow passed between them ... the car behind us as well. Once through the intersection the street elevated and the flood receded and almost by magic the Pontiac spluttered to life. Dad waved a thank you to the car behind for his "help" and we continued home. Although even at that tender age, I seem to recall my parents rather quiet for the duration of the trip.

The '47 Pontiac soldiered along, providing dependable transportation until the winter of 1955. Dad simply wrote it off as winter malaise ... nothing a tune-up wouldn't cure, but despite a thorough check, the condition worsened ... hard to start, stall at every opportunity, no power, wouldn't idle ... it reached the point where we were afraid to venture much further than Bradford. Dad's cousin Bill Magee, always fascinated by cars, was visiting one Sunday and spent a great deal of time trying to diagnose the cause. Plenty of gasps, wheezes, explosions and sneezes were emitted from the Pontiac but little else.

Dad was convinced at this point more serious problems were afoot: valves probably, rings possibly. An engine overhaul could get pretty expensive. Just at this time, Dad's father had taken ill and had been admitted to the hospital. A severe cold had developed into pneumonia and in conjunction with his seventy-five years, Grandpa wasn't doing well. What could possibly be frequent trips to a hospital an hour away were out of the question the way the Pontiac was acting.

Long story short ... Dad purchased a 1950 Pontiac and the '47 was parked behind the barn. Vince Spizalli, our milk transporter at the time, inquired about the old car, and assured it was in need of serious repair, Dad sold it for $150.00. Vince was short on cash so paid half down and took the car, promising the balance within the month.

Shortly after, Vince was replaced by another driver and sort of dropped out of sight. Occasionally he'd surface but never seemed to have any money. After about six months, Dad asked Brock Evans, a Bradford lawyer, for advice. "I'll just send a form letter requesting payment," Evans offered. "Often that's all that's needed." He was right; Vince remitted the $75.00 and Evans never even billed Dad for his services.

Whatever car we were driving, one of my fondest memories was the Saturday night trip to Bradford. These end-of-week excursions five or six decades ago were a regular occurrence during the nice weather, and a much-looked-forward-to event for so many in the rural outreaches. Whether it was the hardware, grocery or drug store, half of the people you met were familiar on a first-name basis. Once the necessities were taken care of came the best part when Dad would treat the family to a chocolate bar or ice cream cone, which we'd enjoy while sitting in the car, observing the people and traffic on the main street.

For me and my brothers the variety of automobiles was our main focus, and we'd take turns shouting out the year and model as they passed by. My parents and older sister were more interested who was walking by on the sidewalk, and again a majority of those passing by, you knew. Depending upon the familiarity of the individual, these encounters would culminate in anything from a wave, friendly smile, simple hello, to a lengthy conversation.

It was a much simpler period, that time in the long ago ... when small independent stores thrived on the main streets of equally small towns that flourished across the breadth of rural Canada. A time when a person could often borrow money simply on their word, a hand shake would consummate most any agreement ... and when lawyers provided service simply from the goodness of their heart.

FIRST LOVE

I was probably about six years old when I kissed Rillie Oertner. The scene was our local one-room schoolhouse on a long drawn-out winter afternoon, when an older student who obviously had nothing better to do whispered to me from across the aisle ... "David, why don't you give Rillie a kiss?" With the exception of my mother, I had never kissed a girl. However, I could see nothing inappropriate with the suggestion and as Rillie sat directly across from me, it would be a simple matter to lay one on her ... which is exactly what I did.

My kiss was audible across the entire classroom and instantly induced giggles from the girls and guffaws from the boys. My teacher, Miss Brown, merely stared in my direction a few seconds. "David!" she finally blurted out. "I don't believe what I just saw ... or heard!" More laughter. Rillie herself failed to show any emotion one way or another. She simply went back to whatever it was she was doing before she was interrupted.

Rillie Oertner I suppose was just a quick fling ... Helen Street was my main woman. I'd initially set eyes on Helen, September 7, 1954. It was my first day of school and I was having a difficult time adjusting to this new way of life. I sat at my little wooden desk, crying softly while my classmates laughed at the big baby in their midst ... except Helen. She turned around in her seat directly in front of me, offered me a Kleenex and a freckled-face smile that promised everything would be alright.

Helen had hair the colour of wheat straw and eyes as blue as Lake Ontario. Eyes that forever sparkled with that "Let's see what we can get into" look. We shared our most intimate secrets and dreams and informed each other on happenings in our respective homes. We even shared lunches. She liked my oatmeal cookies and I her ice-wafer biscuits. The only obstruction threatening to mar this puppy-love alliance centred on the fact her father drove a Ford. For a General Motors fan, that was going to be a tough obstacle to overlook.

Helen's family lived on a farm between the school and our farm, so Helen and I usually walked home together. Occasionally she would invite me in ... especially if her mother was away. One day I was having a difficult time convincing Helen I had to be getting home. "If you stay awhile" she enticed, "I'll show you my new crinoline!" Helen had learned early how to utilize her feminine wiles. Crinolines have long since departed along with bobby socks and jumpers, but in my day, many little girls wore those stiff-lined garments that caused a skirt to balloon outwards at the hem.

Helen was modelling a blue velvet skirt this particular afternoon. "Back up a little," she suggested. I backed a couple of steps. "You're still too close ... I have to spin you know!" No, I didn't know. Anyway, up went the blue velvet skirt to her waist, showing off her white panties.

"What did you think?" Helen asked. I don't remember my answer. I do recall asking for a repeat performance but she refused. "You've seen enough", I was informed ... well for this particular day at least.

One afternoon when I accompanied Helen home, her mother was in the kitchen. It was a hot day and Helen asked if we might have a bottle of pop. We only got soft drinks on special occasions at home, and then just a juice glass, so to be offered an entire bottle was an event noted. I even got to pick my flavour from the refrigerated assortment offered. I chose lemon lime. "Do you want a straw?" Mrs. Street asked. "Huh?" "Do you want a straw?" she repeated. It seemed a strange request. What did straw have to do with pop? Helen handed me a long white thing with a hole in either end. "Maybe David would like a coloured one, Helen?" White ... black ... coloured ... I hadn't a clue what I was supposed to do with it anyway.

Helen placed her "straw thing" in her bottle and I followed suit ... so far so good. I wondered why she wasn't drinking instead of merely sucking on this white thing. Well, I was thirsty, so I hoisted the bottle to my lips and tipped it over. I reasoned the pop must run through this straw thing ... yeah that's it. Out poured the lemon lime over my chin, down my neck, down the front of my shirt and trousers and finally onto Mrs. Street's freshly waxed floor. "Oh my ... " gasped Mrs. Street, grabbing the bottle and reverting it upright, "I guess he doesn't know how to use a straw," she said to her daughter. I have no idea what she said under her breath. I went home at that point ... without my cold drink.

I recall another day when the majority of the school roster was in the process of getting the spring softball season

underway. Even Miss Brown was out on the diamond helping my classmates practice their "flies" and "grounders." A
few of the younger girls who weren't interested in baseball
were skipping rope outside the entranceway to the school.

Neither of these scenarios appealed to Helen or me at
the moment. "What can we do?" asked Helen. "I don't
know," shrugging my shoulders. "I know what!" spoke
Helen after a pause. "We could go out in the woodshed
and show our things!" ... "Okay," I answered. My response
probably would have been little different had she suggested
tiddly-winks or marbles.

The woodshed was attached to the south side of the
school. Since the installation of the oil furnace a couple
of years earlier, it now contained little more than bits of
discarded lumber and a few props and decorations that
were dragged out each Christmas season. Once within its
confines, we didn't waste time with small talk, as I quickly
lowered my trousers. "Turn around so I can see your bum,"
Helen prodded. Following my exhibition, Helen lifted
up her skirt ... it was a blue tartan if memory serves me
correctly ... and slowly but deliberately, almost teasingly,
slid down her underpants with her free hand.

Helen and I visited the woodshed each recess for the
next couple of days and by this time "Woodshed 101" had
developed to full nudity. I sometimes wonder what Miss
Brown's reaction would have been had she happened onto
the scene! But even that became stale, so to renew the magic,
Helen suggested we ask Rillie's sister to join us. Margaret
was in grade three, practically a grown woman! She was
playing ball when we propositioned her ... "Sure" was her
simple response (I guess we had a pretty liberal school) But
even this sexual triangle couldn't sustain the momentum

and following another day the exhibition simply became tiresome and closed down.

After nearly three years at that Simcoe County school, our family relocated to Perth County, some 75 miles away. On the final Friday in March, Miss Brown held a presentation for me and my brothers. She had gathered a modest collection from the students and immediately following final recess, set up three chairs at the front of the classroom for us to occupy. Miss Brown reiterated to the assembly what they already knew, which was followed by a half-hearted rendition of "For They Are Jolly Good Fellows." We each then received a parting gift ... bowties. I remember mine clearly ... yellow with brown polka-dots.

Following the presentation, Helen, her eyes brimming with tears, handed me a picture she had coloured. In crayon along the bottom she had printed "I will miss you." Some idiot began to laugh, taunting her with "boy friend ... girl friend ... boy friend ... girl friend!" Helen then ran out the front door of the school bawling her eyes out ... and I never saw her again. I cleaned out my desk, gathered up my bowtie and left for home.

Next afternoon, as Dad steered our old truck down the familiar sideroad for the last time, I looked long and hard as we passed the Street farm but saw no sign of Helen. I continued to watch in the truck's right hand mirror but finally her place faded from view ... Oh well, I guess it never would have worked. Being from two entirely different cultures ... she Ford, me General Motors ... our relationship probably never stood a chance.

FAREWELL TO WEST GWILLIMBURY

It had always been our father's intention when we moved to our own farm in the spring of 1953 that it would pay its own way ... in fact he'd never considered otherwise. This dream, although commendable, soon proved unrealistic and the "Purina" job at Bradford Farm Supply was undertaken. After a while this job was dropped and another stab at self-sufficiency was declared. Before long, mounting bills again dictated further subsidization. This time, part afternoons at Bradford Shippers in the heart of the Holland Marsh.

Here Dad laboured at a variety of tasks. Cutting celery in the fields and loading the product onto wagons. Another was grading vegetables, carrots and onions mostly, as the marsh had plenty of both. But it hadn't always been so. At the turn of the twentieth century it was basically a 10,000-acre swamp and the only crop harvested was a tall rank marsh grass, utilized mostly for mattress stuffing. It was cut with mowers, pulled by horses with wide planks strapped to their feet to keep them from sinking into the quicksand-like soil.

In 1927, an experimental drainage project grew a successful vegetable crop on 200 acres and two years later a full-scale drainage program was instigated.

In 1934 the first Dutch settlers arrived and by the time Dad worked there some twenty years later, the workforce exceeded 3,000 ... still mostly Dutch. Because the operation followed the techniques used in the Netherlands along with the heavy Dutch influence, many mistakenly figured this was how the marsh got its name. It received its title however from the first surveyor-general of Upper Canada (Ontario), Major S. Holland.

When I was young, a drive anywhere near the Holland Marsh during harvesting season yielded the pungent aroma of onions curing in the hot sun. Although mechanical drying has long since replaced Mother Nature and many specialized implements have replaced hand labour, appearance-wise, the Holland Marsh looks the same as it did when I was a kid ... except for that week in October of 1954.

In the weeks following Hurricane Hazel, both monetary and manpower assistance poured into the flood-stricken community. A giant relief centre sponsored by the provincial government and coordinated by local churches was established at the Bradford arena to help the marsh people. I remember Mom baking pies for her part in the effort. Everything was needed and anything was welcome.

As far as the marsh itself, nothing could be done for a few days until the flood waters receded back into the rivers and streams, but following this, mechanical pumps were sent to the site. A few problems arose at the start because of the huge volume of topsoil and rotting vegetables etc. clogging the pumps, but once a system of filters was put in place, things progressed reasonably.

An unpleasant task for ours and neighbouring townships in the aftermath of Hazel was disposing of the large number of livestock that were drowned when pastures became huge lakes or swollen rivers. Another mission was reviving the countless cars, trucks, tractors and other powered machinery that sat immersed in water for days. Most of these were hauled to the township maintenance centre where all fluids from engines, transmissions, hydraulics, gas tanks etc. were drained and new fluids replaced. Other components such as batteries, coils, spark plugs, wiring and so on had to be addressed as well.

Another huge project was rebuilding the washed-out bridges ... more than two dozen in West Gwillimbury and neighbouring Tecumseth Township alone. So late in the year there wasn't time to replace them, but all "detour" bridges were installed by the time winter set in. The following spring, the temporary bridges were replaced with permanent structures, a job that took two years to complete.

Meanwhile back on the farm, life went on ... Being seasonal, Dad was excused from his job in the marsh when winter approached to resume home duties. Winter was always a battle. We had nothing that even resembled a snowblower so the first snowstorm would block our driveway, forcing us to park our car at the road until spring. Those were cold trips walking to and from that car! And we always seemed to be lugging something with us. The toboggan was our main cargo carrier. It could be utilized to haul a few bags of oats to be chopped at the local feed mill. It also carried groceries, coal, stove oil ... anything needed to get through the winter.

The biggest disappointment would come after a cold walk out to an even colder car only to discover it wouldn't start. Dad or Bill would then have to walk back in the lane, fetch some hot water from the house to pour through the radiator as a starting aid for the tractor, find a chain, drive out the lane, hook onto the old Pontiac and pull it down the road until it finally began to breathe, then take the tractor back ... Only then were we ready for town. No wonder our family had little good to say about winter.

Our house always seemed cold and draughty. I think Hurricane Hazel must have blown away a lot of the mortar surrounding the brickwork, because despite two living room oil burners trying to generate heat, it was never warm. In the kitchen was a combination wood/coal stove, so it and the room directly above where the stove pipes passed through, were the only rooms that even approached a comfortable level. Hot water bottles were a wonderful aid to a bed on a frigid night. Once they'd served their usefulness however, they were kicked out onto the floor where they quickly cooled and if they were fired too close to a window, it wasn't uncommon to discover the bottle frozen solid in the morning.

An old wood furnace was tucked away in the basement but Dad never fired it up as long as we lived there, probably for fear it would blow up. For some reason, as a kid I was just as afraid of our two living room oil burners. Those stoves seemed to entertain a lot of strange sounds and I was certain any minute they were going to explode and launch our family into space.

The best spot in the house on a cold morning was in front of that aforementioned kitchen range. A bit of kindling would get it going, then coal, or a block of hardwood would take over. Depending on what was used, a large amount of ashes or "clinkers" accumulated. Clinkers were the fused mass of spent coal left after burning. They varied in size, were as hard as rock and about as useful. Ashes, on the other hand were saved. We never went anywhere in winter without a bucket stashed in the trunk of the car. A shovelful, strategically placed, had gotten our Pontiac out of some slippery situations.

Some new neighbours moved into West Gwillimbury in the spring of 1955 ... a young English couple, Dick and Mary Price. They managed a farm owned by an absentee landlord living in Toronto. Mom and Dad became close friends to the Prices, offering as much help as their busy schedules and limited resources would allow, and Dick and Mary often hired my brother Bill to help with the milking of the forty-cow Guernsey operation.

Their dream of course was to own their own farm, and remembering the enjoyment he'd known searching for his first farm, Dad often accompanied the Prices in their search for real estate possibilities. Mary commented to Mom one day ... "Harold takes such an interest in looking for farms one would think he was the one buying!"

Little did Mom know her husband was thinking along those very lines ... although I suppose even Dad didn't real-ize it at the outset ... he just sort of became entangled in the excitement. However he eventually convinced himself that the way farmland was appreciating in value in Simcoe County, he could sell for a decent profit and buy a larger more modern farm away from the Toronto area for the same or less money.

There was certainly no excitement of any kind on Mom's part. She had just begun to feel like a part of the West Gwillimbury community, with membership in both the Women's Institute and the Presbyterian Church's

Women's Missionary Society. Furthermore, she and Dad were just a few short miles from the villages of Bond Head and Beeton where they'd lived for ten years and cemented many friendships. To be uprooted now wouldn't be easy.

Throughout that autumn and winter of 1956–57 our parents searched. Orangeville seemed the starting point, with anything west being a possibility until they discovered that large wetland known as the Luther Marsh extending for thirty miles beyond. Wellington County then became the focus. They were now nearly seventy miles from their Bradford home.

I hated that winter when Mom and Dad were looking for a new farm. Instead of coming home from school ready to relate to Mom everything that had transpired that day, I was met instead with a quiet empty house. With Vivien not home from high school and Bill usually in the barn, the house seemed cold and desolate. Those dark days, I'd station myself at the window watching for returning headlights. When a car would appear on our sideroad my hopes would soar ... then sink when it passed by. I'd imagine all sorts of terrible things happening out there.

My brothers and sister were no help in this regard, simply referring to me as "baby." Richard was the worst ... he enjoyed seeing me in tears. I recall one night while tucked in our beds, Richard began to expound on the theory of life and death. "We're all going to die you know! ... Grandma and Grandpa Carruthers ... and Grandma and Grandpa Turner ... then Mom and Dad ... then ... " I was a basket case at this point. "Rich says you're going to die!" I wailed to Mom when she came to investigate. Mom stayed and talked awhile and I began to feel better. The walloping she administered Richard helped as well.

There was no one happier than I when it was finally announced they had found a 100-acre property just inside the Perth County line near a place called Palmerston. "It's got a real bathroom with running water!" Mom related, with surprising emotion. She also mentioned how close the railway tracks were and that the school was just a quarter mile away. Until then I'd never given a moment's thought about changing schools.

Before we could purchase a new farm we of course had to sell the one we had. Before anything official transpired, our neighbour Orville Hughes sent over a friend to survey our place. "The first thing I'd do if I owned this house," he began, "is knock a big hole in this wall and install a picture window ... then I'd knock that wall out and probably this one too. This place needs opening up!" After checking every room with a tape measure he added that he would be installing a bathroom upstairs. "How's your well?" he queried Mom ... "it takes nearly ten gallons every time you flush a toilet you know!" Mom didn't know and cared less. All proved redundant anyway as the prospect never returned, for which Mom was grateful.

When that deal fizzled, Orville Hughes decided to buy the place himself ... the plan being to farm the land and rent the house. There was no turning back now.

March 1957 was a busy month with Mom and Vivien labouring endlessly packing boxes. Delicate articles were appropriately marked and set aside for car travel. There would be no misunderstandings this time! That episode of the shattered crystal during a recent move was still fresh in Mom's mind.

Charlie Cerswell again offered his truck as he had for our move four years earlier. Dad and Bill spent countless hours loading hay and grain for the seventy-five-mile trek. Into bags a shovelful at a time our granary was emptied, leaving just enough to sustain the cattle until moving day. We didn't have much machinery so one load handled it. All furniture and personal belongings plus our milk cooler would go the actual moving day, March 30, with the cattle to follow two days later.

It was a mild March, making it ideal for working outside, but it caused headaches in attempting to get loaded trucks through our mud-infested yard. Mud had been something we simply had to endure; every spring the back roads would be literally boiling with mud holes, some of near quicksand-like consistency.

Just a few days before we were set to move, Jean Hughes phoned to invite us over to watch television. (In the 1950s it was common practice to invite non-TV neighbours to watch a hockey game or something.) Dad wasn't too enthused when Mom related the message. "There's just too much to do right now." After plenty of grumbling, Mom half convinced him that if Orville and Jean cared enough to invite us, it wouldn't kill him to spend a couple of hours away.

The time of evening Mom promised we'd be there, Dad had yet to make it in from the barn. "I told Jean we'd be there a half hour ago!" Mom fumed when Dad finally showed up. "Well," replied Dad, "I still think it's a stupid idea going out to watch TV when we have so many things to do at home!" Following his quick wash and shave, Mom handed him a clean shirt that he put on as he was heading for the door. "Oh blast!" exclaimed Dad, "this shirt's got a rip in it!" ... "Oh Harold, who cares for Heaven's sake ... we're only going to watch TV!" Reluctantly Dad steered us all towards the car. "I really should have changed this shirt!" Dad griped, glancing in the rear view mirror.

Pulling into the Hughes driveway we were met with the sight of a dozen cars parked at various angles about the yard. I remember thinking ... boy there sure is a lot of people here to watch TV! My parents of course understood instantly the real reason for being invited. "And me with a ripped shirt!" Dad grumbled one more time ... "If you don't make a big deal about it," Mom hissed, "no one will notice!"

Orville met us at the car. "We had no idea you were planning anything," Dad spoke. "I didn't even dress up ... in fact this shirt has a rip in it!" While we kids played crokinole, the adults played euchre or just chatted. Somewhere near eleven o'clock Jean managed to quiet everyone down while a presentation was made: a floor lamp with a turquoise shade; it occupied a place in our living room for twenty years. Next, a big picture, a nice pastoral scene that was still around forty years later. There was a cash donation as well.

Following the ceremony, Dad offered the official thank you: "Well", he began. "We sure want to thank everyone involved ... especially Jean and Orville for going to all this trouble. I didn't even dress up, in fact there's a rip in my shirt here ... "

The only down side to the evening as far as I was concerned ... no one ever did turn on the TV!

Moving day dawned cloudy and mild. While the truck was being loaded, Richard, who was two years older than I, decided we should take one last look at our farm. The only proper way to accomplish this according to him was to walk the perimeter. Southerly along the entire length of the "400" highway we went ... then easterly along Ted Edwards' farm ... northward past Herb Hounsome's place ... west along the 9th Line sideroad and back in the laneway. Although just eight with little or no interest in family roots at the time, I vividly recall the experience. In less than an hour we loosened the ties on one facet of our life and looked forward to the challenges of another.

Even without our help the loading operation had progressed nicely. All our furniture was strategically placed on the floor of the truck, while around, on top and underneath were packed cardboard boxes of every dimension. Room was left at the very back for the milk cooler. Dad's brother Doug was taking his car to Palmerston and transported such things as lamps, mirrors and other fragile items.

I don't know how it was decided who rode with whom, but it was Vivien and I in the passenger seat when Dad steered the old truck out of the driveway shortly after noon. In a few minutes, seemingly everything we'd known ... the house, barn, fields, the "400," the schoolhouse, neighbours, friends and classmates ... disappeared.

Tomorrow we would wake in a new house with a new barn surrounded by new fields ... begin classes at a new school with a new teacher and new classmates and neighbours ... a new environment with new challenges and promises ... a new beginning.

WELCOME TO WALLACE

A great many of Ontario's counties can be classified as irregular when it comes to geographical design. Perth County certainly qualifies with its asymmetrical proportions. Its boundaries run on a roughly northwest to southeast axis a distance of some fifty miles and are completely landlocked, unlike the miles of bay and lake frontage that were features of our former county.

In the late 1950s, Perth County boasted approximately 540,000 acres. Just inside the northern boundary of the township of Wallace, Dad and Mom chose their 100 acre parcel, becoming the eighth in a succession of tenants dating back to 1854.

Mom and Dad looked at several farms in the immediate area and the relatively short laneway and close highway proximity were strong factors in the acreage chosen. A concrete silo and automatic water bowls in the barn and furnace and bathroom in the house only added incentive.

It's interesting to note that a majority of Perth County's first settlers emigrated from Simcoe County, so as our West Gwillimbury farm faded from view that March day in 1957, we were merely following a tradition.

According to our father it was an hour and a half trip to our new farm ... by car. In Charlie Cerswell's decade old Chevrolet truck it was at least half that again. The first hour was relatively enjoyable despite our leisurely pace. An endless series of hills beckons drivers between Schomberg and Orangeville and the heavily laden truck was tested on each one. Unlike today's trucks with their multiple gear axles and transmission speeds, Charlie's Chevy was saddled with a simple four-speed unit demanding plenty of gear changes. Over the years Dad had spent thousands of miles behind the wheel this truck however and could coax the maximum potential from each gear selected.

On the upgrade towards Mono Mills ... a two-mile winding incline, no amount of practice could help us as it was second gear all the way. Once Orangeville was passed the land flattened out considerably and we began to make better time. Passing through town, Dad pointed out to my sister Vivien and me the building where he'd attended business college a quarter century earlier.

The road may have levelled out west of Orangeville but it sure was boring! Nothing but bare trees and brown matted grass encased in acres of wetland. We could easily see why our parents had bypassed this particular area. Things improved a bit as we entered Wellington County and before long Dad announced that "Palmerston is right over that rise." Vivien and I paid strict attention as we entered our new "home town." We had plenty of time to survey our surroundings while waiting for a large freight train to shunt across the main intersection.

As much as she disliked leaving the Bradford-Beeton area, Mom did admit to a warm feeling on her initial visit to Palmerston. This appeared to be a place a person could perhaps plant some roots ... permanent roots. Her father took special interest when Palmerston was mentioned, recalling the numerous overnight lodgings and count-less times he'd travelled through Palmerston en route to the surrounding towns and villages while working for the Massey-Harris Company.

Dad's first association with this railroad town was equally memorable. He and Mom had stopped at J. Fred Edwards Drug Store to buy a newspaper. It was an extremely windy day, and as he exited the car a gust caught his fedora and blew it down the street. Dad went racing after the hat, but each time he got near another gust of wind would send it scurrying further. Run ... reach ... grab ... miss ... run ... reach ... grab ... miss ... all the way down the main street. I don't know how much Dad saw of Palmerston that day ... but Palmerston probably saw lots of him!

Plenty of help waited at journey's end. Dad's brother Doug was already there. Mom and my two younger brothers had accompanied him. Wes Nelson, the former proprietor, was there as was his son Murray and a neighbour Harold Cosens. Neither Wes, Murray or Harold had seen a milk cooler I guess, as they thought it was a freezer.

With no milk house or similar building nearby, the cooler was temporarily set up in the implement shed, some fifty feet from the barn. Two sliding doors offered access, and on one I noticed a sign about thirty inches by eight inches tacked to the exterior surface. Professionally printed letters read: **BEYOND THE MOON**. "Beyond the moon?" asked my uncle. "What's the significance of that?" Murray and his father both laughed as obviously Doug hadn't been the first to question the sign's interpretation. The sign we were told had been around as long as they had and no one could recall the story of the sign's origin or the message implied. (Although on a different building, that sign remains as of this writing six decades later and we're still in the dark to its meaning.)

While the cooler was being manoeuvred into position, I surveyed the interior of the shed. Our meagre assortment of farm implements was already there along with a couple I assumed belonged to the Nelsons. An upstairs loft covered nearly half the building's area and from where I stood could just make out an old horse-drawn sleigh. A large cupboard, its usefulness as far as furniture long gone, was located along one wall and held a variety of hardware.

By the time everything was unloaded it was nearly dark but Dad still had to drive back to Bradford. The four AM start that morning coupled with all the other early mornings recently was finally catching up, so after fighting drowsiness for miles he wisely pulled over on the shoulder near Orangeville and "grabbed a few winks."

If the day hadn't been long enough, upon arriving home Dad discovered the cows yet to be milked. "I'll be home by dark" he had promised his eldest son. At eight o'clock Bill wondered if he should start the chores, at nine he wished he had. Dad said he'd be home, so where was he? By ten my brother was sick with worry. Obviously something had gone terribly wrong and there was nothing he could do about it. The rest of the family were at the new farm with Dad most likely somewhere in between. Bill had only been to the new place once and doubted he could find it again. Probably no one would even remember where he was. With no appliances or furniture except for a worn-out cot, Bill could visualize starving to death alone. When the truck finally lumbered in around eleven o'clock, he'd fallen asleep and was long past caring. I would guess the chores were performed relatively conversation-free that night.

Next day, Dad got a chance to catch his breath, for Monday would be another full day when the cows were moved. Both Charlie Cerswell and Orville Hughes offered their trucks and labour for the livestock transfer. Although Orville's Mercury truck was nearly new, events would prove it only borderline in height. Nearing the town of Arthur, one of our more spirited cows "Lady" decided she'd ridden long enough. In his mirror Orville noticed in horror a pair of front legs over the edge of the rack. Stopping as quickly as he could, Orville grabbed a chunk of two-by-four that was handy and "persuaded" the cow back into the truck. Lady gained a few shin abrasions but was a good trade-off for what awaited had she gone overboard.

We all looked forward to the first milking at our new farm. Harold Cosens, the new neighbour who had given us a hand on moving day, dropped by that initial milking as well, but Dad and Bill could have done nicely without him. In addition to the trauma of a long ride, our cows also had to face the challenge of a new milking system.

We previously used DeLaval milking machines, where the bucket that held the milk sat on the floor beside the cow. For some reason Dad decided to buy the Surge units Nelsons used. The "Surge system" utilized an entirely different design with the teat cups and bucket forming an integral unit placed underneath the cow's udder and suspended by a leather strap that circumvented the cow's body. Our cows, unaccustomed to the feel of this new system along with everything else that had transpired that day ... weren't happy! That initial milking proved to be a long and tiring exhibition and not one needing an audience.

Another big change came in the way we handled our milk. Most of the milk output from our neighbour's herds went to the local cheese factory. Owner and manager of the factory, Tye Posliff, manufactured the milk brought in by local farmers into twenty-pound squares of cheese that were shipped to various destinations around southwestern Ontario.

An added feature of the cheese factory, especially if one raised pigs, was the retrieval of the whey ... that watery part of the milk left over when all the good parts were removed. Pigs went crazy over that stuff! Subsequently, Tye manufactured "whey butter," although our family was of the opinion it also tasted like pig feed. However, many of our new neighbours used it as their main spread. "It's something for which you have to acquire a taste," Posliff stated ... I guess!

For our herd Dad chose the bulk milk system. While a new milk house was being constructed next to the barn, our "can" cooler performed admirably from its location in the implement shed. The "milk cart" used at Bradford proved invaluable once again transporting cans back and forth across the yard. When word spread we were in the market for a bulk cooler, there was certainly no shortage of cooler representatives with which to contend.

The only sales personnel more persistent were insurance salesmen. Harold Cosens was one (probably explaining his neighbourliness) although as insurance agents go, he was okay. There was a Mr. Pritchard who'd stand in the stable all evening making glowing remarks about our Holstein herd and the wonderful farm we'd chosen. When the chores were completed, like a pup he'd follow us to the house continuing his sales pitch. Finally, Dad had to tell him as plainly and politely as possible to get lost.

The most annoying insurance agent was Mr. Bender. Nothing you said could shake him and no matter how many times you said "I'm not interested," it simply failed to register.

"We'll duck in here!" Dad urged a couple of us one day when his all too familiar Ford turned into our driveway. "In here" was a tiny cubicle tacked onto the south side of the implement shed. For what service the closet-sized building was originally intended I have no idea, as I can't recall it ever containing anything but scrap metal and discarded lumber. Like fugitives we crouched and waited for Bender to leave, but he obviously spotted us for the next thing we knew there he was larger than life in the doorway. "So ... are you working or hiding?" It would be well understood to say we felt stupid.

In our area in 1957 if one wished to ship bulk milk, there was one choice ... Allan Johnston Transport from nearby Listowel, Ontario. Although Johnston's bread and butter was still his "can" routes, since 1954 he had gradually increased his influence in this burgeoning bulk milk system. When other southern Ontario transporters had sold their routes, Johnston had somehow been able to come up with the financing to purchase many of them. From the outset, his vision had been the lucrative Toronto market and he managed to secure a contract with Silverwood's Dairies to supply milk from the Listowel area.

Johnston was a congenial fellow ... and a good thing too, for he certainly had his hardships and we managed to provide a few of our own. With no adequate means of snow removal, getting the milk truck in and out our laneway that first winter was a bugger! Several times that season we had to transfer milk from the bulk cooler into cans Dad had the foresight to keep and haul them to the road by sleigh. Often in the middle of a blizzard the 100-pound cans would be hoisted to the top of the truck and poured into the tank by Johnston himself.

From his single-axle bulk truck of 1954, his company, still operated by his son and other family members, now numbers a huge fleet of tandem trucks, trailers and tractors. Close to a million litres of milk from hundreds of farms are drawn each day to dairies all through southern Ontario. However, I guess it was all the "little guys" like us that made it possible.

ONE ROOM ... INFINITE
MEMORIES

On September 8, 1954, sixteen-year-old Toronto native Marilyn Bell dove into the water of Lake Ontario at Youngstown, New York, and proceeded to swim towards the Canadian National Exhibition grounds at Toronto, twenty-three miles away. Seventy-five hundred dollars was the prize for completing the marathon and a place in the history books as being the first person to conquer the feat. Twenty-one hours later, after fighting nausea, eels, oily water, polluted water, as well as huge waves causing her to drift severely off-course, and nearly dead from exhaustion ... she arrived at her destination.

While Marilyn was psyching herself up for her translake crossing, another momentous event was taking shape ... I was preparing for my first day of school. Occasionally throughout the summer someone would mention something about "starting to school," but I never paid much attention as there were more important things to occupy the mind of a five-year-old. But as the last hot days of August drew to a close, I realized it was no longer talk. I'd passed my pre-school physical. I had a new plaid shirt and new "scampers" for my feet. As well, I had a brand new "Lone Ranger" lunch box.

To put it mildly, I had some "issues" that first week ... presenting my newly graduated teacher Miss Brown with a major challenge by bawling over the slightest incident and forcing my older sister Vivien to babysit me a good part of each day. Vivien was real impressed! However, things turned quickly around, and I actually began to enjoy most aspects of school.

Once I became settled, I discovered "reading" to be my favourite subject. Learning new words was a real high. "See Dick run. See Jane run. See Dick and Jane run. See Spot run. See Puff run. See Spot and Puff run. Run, run, run!" ... those were great stories!

I had a harder time with printing. Even with that huge red pencil that more resembled a fence post, I found it difficult to make it go where I wanted. Figures were a little easier, but Vivien had warned me of the difficulty in making "2's" ... a digit that proved very challenging for her when she was my age. She was right ... "2's" were a bitch!

Each afternoon I'd hurry home to relate the day's highlights to Mom, who'd patiently listen about the new words I'd learned and look at the pictures I'd coloured. On Mondays, Mom received a special treat. That was the day Mr. McKelvy, our music teacher, made his visit to our school. We'd always learn a new song and I'd perform it a cappella when I got home.

By the start of my third year, I was making steady progress. I could print pretty well. I could read entire stories. We no longer had to be content with writing on any old scrap of paper, as we had real Hilroy notebooks ... or "scribblers" as we called them just like the big kids. Although in the lower grades we were still cursed with that baseline paper ... the type where you had to write around the chunks of wood. And we were still using those fat red pencils that chubby hands could grip. But each day brought discovery and knowledge.

One of the perks of a one-room school was the education you absorbed from eavesdropping. I was a fan of David Livingstone, Ferdinand Magellan and James Wolfe long before I was required to study them. Similarly, we learned our multiplication tables right along with the upper grades, and if extra practice was warranted ... they were all neatly printed on the back cover of your Hilroy scribbler. Along with other items then deemed important, now considered useless, were the legal weights of different species of grain, calculated in bushels or pecks, or how many rods in a mile, or square rods in an acre. By the time of graduation that information was embedded in my brain and fifty years later even if useless ... I still haven't forgotten it.

Before I completed third grade, we moved from Simcoe County to a new school in Perth County. That first morning, Mom herded my two brothers and me inside the school and introduced us to our new teacher, Mrs. Ashmore. At the time she was standing on a stool at one of the side blackboards, putting the final touches on an absolutely overwhelming drawing, in my opinion, of a crayfish. This masterpiece, encompassing the full area of the blackboard, had been accomplished by judicial use of coloured chalk. Mom talked for a few minutes while we stood like fence posts. Most of the class had followed us in and were staring at us from the back of the room. We stared back.

With our appearance, U.S.S. #11 Wallace enrollment escalated to 33 students. At first recess, some of the kids in the primary and middle classes suggested we play hide-and-seek. This is a tough game to play when you know no one's name. We were given a quick introduction then left on our own. "This is Gary and Larry and Harry and Mary and Johnny and Connie and Bonnie and Donnie" … nevertheless, it was a nice gesture of friendship and sort of broke the ice.

A day at our new school pretty much ran along the lines of the former. First, "God Save the Queen," with Mrs. Ashmore pounding out the accompaniment on the corner piano. That was followed by "The Lord's Prayer," then fifteen minutes of Scripture reading. Everyone who could read took part in these exercises. Mathematics or arithmetic as we knew it lasted until recess.

Following recess, spelling and reading … two subjects I enjoyed. Good thing, as our mother would tolerate nothing less than good grades in either … especially spelling. We had about two dozen new words to learn each week. Friday was the big test, with the results being tallied and transferred to a huge sheet of bristle board thumbtacked to the bulletin board wall. A perfect score netted a red star … one mistake, a green. Anything lower, the number of mistakes was simply written in the appropriate space in red pencil crayon … a clear reminder of one's stupidity.

For the best spellers there was an added incentive. Three consecutive red stars earned you one gold star. If I received a couple of gold stars each semester, I was satisfied … and so was Mom.

During the afternoon, Grammar, Social Studies, Science, Penmanship, Geography and Art would be worked into the schedule over different days. I never excelled in penmanship. My grade three report card Miss Brown sent from my former school to Mrs. Ashmore, stated ...

"David's work is satisfactory. He learns easily, although his books are not as well kept as possible. I have to stress neatness with him continually. Otherwise he is clever and well behaved." On a more personal note she added, "I'm sure he will do well in his new school. I'll miss his happy smile!"

As at our former school, a music instructor dropped by each week. That initial week, the school was putting together the finishing touches on their radio debut. Apparently this had been an annual event where a random school was chosen to perform on the local radio station. As we were completely unfamiliar with the music, we missed our chance at stardom.

Saturday morning, we tuned into CKNX 920 in Wingham ... and laughed ourselves silly. There was probably nothing wrong with the performance; it just seemed the thing to do. The following Monday I was commenting on the production to my new classmates.

"It sounded like a bunch of cats with their tails stepped on!" My brother Brian backed me up with a good laugh ... he was the only one who did. "It must have been your radio," one student reacted angrily. "Better tell your old lady to get a new one. It sounded just fine to the rest of us!" I wisely said no more. School spirit was obviously alive and well at U.S.S. #11 Wallace.

Other reflections of public school days ...

Hot lunches: First day after the Christmas holiday break would begin this winter tradition. A strong advocate of nourishment and proper diet, Mrs. Ashmore stressed the need for something more substantial than sandwiches on long, cold winter days of limited sunshine.

Our hot lunches were usually contained in an emptied jam jar, although the container wasn't important, as long as it was glass and easy from which to spoon. Once at school the jars were placed in a roasting pan partially filled with water, and at precisely 11:30 someone would be assigned to turn on the hotplate. By noon, with the water bubbling and boiling, the product would be as good as anything eaten at home. Soup was the mainstay, although there were a few who consistently brought pork and beans. There was nothing wrong with that, provided you didn't sit directly behind them during the afternoon.

Examinations: As a rule, Mrs. Ashmore wrote the exam questions on the blackboard the previous evening. Next morning she'd unroll the series of world maps … remember them? … they were sponsored by Neilson's and advertised a chocolate bar at each corner. The maps were just the right dimension to cover one complete blackboard. It was always kind of dramatic as the maps were re-rolled the following morning, exposing the exam questions, one by one.

There was one announcement Mrs. Ashmore would make each month, sending a resounding cheer throughout the room. "Film Day!" A series of films approved by the Board of Education made a regular circuit of all the schools in the district. Someone's parent would be assigned the task of retrieving the batch of films from a neighbouring school. It was the grade 8's job to operate the Bell & Howell projector, while the grade 7s observed. The following year, they would be ready to take their turn at the controls and the cycle would continue.

Within the collection of reels, there'd be a "Health and Hygiene" film, a Geography film and a couple of "Industry" reels depicting a commodity's journey from raw material to finished product. There would inevitably be one on some famous explorer. We were supposed to keep notes during the presentation for further discussion, but mostly we viewed the entire episode as simply a day away from the monotony of regular school subjects. If things appeared to be progressing too rapidly and we might run out of material before the day was through, the grade 8s had learned from their predecessors how to discreetly break the film and waste a good proportion of time splicing it back together.

On Friday, June 29, 1962, I bade farewell to the one-room school at U.S.S. #11. The previous evening as in years past, our school presented a "bon voyage" to the grade 8s, plus a welcome to the first graders who would begin in September.

As president of the students' council, I was expected to chair the evening's programme. At noon on graduation day, Mrs. Ashmore presented me with a two-page account to be memorized for the show, just hours away. I stared at the sheet. She hadn't missed a thing ... It began with an introductory message to the community on behalf of the school; an itinerary of the previous year's curriculum, including the destination of the annual school bus excursion and how we fared at the annual Field Day. Any achievements in music or public speaking were duly noted. The donation of a book by the Women's Christian Temperance Union was acknowledged, as well as New Testament Bibles by the Gideon Society.

(This is a highly contentious issue nowadays, but back when I was in school every student upon reaching grade five received a Bible. Started in 1947, the Gideon Society's objective was to spread the word of God by placing Bibles in schools, hospitals, seniors' residences, hotels, prisons etc. ... I still have the pocket-sized Bible presented to me ... dated November 5, 1958.)

"There's no way I can learn all this on such short notice!" I said to Mom on reaching home. I was bawling like a baby at this point. (I cried the first day of public school, why not the last?) "Nobody says you have to memorize it totally," Mom answered reassuringly. "If you have any trouble, you can read some." She then injected a dash of maternal psychology. "But I know you ... if you put your mind to it, you can learn it easily by tonight."

Mom was right ... but I certainly didn't believe her at the time. Following the event, Mrs. Ashmore commented to Mom how proud she was of me. Mom admitted I had some "doubts," but just needed my confidence restored. "I knew he could do it," said Mrs. Ashmore. "David's got a great mind!"

That "great mind" can remember not one word our guest speaker offered to us that June evening as we took the giant step from one-room elementary to the unknown world of secondary education ... great mind indeed!

THE SHOW MUST GO ON

In the multiple-grade, one-room school system in which I was raised, confusion never seemed far away at the best of times. Factor in something as special as the annual Christmas concert and confusion quickly graduated towards chaos. Depending upon the talent of the students and the originality of the teacher, these concerts could vary from wildly entertaining to dreadfully dull. At Fishers Corners, the Simcoe County country school where I began my academic education, the ordeal began sporadically in early December. Some minor decorating ... windows, blackboards etc. ... then a few days before the concert a more concentrated effort, when the classroom would be strung with red and green crepe paper from wall to wall. These streamers had an annoying habit of falling down over the next few days as the scotch tape dried out.

Finally the big night, when the community would fill every chair in the place and as well there'd be a few men supporting the back wall. (If the show simply became too boring, they could slip outside undetected.) For an hour and a half the concert would continue, with children constantly entering and exiting through "bed sheet" curtains in order to perform their recitations, skits and songs.

What I remember most about those early concerts was always being cast as a shepherd in the "First Christmas" pageant; never Joseph or one of the three wise men ... just a dull shepherd. I wished to wear a colourful robe and crown as the men of the east, instead of the greys and browns dictated by the sheepherders. The wise men got to present nicely wrapped gifts to the baby Jesus, while the shepherds just stood and dumbly stared at the manger. One year, I unintentionally provided a degree of levity to this solemn occasion by waving to Mom and Dad from the stage. Totally out of character for a shepherd!

The best part of the show of course was the arrival of Santa. To the cue of "Jingle Bells" he'd come stomping in with a suit that chronically never fit, a beard that never stayed in place and rubber boots scrubbed as best they could of nature's fertility.

At Fishers Corners, Santa Claus always sounded suspiciously like our next-door neighbour Orville Hughes, who'd dole out the presents we'd been eyeing all evening. Every student received a bag of candy along with their gift and every year it was the same variety stuffed into that aforementioned bag; an orange, a few hard candies, some licorice "all-sorts," peanuts in the shell and perhaps a chunk of home-made fudge. And every year without fail, the hard candies and licorice would melt and glom onto the orange.

I always worried that somehow my name would be missed and I'd face the humiliation of heading home empty-handed, but Santa always came through. I recall one Christmas concert's gift was Chinese Checkers. It was a metal play board and the marbles orchestrated a delightful clatter as they were moved across the board. But nothing came close to the racket my metal drum made from another school concert. "Not here!" was Mom's comment as I struck up the band. "Take it outside ... or wait until we get home!" I figured the back seat of the car on the way home was close enough, but Mom and Dad failed to agree. When home, I really cut loose, sounding like the drum major in the twelfth of July Orange Parade, I thought. No one else did. "Take that thing upstairs!" Mom hollered. As I made my way up the stairs, I recall Mom saying to someone, "I'd sure like to get hold of the kid who gave him that drum!" I beat that drum consistently for the next day or two, then it mysteriously disappeared.

When our family moved to Perth County and a new school, some things didn't change. As at Fishers Corners, bedlam prevailed the two weeks preceding the Christmas concert. Every season, Mrs. Ashmore would begin with grandiose plans for her students. Two dozen songs, a number of small skits, a dozen recitations, a couple of piano recitals, the nativity scene and of course the main three-act play. And every year Mr. Gedke, our music teacher, would delicately suggest that she cut the program by half if she hoped to meet the ninety-minute timetable.

As well as everything else going on, "drills" played a major role in concerts of yesteryear. Wearing a variety of costumes and doing a number of exercises and formations, these events were scheduled mainly before major skits or the main play. Generally, they provided a distraction more than anything from the commotion taking place in the wings.

What kind of concert would it be without the story of the first Christmas, and once again I'd be cast as ... yeah, you guessed it.

Some afternoons, Mrs. Ashmore would become completely frustrated with her dumb, apathetic crew. "Alright!" she'd explode. "If nobody is going to take this concert seriously, we'll just forget the whole thing. I can certainly do without it! We won't waste a minute's more time!" Her outbursts, although frequent, passed quickly and next afternoon we'd resume practice. The final day we'd run through the entire production from start to finish. Songs, skits, recitations, the rhythm band, the big play … everything … with costumes.

The only year we'd didn't engage in full dress rehearsal was the year the main play was done in "blackface." It was a throwback to the old minstrel shows that had originated in the late 1800s and continued well into the next century. Basically it featured white performers, blackening their faces to take on the appearances of Negroes. Stephen Foster songs would often be integrated into these shows, while "black" performers with names like Rastus, Sambo and Otis would tell stories and jokes.

It all sounds so politically incorrect and even racist now, and even in 1960 it was well past its time. Originally, burnt cork was used for the blackening effect. Mrs. Ashmore utilized some sort of black paint. I guess it looked "real" … but what a challenge to remove!

Finally the long-awaited, or dreaded, night depending upon your perspective. At eight o'clock, the chosen master of ceremonies would welcome all, and the show would be on. For the next ninety minutes, conditions on and off stage would cycle between moderate bedlam and total chaos. All recitations were performed in front of the bed sheet curtains while the next act was setting up behind the scenes. Mrs. Ashmore stood just out of audience range, script in hand, ready in a second to prompt a student with a forgotten line. All around her in the wings, confusion reigned. Laughing, giggling, crying, coughing, whispering and vomiting could be heard from most anywhere in the room.

One of the most difficult aspects of staging a show such as this is trying to co-ordinate a couple dozen kids in and out of costumes, while working in a cramped environment. No matter what plans had been put in gear, stipulating whose costume was whose and where it was ... it just never seemed to be in its proper place come the big night.

I recall a drill which required our clothes to be worn in reverse ... shirts buttoned up the back, trousers on backwards. Halloween masks were affixed to the back of our heads to complete the charade, and a sort of cheesecloth type material was draped over our faces and secured with the same elastic band that secured the mask. Everyone was searching through the costume pile like rummage sale customers, among conditions less than favourable as someone had thrown up on the dressing room floor.

I finally found my shirt and pants which I speedily pulled on over my regular clothes. We all fastened one another's buttons. I secured my face mask but couldn't locate the face shroud. Panic gripped me as Mrs. Ashmore whispered the stand-by signal. Just then I discovered it on the floor. "How in the heck did it get on the floor!" I hissed at someone. I grabbed it then recoiled as it was spattered with vomit! It was too late to do anything but wipe it off. The drill lasted just a few minutes, but seemed like months with that stinking piece of cloth dangling in front of my nose.

After an episode such as that, things could only improve, and finally it was the last act of the last play and the last song sung. It was at this point that the anticipation and excitement of Santa's arrival really came into focus. Santa always made a grand entrance at our school, bounding up the porch steps and into the schoolroom. This particular night, however, as he raced into the lobby his rubber boots lost traction on the slush-covered surface and he careened across the wet floor and crashed into the far wall. As he glanced off the door frame, he dislocated his beard and knocked his hat off. A couple of men leaning against the back wall were later heard to comment that Santa's language during the incident wasn't all that conducive to the holiday spirit. However, true soldier that he was, our St. Nick gathered himself and continued up the aisle, albeit slightly less energetically. By the time the gifts and candy bags were handed out ... with the exception of Santa himself perhaps ... the embarrassing incident had been largely forgotten.

OLIVER

The ringing of the telephone interrupted my sleep that September morning. From my upstairs bedroom I could hear Mom talking to someone. Following probably a five-minute conversation, the closing of the screen door signalled she had gone outside. I arose and walked down the hall to the bathroom. From the window I observed Mom walking across the yard towards the barn. I wondered who would be wanting Dad this early, or what was so important that couldn't wait until breakfast. Not worthwhile returning to bed, I dressed and went downstairs. Mom was back in the kitchen at this point, the familiar odour of oatmeal greeting my nostrils as I entered. "Uncle Eldon called," said my mother, stirring the porridge. "Grandpa died last night."

I think it was that moment ... when the reality of young and old and life and death struck me. I knew Grandpa was old ... well, to an eleven-year-old he seemed old. He was seventy-nine. In a way, Grandpa had always seemed old. I always wished I'd known him better ...

But then, few people actually knew Oliver Turner well ... as he entertained a quiet, reserved manner. Never talked much unless he figured it was important, and then made his point quickly and clearly. He was generous, gladly lending anything he might possess, expecting no payment for favours except a simple thank-you. He was a believer in the axiom that all people were honest, trusting everyone unless they gave him reason otherwise. More than a few times, he'd helped neighbours and friends out of a financial jam by co-signing notes or mortgages.

Oliver Turner was not the visible type of friend and neighbour, much preferring to contribute from the back row of the crowd. He took great interest in local politics, forever backing candidates whom he believed could make a difference in township and county development. He loved music and was an avid reader, poetry especially. My Dad recalled his father lifting him and his sister onto his lap often at bedtime, while he recited, from memory, lines from his favourite authors.

He also took an active interest in church affairs, being Sunday school superintendent at the Eugenia Methodist church, while also giving assistance to other congregations. When the Rock Mills Baptist church was in need of a new roof, Oliver donated $20.00 … a lot of money in the 1920s. In those days, one generally left a quarter on the collection plate. My father recalls one church member placing a dollar on the plate and taking back three quarters in change.

Despite his other interests, Oliver was a farmer, learning agriculture at the side of his father, which in the late 1800s and early 1900s added up to simple hard work. He knew one never went for the cows without a rifle, as he'd often heard the screech of a wildcat in the bush, and the mournful howl of a wolf pack would send a chill up your spine. Occasionally during the early morning hours, he witnessed a bear licking the salt block set out in the pasture for the cattle.

When in his early twenties, my grandfather joined the Western Canada harvest excursions sponsored by Canadian Pacific Railroad. The CPR had been assembling special trains to the west for years and Oliver decided it was time, joining other harvest hopefuls at Toronto's Union Station. Like all first-timers, he was completely taken aback by the sheer magnitude of the prairies. Equally impressive was the custom operator's portable threshing unit.

The largest steam tractor he'd ever seen was hooked to a thresher unit and that to a water supply tanker. Hooked behind that was a "cook car" that would seat a couple dozen men and beyond that, other bunk cars where the workers slept. Bunks were the minimum of comfort, a blanket spread over a layer of straw with two or three blankets on top. Those blankets would be needed during the cool prairie nights. Both rats and lice were major problems.

Because of his farm experience, Oliver played a hand in all aspects of the harvest operation. Each harvest day began at five AM, signalled by the steam tractor's whistle. Get up, wash in the icy cold water of a basin, dress and head for the cook car. Pancakes were the focus of each breakfast. Very seldom was morning dew a factor on the prairies so by six o'clock the harvest was ready to commence, with the horses fed, watered and harnessed and tractor up to full steam. Fuel for this mighty steamer was the cheapest available ... straw. It kept one man busy just forking straw into its fiery belly.

Whatever the task, those with experience taught those without, and by season's end the crew was harvesting 2,000 bushels of wheat a day. The routine was unrelenting but scheduled ... midmorning refreshment right in the field. At noon, a full course meal back at the cook car, then another midafternoon field break, followed by supper at six. After the evening meal, some played cards, others shared a bottle, while some just sat and talked or told stories from home. If anyone had brought a harmonica or guitar, they played it, or if you were too tired from the day's work, you simply dragged your ass to bed.

And so it went for six weeks. From field to field, farm to farm, through twelve-hour days of sun and wind and dust, the monotony broken only by the occasional rain. At the end of their six-week term they were paid the $100 they'd been promised. To most of these young men, this was more money than they'd ever seen ... but they'd earned it.

In 1910 when my grandfather was thirty, he married Janie Magee, daughter of a neighbouring family. Initially the newlyweds planned to move into a rented house south of the home farm. One cold, late autumn day, Oliver took over their first load of belongings, kindled a fire in the kitchen stove to remove the chill and left for a second load.

Upon returning, he discovered the house ablaze. The brisk November wind had fanned the flames beyond control by this time, so Oliver could do nothing but watch the house crumble to the ground and his plans with it. After this disaster ... plan "B" was put into effect. His father owned the farm across the road and on this farm was an uninhabited log house. It was here Oliver and his bride finally began married life and where my father was born.

The Turner and Magee families were as different as dark and light. The Turners, calm, cool and collected ... the Magees, the epitome of the "fightin' Irish." Janie's parents, their son and daughter-in-law, plus two unmarried daughters all lived under one roof. To say this made for chaotic conditions was understatement unequalled. Somebody was always angry with someone and quarrels were frequent.

Granddad William Magee seemed forever on opposite sides of the female connection. The pattern was well formulated. A disagreement would surface, followed by a shouting match, often with such intensity all three women ... his wife and the two unmarried daughters ... would walk out of the house. They always went to the same place ... Oliver and Janie's. Sometimes they'd stay just a day or two, other times a week or more, depending how violent the parting. Inevitably tempers and feelings would soothe and back home they'd go until the next explosion.

William often blamed Oliver for many of his frustrations, especially when it came to harbouring the "no good spoilt bitches." On one occasion the elder Magee became so agitated he grabbed his rifle and shouted ... "I'll quiet the lot of you!" Everybody ran for the family car parked in the driveway ... except Oliver. "Hurry up Oliver!" someone yelled. "He's going to kill us all!" Oliver stood his ground and answered evenly. "You'll never see the day I run from William Magee." The rest didn't wait around for the outcome and headed for Oliver and Janie's, a mile away. A short time later, Oliver walked down the road, his stand-off evidently successful.

One task expected of every rural taxpayer in the early part of the twentieth century was aiding in the township's ongoing project of road maintenance. For a couple of days, spring and fall, each farmer donated his time and labour and usually a team and wagon, to load, haul and spread gravel. One particularly hot season while shovelling gravel, Oliver was overcome by sunstroke, its side effects lingering in varying degrees for years. Frequent nausea, often quite violent, followed whenever he was exposed to sunlight. Years later would still find Oliver stooking grain by the light of the moon, rather than facing the daylight sun.

Another unrelated problem was cataracts. The medical world didn't routinely operate on cataracts like today, but over a period of a summer, a doctor in Owen Sound by a bizarre combination of medication and pupil stretching, supposedly cured his affliction. In the interim, Oliver walked around with pupils resembling a cat ... much to the amusement of his children.

Janie Turner, while always delicate, incurred developing health problems of her own when still in her thirties. With x-ray technology in its infancy in the 1920s, the best medical information available pointed to heart valve complications. "Thorough rest and medication" seemed to be the best offer of hope.

At first, friends and family refused to accept the heart theory. It was easier to believe that Janie was simply "run down" and all offered personal advice on diet and nutrition. Later, with the realization of more serious problems, they traced it back to that day two or three years earlier when the horses ran away with the buggy in which Janie was riding, throwing her onto the roadway. But the reasons weren't important anymore. By the end of the year, Janie's heart was so weak she was confined to bed full time. Oliver, feeling helpless, consulted a second doctor's opinion, who except for a slight change in medication could add nothing. The regular visits and prescribed medicines seemed to do little except inflate an already large medical bill.

In the early hours of a cold February morning, the doctor stated Janie had only a few hours to live. My dad and his sister, just nine and ten respectively, were brought to her bedside, while Oliver went out to the barn to do the chores early so he could be with her in her final hours. However, she died before he could return.

A frugal man in many ways, my grandfather had allowed himself few luxuries throughout his years, so it was a surprise to most everyone in the community when he bought a new Ford Model T. Surprising because, like many of his generation, Oliver found the transition from horse power to gasoline difficult. On one occasion he drove over to his sister's place, and as he prepared to stop, became confused with the procedure. Hearing the disturbance, she peered from her window to see her brother rotating in circles around the yard, all the while hollering ... "Whoa ... whoa!"

Although it was none of their business, a few neighbours questioned the logistics of such a purchase at this time, reasoning Oliver shouldn't have been "wasting his money" with so many medicals bills yet to be paid. Oliver, never one to be concerned by idle gossip, saw no reason for defence. It was obvious to anyone with half a brain anyway. He'd promised his wife and kids a new car and with all the worry and sadness borne over the preceding months, something new and fresh and yes ... maybe just a little frivolous ... was needed to regain some of that family spirit!

The Christmas of 1925 was a tough one for the Turner family, but they'd followed tradition and gone to the in-laws for the holiday feast. My grandfather always seemed out of place at these gatherings. Very religious, his nature didn't always mesh with the more free-wheeling Magees. Above all else, the Magee family enjoyed hunting, good cigars, and fine whiskey. As Oliver neither smoked nor drank and "sport" hunting held little appeal ... it made for a long day ... and on this particular Christmas ... even more.

My older brothers and sister experienced the warmth and companionship of a grandfather when he was still relatively young and in good health. They had often talked about weekends and holidays spent on the old Artemesia Township farm, "helping" Grandpa with chores. By the time I was getting to know him, the years were taking their toll, especially since a severe bout with pneumonia five years earlier. He never fully recovered from that ordeal. At his birthday the previous December, Grandpa was very frail and his eyesight poor.

But on that second Sunday in September, he had felt the best in a long time. So much so, his son and daughter-in-law decided to take him on a drive through the Beaver Valley. The leaves were nicely into their glorious colour change, and Grandpa remarked on their beauty. Around ten o'clock that evening, he suffered a stroke and died instantly.

When Mom and Dad were heading for Eugenia on Tuesday for visitation, Dad stopped for gas at "Smitty's" Texaco in Palmerston. Smitty, who knew both Dad and our ten-year-old Pontiac well, offered a '55 Chev that he had for sale. "Take it and see how it runs." Smitty was always trying to update Dad to a better vehicle. His most recent campaign had been the previous summer when he tried to interest our father in a couple of Fords.

When they got back that evening, I was all excited about the "new" car they were driving, asking Dad all sorts of questions about its performance and features ... questions he could certainly have done without. Changing the subject I then asked ... "How did Grandpa look?" ... "Just like he was sleeping," Dad answered. "You'd think he was taking a nap." That answer seemed to satisfy my curiosity and I didn't bother him further.

On Wednesday, the day of the funeral, I was hoping the Chevy would be providing the transportation, but Dad returned the car that morning. Apparently it had jumped out of second gear on occasion. With possible transmission problems, Dad wanted no part of it.

Before going out to the farm at Eugenia, we stopped at the funeral chapel in Flesherton. Unfamiliar with our surroundings and sensing our reticence, Dad took us younger kids by the hand over to the casket. I had to admit, Grandpa did appear to be simply having an afternoon nap. However, I was eleven years old and knew better. A couple of memories, like the feel of his whiskers warm against my face, or the stiff fabric of his overalls while seated on his lap, brought wetness to my eyes.

Out at my grandparents' house, a light lunch was served after the funeral. As I sat in the living room, my gaze was drawn to a large portrait of three young men. Noting my interest, Dad informed me the photograph was of his dad and Oliver's two brothers. Until this moment, it had never really occurred to me that Grandpa was once young, yet there he was looking barely out of his teens. I was once asked if there was a particular spark that ignited my interest in our family's history. I sometimes wonder if perhaps it was that turn-of-the-century photograph.

" ... Oliver Turner resided all his life in this community. He was a congenial friend and neighbour." So ended the obituary in the *Flesherton Advance* the following week; a simple tribute ... but in its simplicity, I guess it said it all.

THE FIVE COMMANDMENTS

B efore I began writing this story I researched the word "sin" in my Webster's dictionary ... "the willful breaking of religious or moral law." That's a rather general explanation isn't it? Open to all kinds of interpretation. My thesaurus came up with an entire column of dreadful synonyms ... evil, wickedness, depravity, immorality, debauchery ... it just got worse. During my public school days in the 1950s, sin generally fell into five categories, which depending upon one's perspective could vary greatly in severity. In no particular order they included alcohol, tobacco, sex, profanity and even card playing.

A small but important segment of our neighbourhood community belonged to the United Missionary church, an offshoot of the original Mennonite Brethren in Christ of Pennsylvania. This sect shunned cards almost completely. Euchre was definitely out. To them it was the "devil's game," a one way ticket to Hell. They could play "Lost Heir" however ... a game that traced its routes to the beginning of the twentieth century and was manufactured in British, American and Canadian versions. Whatever version, the cards utilized cities instead of kings, queens, aces etc.

Their "non-euchre" rationale always seemed a little foggy to my way of thinking. The cards were the same size; like euchre there were four suits, "trump" cards were part of the game, one played for points etc. ... but for some reason Lost Heir was okay simply because it didn't have those "devil pictures."

Sex? ... well except for that woodshed exhibition with Helen Street when I was five or six and really too young to pay attention ... I knew nothing. Even at ten or eleven I was still under the impression my penis was for peeing and nothing more. At home, the closest we came to sex education was the Eaton's catalogue women's underwear section.

Profanity? ... I recall my school chum Larry saying: "You guys didn't know how to swear until you came to this school." Although eight years old when I moved to our new school, Larry was right ... I don't recall hearing a swear word at our old school. Again, I probably wasn't paying attention. Larry taught me a little song soon after my arrival ...

Two Irishmen, two Irishmen were working in a ditch, one called the other a dirty son of a bitch. One had a daughter, she was fair and fine and fit and one day she said would you like to feel ...

... Well the rest isn't important as it got progressively more tasteless as I recall. It may have lacked class but it was a catchy number we sang for years.

We seldom heard expletives at home. Even a direct hammer hit on the thumb would yield little more than a "dash the hammer!" from our father, at least when we kids were around. Dad would sometimes begin a slightly off-colour story only to be stopped by Mom with "Now

Harold ... don't be vulgar!" I can't count the times I heard that phrase.

Nowadays even elementary school kids have access to almost every drug imaginable. In my day of the one-room school, tobacco was it. And since its link to lung cancer, emphysema and heart disease etc. hadn't been established ... smoking was just good old-fashioned sinful. Because of budget constraints, dry leaves often had to substitute for tobacco. Occasionally someone would bring some "real" tobacco to school they'd bought or stolen. Neither my brothers nor I ever smoked in the school yard ... no we weren't almighty pure ... we simply didn't trust one another not to rat.

I smoked my first "leaf" cigarette underneath the maple tree at the end of our laneway. I'd probably be about ten. What I remember most is nearly expiring from a coughing fit as well as setting fire to the dry September grass beneath the tree. To be a real man I had to have a real cigarette. The easiest way was to steal them. As Dad didn't smoke an alternative was necessary. The temptation presented itself that Christmas at my grandparents' house. Grandpa Will Carruthers had smoked "Export A" for sixty years. He had a small workshop in his basement where he puttered around and one could usually find a partially used pack there.

I stole three cigarettes and stuffed them in my shirt pocket beneath my vest. I recall my brother Richard slugged me for something I did or said on the way home and busted one of them, which I later had to tape back together. Next day I borrowed a couple of matches from the kitchen cupboard and headed for the loft above the implement shed. I just puffed, as inhaling and coughing to death hadn't been much fun. I had to wait until mid-February before we went to Toronto again. This time I lifted an entire pack. It's true ... stealing gets easier as you go along!

I guess I wasn't the only thief that day. While my younger brother Brian and I were playing dominos on the living room floor, a couple of cigarettes tumbled triumphantly from his shirt pocket onto the carpet. "How did these get here?!" a totally embarrassed Brian fairly shouted. "I'll take them back right now!" While my brother high-tailed it to the basement, his face crimson as an ocean sunset, I was sitting smugly with mine stashed safely in my own shirt.

Those cigarettes lasted me until spring. My friend Larry stole a pipe for me and I tried that for a while, but always had trouble keeping the blasted thing lit. I even gave cigars a try: "Old Port" ... rum flavoured, wine dipped ... or was it wine flavoured, rum dipped?

That left drinking; Dad bought one twelve-pack of beer a year. "I like a bottle of beer during haying," he'd say. "It cuts the dust better than anything else." If it was an especially short haying season there'd be a couple left over, but when they were gone ... that was it. Back then the insurance company with which Dad had a policy offered a discount for non-drinkers and each year when he'd fill out his renewal, Dad would write "yes" for the discount. And every year as if to justify his answer, he'd say, "I guess a bottle of beer during haying doesn't really count."

With just one case of brew available each summer, it was difficult for a young lad of inquisitive nature to get a taste of this corrupt liquid. Well wasn't that what the Women's Christian Temperance Union tried to teach us during those long boring winter afternoon school sessions? Just one drink and you'd experience a complete lack of co-ordination, slurred speech, double vision, blurred vision ... no vision.

Incidentally, the WCTU, if not familiar, was founded in 1874 and still survives today. For a major part of their first century "total abstinence of liquor" was foremost in their crusade. As time progressed they gradually shifted their focus to more worthwhile and meaningful world causes ... women's shelters, voting rights, stiffer penalties for sex crimes against women, equal pay for equal work etc. ...

However during those teaching sessions we endured fifty or sixty years ago, "Lead us not into temptation but deliver us from the evils of alcohol" was the message drilled into our subconscious. Well ... to hell with the WCTU, I was ready and willing to stare into the face of the devil himself for a sample of this most forbidden nectar!

My chance arose when my Uncle Mac left behind three or four bottles of "Labatt's 50" when his family had vacationed at our place earlier in the summer. In addition to the two or three Dad had left over, I felt quite comfortable in stealing one without arousing suspicion. It was a blazing hot August afternoon when I slipped into the cool semi-darkness of our basement. I wore my rubber boots so I could hide the bottle within and leave the house undetected.

My plan was to hike to a huge maple tree that grew on the boundary of our property near a large woodlot. It would be nice and cool, plus offer complete privacy. The walk consisted of well over a mile and man was it hot! As I trudged along in my rubber boots, I tried to imagine how beer would taste ... like triple-strength ginger ale perhaps? I was thirsty down to my toenails by the time I reached my destination and the vision of that cool amber liquid, topped by that snow white foam that was a feature of every beer advertisement, had me filled with anticipation.

I sat down within the inviting shade and kicked off my rubber boots. My socks were drenched with sweat and the bottle itself was the temperature of urine. However at this point I didn't really care as long as it quenched this powerful thirst. It was at that moment it occurred to me ... I'd forgotten the goddam opener! I stared at the bottle in my hand as if willpower might somehow dislodge the cap. After a couple of sentences of expletives that Mom would have rinsed my mouth with Javex had she heard, I headed back home ... I swear I could hear those old biddies from WCTU laughing their heads off!

If I thought it was a long hot trek to the bush, it was nothing like the return. I don't ever recall being so thirsty! Mom was digging carrots out of the garden when I approached the yard. "Why on earth are you walking around with your rubber boots on? It must be a hundred degrees!" I mumbled something about "going for a walk" ... "with your rubber boots? The sun must be frying your brain! For heaven's sake put on your running shoes and if you've got that much ambition to go traipsing off to the bush, you can expend some of it helping me in the garden!"

Totally frustrated and dejected, I headed toward the house where I'm sure I drank five gallons of water. But I guess it could have been worse ... Mom could have asked me what that lump in my boot was!

CHARACTER STUDY

In a recent discussion with a friend of mine, the subject of movies surfaced and I mentioned I rarely attend movies as most hold little interest. She then asked what kind of movies I did like and I answered "character studies." She laughed then added, "Well ... if the current movie trend is any indication ... good luck with that!"

It reminded me how few screenplays actually fall under that category and it also got me thinking about "interesting characters" in real life. For no reason in particular I recalled a couple of characters that at first glance appear insignificant, but in their own way helped weave the fabric of our family's rural heritage.

There was Curt Samson, uncle of my father. Curt among other things was custodian for the one-room school Dad attended in the 1920s. During the winter months, one of Curt's jobs as caretaker was to make sure the schoolhouse was reasonably warm by ensuring the wood stove was fully stoked and burning brightly when teacher and pupils arrived for class. Unfortunately this was not always the case as Curt wasn't noted as an early riser even though he lived directly across the road from the school.

As many of that era, life was hard so as a result Curt and his wife Maggie never earned much from their Artemesia Township farm. The farm had originally belonged to Maggie's parents and was sold to them when they married. Originally a hundred-acre parcel, a large portion had been flooded as a result of the recent Ontario Hydro Eugenia Dam construction project. Making up for the agricultural land lost, Curt compensated by boarding fishermen who travelled from Toronto every weekend from April through October to try their luck in the newly constructed "hydro lake." The trees and stumps left standing when the water rose had created a mecca for sport fishermen, and the Samsons as well as other neighbours had welcomed the opportunity.

During winter, times were especially lean, but Curt was a good hunter so even if the cupboard was bare he could be counted on to bring something home. If things were really tough, pigeon sufficed for chicken. Wild duck was another alternative. They didn't have much meat but were rather tasty. One minor inconvenience was retrieving the excess buckshot from the carcass.

What the Samsons lacked in monetary rewards they gained when it came to community affairs. Dances or house parties were seldom missed with the duo providing the entertainment. Maggie was a fine piano player and Curt was equally talented on the harmonica. He even competed successfully on local radio station CFOS during their "talent search."

Few would disagree that he was the neighbourhood's best square dance caller as well, although these outings weren't without incident. Maggie had a fiery disposition, augmented by a matching jealous streak. Returning home from these Saturday night gatherings, Curt would face a volley of accusations. "I saw the way you were looking at that whore!" Maggie would begin. "You don't know what the hell you're talking about!" Curt would growl in return. "You're so blind you wouldn't recognize yourself in a mirror!" These shouting matches were regular Saturday night occurrences and lasted a lifetime.

Storytelling was a speciality of Curt Samson; there was the one about the youngster who was violently tackled during a high school football game, ripping open his intestines and spilling them out onto the playing field. According to Curt, the doctor arrived with a basin, simply washed off the intestines, shoved them back in and sewed him up. "And he was fine ... no infection at all!"

Curt barely scratched a living from the fifty-acre parcel of stones and gravel disguised as a farm, so was forever dreaming of an easier life and his stories reflected that desire. There was this guy Curt knew who had a job at a factory in the city removing caps from beer bottles so they could be recycled. "That's all the dang guy had to do all day", Curt said wistfully. "And some of the bottles even had a little beer left in them which he got to drink!"

Because he was forever strapped for cash, Curt sometimes crossed the line when it came to honesty. One day while observing a man crank his Model T Ford on a village street, Curt noticed a dollar bill fall from his pocket. One dollar was a day's wages during the Great Depression so Curt simply walked over to his car and on the pretext of chatting with the gentleman, stood on the dollar bill. Once the individual drove way, Curt retrieved the currency.

Curt loved spinning yarns to kids as well and no one was more receptive than his own son Lester. Lester's favourites were of his father's hunting exploits. "Tell me another bear story!" he'd ask all wide-eyed and Curt would launch into yet another version of some bygone event, real or imagined, adding just enough new material to keep the account exciting.

Lester and my father were three years apart in age and the closest of friends, although their character differed as darkness and light. Lester was wild, uninhibited and forever skirting trouble's fringe, while Dad was shy, polite and reserved. Lester's mother confessed she didn't worry when her son was out with my father, certain he was a good influence. Dad certainly had lots of time to influence since the two were seldom apart. If he biked into Eugenia, Lester went too. Groundhog hunting, Lester was there. Lester ate as many meals at my grandfather's as at home. He often rode back and forth on an old fat mare that he liked to run at full speed. You could hear the horse's hoofs a half mile away. How Lester ever stayed on the barrel-bodied nag, Dad could never understand, as he rode bareback.

The only time they really saw little of one another was during school hours as Dad was in grade twelve (fourth year) when Lester began high school. Whereas my father enjoyed every minute of school, Lester simply didn't apply himself to learn anything that even remotely resembled an education. He spent about six years in the secondary school system but the result was about two where it counted. The first couple of years Lester attended Flesherton High until he got expelled. He then graced the classrooms of the neighbouring high school town in Feversham for a while but got kicked out there too. Chronic absenteeism and general insubordination seemed to be the deciding factors with each dismissal. Following the Feversham expulsion, Lester stayed home on the farm for a while before once again attempting a couple more sporadic periods at Flesherton.

When my father got his driver's license, Lester was excited as they could now travel farther afield, providing they had a quarter for a gallon of gas. If not, there was always that magical link to the world ... radio. As mentioned, Lester's father rented out a cottage to fishermen and when they left for the city on Sunday nights they left their radio behind. The pair would break into the building and spend long evenings listening to the country music stations that beamed their signals out of the U.S.A. Weather had a lot to do with what you received on any given night. Some nights ... nothing but static ... others, the air waves were as clear as a bell. Generally later the hour, better the reception.

While Dad left for a couple of years to try his hand at city living, Lester drifted around doing odd jobs, which was about all one could find in the midst of the Great Depression. However a few years later Lester stumbled onto a position working at a large dairy farm on the edge of Brampton, just west of the city of Toronto. By this time Dad's stab at a business career in the big city had long since folded but Lester insisted there was work for him at this farm if he chose. The war was on now so the job opportunity had completely reversed as tens of thousands had gone overseas to fight Hitler's armies.

When Lester began his stint at B.H. Bull's dairy operation, he began a trend of sorts. Besides my Dad, who was married by this time, several neighbours from "back home" in Artemesia followed over the next year or two. Lester's parents even gave it a try. Curt was still dreaming about a city job that paid handsomely without much physical activity ... "You know there's this guy I know ... and all he has to do is count how long each worker spends in the bathroom!"

Curt's new job didn't quite fulfil that dream. Although tractors had taken over major field work, B.H. Bull's still kept a few horses for certain tasks. Curt filled a vacancy for teamster, his main job hauling manure from the four dairy barns. Not too glamorous perhaps, but at least it was regular pay, which was more than either Curt or Maggie were used to back home. Maggie got on the payroll by operating a boarding house. Lester boarded there as well as two other men.

With the war raging full force in Europe, draft notices were common items in mailboxes all over Canada. Lester received his notice to report to Camp Borden near Barrie, where he undertook three weeks of extensive military training. This included the usual army ritual for getting in shape, one of which involved running full speed at earth-filled bags with bayonet-equipped rifles. His mother was in a dreadful state, agonizing how her "poor wee Lester" and hundreds of others, had been herded off to the army base "like cattle." Maggie heaved a sigh of relief when Lester escaped induction, B.H. Bull's signing an affidavit he was "an essential person" to the organization.

This declaration caused more than a few snickers among co-workers, as Lester was probably the least dependable person on the place. He was forever shirking responsibility and never any good to get up in the mornings as he was often out carousing late into the night. Dad covered for him often, and once during a heated argument pointed out that perhaps overseas would be just the place for him. "You're one to talk!" Lester fired back. "You got married and had a kid every year to keep from going!"

Lester, especially as a teenager, simply did not see eye to eye with his parents. Things had smoothed somewhat in the intervening years but now that he was back with his family, arguments erupted with regularity. It was with Curt that Lester continually found himself on opposing sides. His father would give Lester hell for something, Maggie would intercede to protect Lester, then Curt and Maggie would have a yelling and swearing match. Other times, Curt would kick Lester out altogether, Maggie would blame Curt and another round of insults and name calling would ensue.

One particular squabble would mark Lester for life. To put it bluntly, Lester for some time had been screwing the wife of a co-worker. One evening Curt and Maggie came home to discover the couple going at it in overdrive on the living room sofa. It all hit the fan then ... and nobody within a thousand feet missed what followed!

First a scream, then a partially dressed woman running from the house; next was Curt hollering and swearing at Lester, who in turn was hollering and swearing at his father, while Maggie tried to referee. Interspersed was what sounded like furniture being tossed about, then finally Lester bursting out the door and shouting that "someone is going to get hurt around here!" With that he jumped into his car, jammed the Dodge into gear and sped away into the darkness.

Next morning Lester failed to appear for milking, not an entirely unusual occurrence. At breakfast, seeing no sign of Lester or his car, Dad questioned Curt and Maggie, who assumed he was out in the barn or with my parents, where he usually went after being thrown out at home. Just then a police car pulled up to the Samson doorway. Hysteria reigned supreme for several moments as all possibilities were considered. Maggie just knew Lester was lying dead somewhere and Curt was the cause, so several well-timed four-letter remarks were hurled in his direction. Once saner heads prevailed it was learned from the police officer that there had been a head-on collision during the night and two accident victims had been brought to the Brampton hospital, one with minor injuries, the other major. A hurried trip to town confirmed the worst case was Lester and he was barely recognizable.

As Curt, Maggie and my father entered the room, they recoiled in shock. Lester's face was completely black and blue and swollen terribly, and his nose was smashed flat into his face. Maggie couldn't stand it and vacated the scene crying. Besides the obvious facial injuries, Lester was also diagnosed with broken ribs and a ruptured spleen ... Lester's parting phrase to his parents the previous evening had proved eerily prophetic!

Before leaving for home, Dad and Curt drove to the police compound to see what was left of Lester's old Dodge. A graphic reminder of the severity of the collision was a dent where his nose had impacted the steel dashboard. Lester would recover from his internal injuries, but the accident left him permanently scarred as plastic surgery hadn't evolved to the point where it could do much for his facial trauma, particularly nose reconstruction.

The year 1943 dawned with Curt and Maggie calling it quits and heading back to their Artemesia farm which they had simply left to grow weeds for a couple of years. Lester then boarded with Mom and Dad for a while but that too was bound for change when Dad secured a herdsman's position at a dairy farm in Simcoe County. Without Dad to shield him, Lester was soon fired and returned home to live with his parents.

It was during that year that Dad received his draft notice, and unlike Lester was indeed considered "essential service." During the 1940s, agriculture packed a lot of clout and anyone directly involved with food production was considered essential and exempt from military duty. In fact it wasn't an uncommon practice among farmers especially if they were financially sound, to purchase a neighbouring farm for a service-aged son. This practically guaranteed absolution from an overseas hitch.

Curt and Maggie even scraped enough together for a small down payment on a fifty-acre farm for Lester. This was one poor excuse for a farm. With the proper machinery and a few dollars for fertilizer, the acreage probably could have formulated a modest showing. Lester had neither. Curt couldn't offer much in the way of relief as he had a full-time task restoring his own twitch grass-weed infested acreage to some semblance of a working farm.

Dad visited Lester shortly after he'd taken possession and never felt so sorry for anyone in his life as this farm seemed beyond help. There was Lester, enveloped in dust, riding a rickety cultivator that appeared held together with little more than hope. Transporting the implement over the barren rock-strewn field was a team of tired worn-out horses. Upon leaving, Dad wondered to himself if military life could possibly have been much worse than this!

Maggie of course needn't have worried about Lester being drafted. Following his accident, automatic denial would've been a certainty. She did have one other reason for trying to keep Lester home. Following his dismissal at B.H. Bull's, Lester wandered aimlessly for a year or so until he found himself in the Hamilton area. Here he met his future bride, daughter of a Saskatchewan farmer. She talked often about the section her father owned, and perhaps it was the fear that Lester would "go west" that hatched the farm idea. Lester didn't go west but he didn't hang around that sorry-sight farm for long either. He headed back Hamilton direction and eventually secured a good job working on a government-operated farm near that city.

Maybe it was married life that finally settled him down for he stayed nearly twenty years and apparently became a respected and dedicated employee. Due to the accident, however, he was plagued with difficult breathing. That in conjunction with a lifetime of cigarettes shortened Lester's time on earth and he passed away at the relatively young age of sixty-one.

Meanwhile his parents soldiered on until they reached pension age. At this point, Curt and Maggie sold the farm and bought a house in the village of Flesherton, finally living in some state of financial comfort after a lifetime of economic challenge.

The last time I saw Curt Samson was at some family function in the late 1960s. He was probably in his mid-seventies then and I recall him having a discussion with my brother Richard, who had recently started working for Bell Canada as a lineman. Except that Curt thought it was Hydro. "I guess we both climb poles," Richard responded. "Yes ... but the telephone is a lot safer," added Curt.

At this point Curt lit his pipe, which always signalled a story was on the way. "In fact there was this guy I knew who worked for Hydro and he was up a pole ... and there were two wires behind him. I guess the one was turned off but he must've forgotten about the other. He leaned his head back against the wire and was instantly electrocuted ... fell to the ground in a pile of ashes." Curt took a drag on his pipe ... "That's all that was left. They didn't even bother digging a grave. A farmer just happened to be digging post holes in a field next to the cemetery that day so they just hired him ... I think he only charged a dollar ... Well anyway, they just dumped the guy's ashes in the hole and that was it!"

SHORTCOMINGS

One Sunday afternoon returning home from some family gathering, we turned into the laneway and descending the gentle grade to our yard saw a familiar green Buick. Mom and Dad almost in unison sighed ... "Not the Shorts!" Luther and Mina were neighbours Dad had grown up with in Grey County. Now living in Whitby, their frequent visits had become somewhat tiresome.

Luther and Mina Short had three kids. Floyd was my age, Nick a couple of years older and Emma another two or three years above that. A more dysfunctional unit I never met.

Luther was muscular, tall and broad-shouldered and walked with the conviction of an army man. Luther's family had a long lineage of military involvement; his great-grandfather had joined the cause to bring Louis Riel under control in the 1870s. His father had fought Kaiser Wilhelm in Europe and Luther had done likewise against Adolf Hitler.

Luther actually had a well-paying job as a secretary/ courier for some government diplomat in Toronto, but after a couple of instances of insubordination ... plus that incident concerning the diplomat's wife ... Luther found himself on a boat headed for Sicily where he joined up with the Italian Campaign and spent the remainder of the war in Europe fighting for world freedom.

As a kid, I always thought Mina seemed a funny name for a woman as we had a cow named Mina. In fact in my opinion, her angular face and large brown eyes bore more than a passing resemblance to her bovine namesake in our stable.

From the moment Luther and Mina entered your house they never stopped talking ... or arguing. Mina was forever cutting Luther off when he would offer some comment and seemingly found great satisfaction pinpointing his ignorance on any given subject. Mina was a large-framed woman and when she laughed her entire body seemed to vibrate and ripple from head to toe. And she laughed a lot; a laugh that began as a high-pitched cackle then gradually wound down in decibels before culminating in a highly audible sucking sound as she ingested a large draft of air into her diaphragm. According to our father, this comical (and after a while annoying) suction uptake merely meant Mina was readying herself for the next outburst.

Gardens and books were Mina's favourite subjects and she could talk non-stop about either. "My beans weren't worth a ding this year ... Luther says it's blight but of course that's wrong ... I think its aphids, although my brother believes it's flea beetle." The tomatoes were great though ... I put down twenty-five jars of chili sauce. I guess the tomatoes liked the hot weather. That's why I can't understand why the beans failed so miserably! Beans like hot weather. I'm still convinced it was aphids."

Mina read only mysteries and liked to compare notes with Mom on a certain book's contents. Mom's taste in books more favoured historical fiction or biographies, but she did enjoy Agatha Christie novels so had some common ground there. Mina never missed a chance to put her husband down when it came to books either. "Luther of course thought it was the butler who killed the old man (laughter) but I knew it was the daughter ... the one you'd least suspect."

Perhaps because Luther stood little chance against his own wife, he seemed to delight in finding fault or making fun of others. "Mina's brother is so bald now you can't tell his face from his ass!" At some school board function on a day hotter than hell, a shy neighbour of Luther's couldn't stand the heat anymore and although dreading getting up in front of everyone, walked to front of the room to open a window. Between paint and humidity, the window was stuck and wouldn't budge. After several futile attempts and crimson-faced with embarrassment, he returned to his seat. At that point Luther hollered out ... "That sure feels better, Bob!"

Luther also liked to test our mother's patience. It didn't matter whether it was Aylmer soup, Club House peanut butter, Swift's meats or Silverwood's ice cream ... if Luther consumed it ... then it was the only product to use and anyone who didn't ... including Mom ... was simply stupid. Another favourite burr was politics. Luther honestly knew little of the subject and seldom voted, as Mina made it clear she would "cancel his vote" at every opportunity anyway. Luther was well aware of Mom's undying support for the Liberal party, however, so went to any length promoting

Conservative policies whether he knew anything about them or not.

Luther seemed to have a different job every year. He sold sporting equipment and electric tools. He sold used cars, drove trucks, laboured as a windmill mechanic, clerked in a grocery store and at one point was part owner of a hobby shop. He even worked on the assembly line at General Motors in Oshawa in the late 1950s installing seats on new Chevrolets. He never stayed at any job long. One reason may have been his habit of taking his work home with him. Opening his trunk one time to reveal a new power drill, Luther with no embarrassment whatsoever simply stated ... "That must've followed me home!" Another time a circular saw graced his trunk. I borrowed that last week to build a verandah and I guess I forgot to return it."

Luther often vented his frustrations with life and wife on Nick and Floyd. He was forever threatening them with a "fat lip" or a "fat ear" if they got out of line or talked out of turn and both boys always seemed a little scared of him. "I don't remember asking your opinion!" was his favourite line if either issued any statement without permission. He was never at a loss for a quick remark to anyone else either. One day while I was sitting on the porch picking my nose (do kids still do that?), Luther walked by. "Got something in your eye Dave and trying to get it out the hard way?"

Luther never bothered with Emma much at all ... no one did. To me, both parents seemed at a lost to get through to their only daughter. Unlike her two brothers who were characterized by a skinny sawed-off appearance, Emma was a rather pretty girl, employing her father's height and her mother's heavier build. Emma also had Mina's big brown eyes but without the "cow-like" countenance. Her eyes were her best feature I thought, but always seemed as though they were staring at something in the distance no one else could see.

I don't ever recall Emma taking part in any discussion. While the rest of the family hollered, laughed, argued and quarrelled, Emma sat quietly in some far off room reading a *Seventeen* or *Movie Screen* magazine, adrift in the calm waters of her own little world ... a world seemingly disconnected from the chaos and disorder that swirled about her.

Luther didn't enjoy a long life. Developing heart problems in his fifties claimed him by the time he was sixty. Luther always declared the four years he spent fighting in the war in Europe stole ten years from his life, but in his case perhaps it exacted even more.

Mina outlasted Luther by thirty years, living well in to her late eighties, still in her own home and still tending to a small garden. For Mina, the end came quickly but happily I guess. Over a cup of tea sitting at the kitchen table with a neighbour, Mina was reminiscing about the old days ... "Remember the time I sent Luther out to the garden to get beans and cucumbers and the fool came back with peas and zucchini!" She began her patented laugh as she had done thousands of times before, that familiar high-pitched cackle gradually lowering in scale until ... except this time just before the "air suction" finale, Mina simply keeled over onto the linoleum floor.

While both Floyd and Nick had long-standing parental issues growing up, they also entertained a healthy appetite for trouble outside the home. Floyd was always reminding us "farm kids" how things were done in the city. We were told to always wear long-sleeved shirts and trousers with plenty of pockets when entering a store and Woolworth's was one of the best places to shoplift. "They sell a lot of small items that are easy to hide," Floyd summarized. "It's surprising how much stuff you can get in a few pockets!"

By age twelve, Floyd had captured the entrepreneurial spirit of stealing bicycles from school and other neighbourhood institutions, disassembling them before selling the parts at some vacant lot across town. It wasn't long before he was caught, but because of his age got off easy, provided he enroll in some community involvement program as part of his payment to society.

I recall as early as eight or ten, Floyd excelling at card and board games. He had the art of deceit down to a science and we'd have played a dozen board games before it sunk into our country brains he was making his own rules. Cards were even worse odds ... particularly when he dealt. One time we were playing rummy and Brian and I both had two aces and discovered Floyd did as well! When you finally figured it out and accused him there was never a glimpse of shock, denial or repentance. He'd just give you a ... "So what's the problem?" look.

Floyd followed in his father's footsteps when it came to variety of employment. He sold kitchen appliances, artwork and aluminum siding, worked in the record department at the local Eaton's store, spent one summer at a landscaping business, another at a golf course and expended a winter at a logging operation in Northern Ontario.

By the early 1970s Floyd was married and had bought a home somewhere east of Toronto. It was about this time he showed up at our place with a new Corvette. In the interest of conversation someone asked how he could afford such a car. "Oh it's easy ... we just put a second mortgage on the house and stretched the payments out a little." I suppose there's nothing wrong with a second mortgage for someone with a steady job ... but of course Floyd was soon without work and in due time lost the car, the house and his wife.

I saw him a few years later at some function in Toronto. He'd thumbed his way from Nova Scotia and was heading west to Alberta. Somehow the subject of the Corvette came up and Floyd said ... "You know the bank was pretty good about that ... I probably drove that car for three months without any payments before they took it!"

Following that episode he bought an eleven-year-old Volvo. "It had over two hundred thousand miles on it but that's nothing to a Volvo." So what happened to it?" I asked. "I was doing some hill climbing in a gravel pit behind the place where I was staying and I'm not sure what happened because I'd climbed that particular hill before. Anyway, long story short, I rolled it down a steep embankment. Volvos are pretty tough, but the roof was kind of flattened so I just sawed it off and drove it the rest of the summer as a convertible."

Nick was the most complicated of all the Shorts, having what some people would describe as a "dark" personality. Nick was always daring us younger kids to stick our hand into an electric fan or ingest carbon monoxide by sucking on an automobile exhaust pipe or something. When he was only five or six he'd tossed a doll belonging to the little girl next door through the lawn mower, "just to have a little fun." Some neighbour kid on his bicycle accidentally knocked over their garbage can placed at the curb so Nick rammed a baseball bat through his spokes, the kid consequently running into a hydro pole and suffering a concussion. I heard the parents planned on suing so I'm not sure how that turned out.

Nick had a "wandering eye" ... I don't mean when it came to women ... I mean he literally had a wandering eye. It just sort of drifted around and never really transfixed on anything in particular. It was sort of mesmerizing until you got used to it, and he was sensitive about it. A neighbour kid of ours, Freddie Jackson, made an innocent remark and instantly found himself flat on the ground with Nick's foot planted squarely in his face. "I should squash your nose right into the back of your head!" Fortunately for Freddie, someone drove into the yard at that moment so he was spared any further assault, perhaps even his life.

If all things went as planned, Nick would've been a cowboy. He was forever talking of the "old west" and the good old days when everyone carried a gun. "People had respect for you then." Nick's hero was Matt Dillon of *Gunsmoke* fame, in fact Nick figured a U.S. Marshal to be the best job in the world. "A U.S. Marshal can go anywhere and do anything he wants." ... "Well, I guess even a Marshal has to abide by some rules", I ventured ... "No ... not Matt Dillon," Nick countered ... "Nobody can touch him."

Nick had a lucrative business stealing hub caps, mud flaps, aerials etc. ... then selling them to the highest bidder around Whitby. He and a couple of associates would make their rounds on weekends, scouring the parking lots of rodeos, fall fairs, music concerts, car shows ... anywhere there happened to be a substantial gathering of vehicles. When someone recognized something Nick was trying to unload as their own property they called the police and it was game over. Nick paid a fine and did some community service cutting grass at the park and cemetery for the balance of the summer.

Fines and community involvement couldn't cut it when Nick branched off into selling bootleg booze to minors. "Nick has gone away for a while to visit relatives" we were told. He resurfaced two or three years later in Northern Ontario driving trucks for a construction company that built roads into mining and forestry camps. Here he apparently assaulted a co-worker who'd insulted his girlfriend. Nick was still on parole so had to do some additional time. Many years later we heard he landed a job on a cattle ranch somewhere in Alberta, so despite his past problems perhaps his cowboy dream was nearing fruition. With his criminal record, however, Nick's chances of following in Matt Dillon's footsteps were probably pretty slim.

That left only Emma ... whose isolated life no one seemed to take time to understand or recognize. "She's just a quiet girl," was the explanation her parents had always given to anyone who bothered to inquire. During four years of high school, Emma made no close friends and the one or two who tried were kept at a safe distance. Well into her twenties she continued to live in her magical world where divine romance and everlasting love were a certainty if one wished hard enough.

Then finally the pieces of Emma's dream began to fall into place. As secretary in a financial services office, she met and fell for one of the managers, an energetic rising star ten years her senior, ready to make his mark on the world.

Lance was handsome and successful with an extensive record of girlfriends to his credit, but Emma saw only the stars in the sky and a full moon rising. In her mind even his name conjured up images of "Sir Lancelot" of King Arthur fame. Emma had no doubt this was the knight in shining armour for which she'd spent her life waiting and surrendered completely.

In return, Lance lavished her with jewellery, took her to the finest restaurants, jetted her away on weekend holidays to New York, Los Angeles, even Paris and London; and the keys to his T-Bird convertible were hers anytime she wanted. Emma spent hours planning and dreaming about that mystical wedding day she could envision so clearly; the bridal dress, the church ceremony; the promised house tucked away in the hills of the countryside. The appropriate paint, wallpaper and carpeting choices for each room of their castle had been thoroughly analyzed and debated within her mind. Decisions on furniture style, lighting and appliances, even the projected number of children their union might produce were calculated with utmost care and forethought. The transformation from dark isolationism to the glamour and glitter of Broadway and beyond was nothing less than dramatic ... until after a few months when "Sir Lance" declared things were getting "too confining" and decided to move on.

It can be tragic what life can sometimes do to a fragile mind. As legend goes, the night Lance split, a shattered Emma went home and picked out her favourite Harlequin paperback, reading it front to back non-stop. Then she read it again ... and again ... and again. After two or three days of continuous reading of the same book with no sleep or food, Emma was institutionalized for obvious concerns.

Except for the occasional failed experiment of supervised "home care," it was here Emma would spend the next twenty years. She barely spoke or even offered a flicker of recognition to anyone who visited, and on the rare instances she did speak the conversation concerned only "this great book" she was reading.

Emma passed away in her late forties, sitting in her favourite chair by the window, a book in her hands and according to the nurse who discovered her ... a smile on her face.

In the end, the repeating message nestled within its pages had been all that was important or mattered. A book that featured contentment, reassurance, encouragement and promise; a book wherein all dreams, wishes and hopes were fulfilled and everyone lived happily ever after ... If only real life could have been even remotely connected.

HAIL TO THE CHIEF

It was a 1950 Pontiac, and already four years old when delivered to our door that Saturday morning. However, with its medium blue paint shining bright and the chrome "silver streaks" that graced both hood and trunk reflecting the April sun, to a five-year-old, a new one couldn't have looked finer. Those silver streaks had been a Pontiac styling tradition since the mid-1930s.

Another trademark was the "Indian Head" hood ornament. Hood ornaments were important brand identifiers in this era. Like Dodge's "ram," Plymouth's "Mayflower" and Chevrolet's "bowtie," Pontiac sported "Chief Pontiac," the Ottawa-born native who became leader of the Chippewa Indian nation. As an added bonus, the "chief" even illuminated when darkness descended and the head lights were switched on. While Dad was finishing up the paperwork with the salesman, I noted with approval the four doors, gas cap hidden behind a hinged door, push button door handles and push button starter ... all novelties our previous Pontiac had lacked. The parking brake even worked for a while.

Later in the day when the initial excitement had died down, I wandered out to where our brand new used car sat on the lawn and climbed into the driver's seat. I absorbed the beauty of the dashboard stretched out before me ... the steering wheel complete with semi-circular horn ring, and behind it a semi-circular speedometer. Pontiac was obsessed with semi-circles that year as the fuel, battery, oil and temp gauges, grouped either side, were ... you guessed it. Dead centre of the wide dashboard was a clock (round). It didn't work as long as we owned the car, but it looked nice.

Just a couple of weeks following its purchase, the Pontiac began a series of coughs, splutters, burps and other unflattering sounds that grew steadily worse until it died completely on our side road in broad daylight ... a devastating blow to our pride. This was an era when cars dominated practically every conversation when boys as well as girls got together. It was bad enough we had to abandon the car that morning and walk the rest of the way to school, but the real emotional blow came later that day, when along the road in front of the school came our Allis Chalmers tractor, and towed ingloriously behind, our Pontiac. Our peers had a great time laughing and pointing as the pitiful exhibition rolled by, especially the "Ford" kids.

One day shortly after that incident, I was fiercely stating the high qualifications of Pontiacs and running Fords into the ground, when Carol Steers, a Ford girl, had heard enough. "Oh, Pontiacs are great cars alright. Do you take your tractor with you everywhere in case you have to pull your car home?" My face burned with embarrassment as a dozen kids laughed their heads off. When the laughter subsided, Irene Jackson, a Dodge girl, spoke up. "What *was* wrong with your car David?" "There was water in the gas," I answered. "Well," continued Irene, "That's not the fault of the car, that's the gasman's fault." I glared straight at Carol. "Yeah!" With more time I could've had a better retort I'm sure.

But that was the problem ... except it wasn't the "gasman's" fault. During winter, due to the condition of our laneway, our car was consistently parked at the road where Dad left a couple of forty-five gallon barrels of gasoline to refill the tank when needed. Accumulated snow on the barrel surface, melting and freezing in a continuous cycle throughout the winter, slowly seeped into the supply. Stan Copeland, our mechanic from nearby Newton-Robinson (the name was larger than the village), diagnosed the problem and drained the fuel system, which included removing and draining the gas tank as well.

Our mostly faithful Pontiac motored on, but was in a rusty state by 1958 and since too many other expenses prohibited a trade, Dad did the next best thing ... a paint and body job. It was like a new car when returned from the shop. All rusty panels had been replaced, several holes in the trunk were patched and a new rubber mat covered the floor. Red plaid seat covers brightened the interior and the exterior was repainted light grey. I recall Mom wasn't enthused with the colour change, as blue was always her favourite hue. My father's argument: "Well, they had lots of grey in stock and gave me a deal."

Things picked up a bit over the next few years. A '54 Plymouth followed by a '56 Ford and then a '59 Chevrolet. Throughout this turnover of vehicles our Pontiac soldiered on with its back seat removed, routinely hauling grain to and from the feed mill, plus the occasional bull calf to the livestock auction in Listowel. Dozens of cars and trucks that were just a few revolutions short of the scrap heap would roll into town for the weekly sale. Rusty fenders flapping in the breeze, a few without brakes, many without lights, some with interior holes so large they had long ago been forced to quit hauling pigs. For most of these relics, Tuesday was their only day out.

The Department of Transport spoiled this weekly exercise when they began issuing "unfit" citations and confiscating license plates. A DOT officer stopped Dad and me one Tuesday. Our old Pontiac had definitely fallen into the "rough" category but was still a notch or two above many Tuesday specials. "Has it got lights?" Dad proudly showed how both headlights worked, even if one was dangling by a wire. "Brakes?" Dad pumped the pedal and by the third push had reached a satisfactory stage. "How about the emergency brake?"

The inspectors always left the best to last. They knew full well not one in twenty would pass this test. Ours was no different, but my father pulled the lever under the dashboard, and rather ingeniously I thought ... without the officer noticing ... placed the gear selector in high instead of low. It was an impressive manoeuvre, with the clutch burning as the car struggled to launch itself; then it stalled and as always when hot, refused to restart. The officer helped Dad push the car onto the shoulder of the roadway, then quickly lost interest. Once the engine cooled, Dad quietly slipped away.

The Pontiac's days as a licensed vehicle ended on February 28, 1962, but a month before, as sort of a grand finale, we used it to deliver a calf to Bond Head, a seventy-five-mile trip. The calf was several months old ... well past the stage of riding in the back seat of a car, but I was assured by Dad that once under way the calf would settle down and cause no problems. Ha!

We were scarcely out of sight of home when it proceeded to jump into the front seat and I had to wrestle it back where it belonged. The calf obviously had no intention of lying down, so I ended up spending the entire trip bent over in the back seat holding onto this fool calf. My back still aches when I recall that day.

Although sunny, it was a bitterly cold day. The Pontiac's mediocre heater was severely offset by a passenger door that wouldn't latch. A length of baler twine secured to the steering column kept it from flying open, but wasn't near snug enough to prevent January's frosty blast from entering. The driver's door was only slightly better. The door closed, but a sizeable hole in the floorboard allowed a continuous blast of air. As a result, Dad's foot was numb with the chill by the time we arrived and he literally fell out of the car when disembarking. As for me, it was awhile before I could fully straighten up. I recall the ride home wasn't any warmer but at least more comfortable.

After the license expired, the Pontiac was relegated to around-the-farm jobs such as fencing, getting the cows or hauling garbage to the dump site back in the bush. At this stage it was also my "practice" car. By the following year it was consigned to a location behind the implement shed. After another year and some prodding from Mom on what an eyesore the rusting machine was, it was driven to Shoemaker's Wrecking lot, five miles away.

"Thirty-five dollars," said Carl Shoemaker. "I thought it might be worth seventy-five," argued my father. "The engine's real good." Shoemaker shook his head. "We've got just two prices ... thirty-five if it's running ... twenty-five if it isn't." Dad thought for a minute before answering. "Well since we're already here, I guess we may as well let it go."

Just then ... almost as if it heard the death verdict, the Pontiac stalled and as always when hot, flooded and refused to restart. At that point the "chief" was simply and unceremoniously pushed off to the side of the driveway, joining a row of equally disabled veterans of the auto world awaiting their fate.

DON'T CALL ME BILLY
ANYMORE

Thursday, October 8, 1958, my brother Bill turned sixteen and immediately set about obtaining his driver's license. In my brother's case this was more formality than official fact as he'd been driving some variation of motorized vehicle since he was eight or nine. While Dad worked as cattle herdsman for Charlie Cerswell at Bond Head, Bill was negotiating Jeeps and tractors up and down the farm's steep inclines with regularity.

When we began farming on our own in 1953, Dad purchased a new Allis-Chalmers tractor and eleven-year-old "Billy" (as Dad always referred to him) received a large share of the driving. Because most of our machinery was essentially "two-men horse implements," Billy drove the tractor while Dad operated the controls from the implement's bumpy steel seat.

Despite my brother's struggle to advance from "Billy" to the more mature sounding "Bill," his father would continue to refer to him as "Billy" even when in his twenties and thirties. Conversely, the remainder of the family, as well as relatives, friends etc., seemed unable or unwilling to accept this evolution, preferring instead to concoct their own derivatives such as "Wilbur," "Wilbert" or "Willy."

By whatever name my brother might be referred to ... let's call him Bill for the sake of this story ... he enjoyed most aspects of tractor driving with only the occasional weak moment. Cultivating at the back of our farm one evening, the closer Bill drew to the tree-lined fence the more nervous he became. Just fifty feet from the fence and darkness settling, his nerves were unable to withstand it any longer and he quickly headed for the barn. Bill didn't tell Dad the reason for not finishing the field was he was certain there were monsters lurking beyond the trees.

Five years passed and sixteen-year-old Bill at long last was ready to obtain his legal right to drive on Ontario's roads. The early December day chosen for the driver's test arrived cold and blustery. There were no specifically designated Department of Transport examiners in the 1950s, the town police chief providing the service as part of his job description.

Palmerston police chief Forrest Inch slid into the Pontiac's passenger seat motioning Bill to make a right turn, then a left onto the main street leading westward out of town. Whether environmental conditions or fear intervened, just two or three minutes later, Chief Inch announced, "That's enough ... turn around ... I see you can drive."

Perhaps Bill might have been better served with a more thorough test, for he obviously didn't know *all* the rules. A few weeks later the deputy police officer witnessed my brother run a stop sign near the high school. The cruiser followed the Pontiac for a couple of blocks while Bill nervously watched through his rear view mirror ... and drove through another stop sign.

This time, the cruiser activated its lights. "When you went through the first stop sign I thought maybe it was just a slip," said the cop as he stood at Bill's side window. "When you went through the second, I figured it must be a regular habit." While the officer was talking he was also taking note if Bill had been drinking. "You were driving kind of erratic!" Bill, who had never consumed a sip of booze in his life, shot back angrily, "That's because of all the pot-holes in the street!" That remark was aimed directly at the person riding in the passenger seat of the cruiser, who worked for the Town of Palmerston. (There was always someone riding around with the cops in those days.)

Whatever reasons or excuses were given, the officer had plenty of material to write up a $16.00 citation. Bill was afraid if Dad learned of this infraction he'd take his license, so posted his sister at the mailbox for the duration of the week until the summons arrived. Bill may have gotten off easier if it had been Chief Inch on patrol that day. The chief owed him a favour as Bill had rescued the cruiser from a ditch with the tractor earlier in the winter.

Unlike today where every farm is home to a pickup, when I was a kid, generally one vehicle … the family car … provided all duties. Cattle feed, fencing supplies, small livestock, fertilizer and seed were hauled courtesy of the family sedan. When Dad began his career as a farm owner in 1953, it's not surprising that the idea of owning a pickup would surface from time to time. More pressing financial commitments always relegated the pickup dream to the back burner until the spring of 1959 when our farm finally received that elusive truck when Bill bought his first vehicle, a dark blue 1949 Chevrolet.

Although a decade old, mileage was low and the body solid. During the first winter of ownership, Dad was heading to Harriston when he became entangled with a petroleum truck on an icy hill. "There's a little bump in the door," Dad informed his son upon return. Upon investigation, Bill discovered a large dent in the rear fender and most of the door stove in, the result being it would barely open. Farmers never worried too much about collision insurance in those days ... the rates seemed so high especially for teenage drivers ... so Bill, as anyone else who drove the truck from that point on, merely endured the mangled door and fender.

That truck was the first vehicle I ever drove ... sort of. I'd be ten or eleven and Bill and I were picking up bales of hay from the field. The bales were in "stooks" ... a pyramid of six bales ... and my job was to simply move the Chevy from one to another while Bill threw them in the back. Although the truck was fashioned with a hand throttle as well as the regular floor pedal, I seemed unable to co-ordinate the clutch, and following a dozen stalls and restarts, Bill lost patience, informing me I was going to ruin the battery, and kicked me out.

In the fall of 1960, Charlie Cerswell asked Dad if he could hire "Billy" to help out at the Royal Winter Fair. (Knowing him since a baby, Charlie would always refer to him as so.) It was on the way to Bond Head in early November that a connecting rod gave up the ghost on the old Chevy and Bill was forced to hitch-hike the rest of the way. Dad and Richard drove to Arthur and retrieved the disabled truck, placing it in the upstairs of the barn where our soon-to-be brother-in-law Glen Cober, perhaps trying to score points with the family, elected to do the repair free of charge.

Once back together, Glen's father, who was a mechanic at a small garage in the village of Fordwich, set the timing and got the engine running on all six cylinders. It maybe didn't sound 100%, but all agreed after a little run, the Chevrolet would be purring like a kitten. It never did reach the purring stage. First trip out ... another rod failed. Obviously there was a problem here!

Meanwhile, Eldon Lobsinger, who operated the local whitewashing business, inquired about the truck when he was spraying our stable. When told it wasn't running, he said, "I thought you fixed it ... what's wrong ... no oil in it?" "Lots of oil," someone answered. His curiosity aroused, Lobsinger pressed further, "Maybe the oil line's plugged ... did you check it?" His question was greeted with blank stares. "If you've got a wrench handy we can sure find out." A wrench was retrieved and he set about loosening the main oil line where it joined the filter. "Now, turn it over a couple of times." As the engine revolved, oil simultaneously spurted from the open line.

Satisfied the pump was in good order, he cast a disapproving glance at the greasy and dirt-encrusted oil filter assembly. "You changed the filter of course?" More blank looks: once the metal canister was opened, the enclosed filter was completely plugged. The reason the engine was being starved of oil was obvious. Lowering the hood, Lobsinger added one final remark. "I'm glad I don't have you fellows fixing my airplane!"

In Glen's defence, the oil pressure gauge didn't work and many engines of that era were manufactured without oil filters, but it was an unfortunate lesson nevertheless. Dad, who had financed the initial repair, figured one overhaul sufficient, so without fanfare the truck was carted off to the local scrap yard.

So not only was our farm without a truck, Bill was without wheels of any kind. In the meantime, Dad had purchased a 1954 Plymouth from a neighbour to replace our aging 1950 Pontiac. In need of a vehicle, Bill took a shine to the Plymouth ... after all how could he find any girls to date driving a ten-year-old bashed-in pickup? Dad sold it to him for $600.00 and consequently had to search for another car of his own.

This particular Plymouth was a top of the line Belvedere model with several options, one being power steering ... the first year that feature was even available on a Plymouth. My sister Vivien had decided at this point she wished to obtain her driver's license, and the Plymouth with its "magic steering" seemed the ideal candidate on which to practice.

Bill was her instructor, and just a couple of weeks into her driving studies the two were heading to Palmerston. The first indication of trouble was a gentle swaying of the car on the freshly gravelled sideroad. Quickly the swaying multiplied as Vivien fought in vain to correct the situation. The "zero" feel of power steering–equipped cars of that era afforded my sister no idea which direction the car's front wheels were pointed. Bill grabbed the steering wheel, but it was either too late or he simply magnified the situation, as the Plymouth headed for the ditch sideways, slid down a shallow embankment, made a half roll and came to rest on its roof.

Good news ... neither my brother nor sister were injured. The Plymouth however was a write-off and Bill carried no collision insurance (the rates were still too high) The O.P.P. officer who investigated the accident needed an engine for his personal car, so offered Bill $65.00 for the engine and the remainder of the Plymouth went to Shoemaker's Wrecking Lot ... the second time within a year my brother was forced to watch his wheels carried off to the auto dump.

Bill's third swing at the ball appeared in the form of an olive green 1953 Volkswagen. 1953 was just the second year the German car was even available in Canada, and being early in its career, the little car had all sorts of quaint curiosities, unfamiliar to North Americans. Like an auxiliary gas tank that held one gallon for emergencies, a useful item as Volkswagens of that era had no fuel gauge. The reserve tank was activated by a lever beneath the dashboard

The accelerator pedal wasn't a pedal at all but rather something that more resembled a roller skate wheel. The car had originally been fitted with European style indicators, which were merely short luminous rods that dropped down either side of the car, depending upon choice of direction. This particular vehicle had been transformed to meet North American signal light regulations, leaving just the empty slots which had housed the signal feature.

These signals contained no automatic flashing mechanism, necessitating a person to pulsate the lever up or down depending upon turning direction. This procedure was complicated further as the car had a manual transmission; stroking the signal lever with your left hand while approaching a corner, while your right hand geared the transmission down didn't leave much with which to secure the steering wheel. To compound the problem, third gear had to be manually held in position, or the transmission would disengage.

One cold winter day the car caught fire somewhere underneath the dash, so Bill reached through the smoke, yanking out any wire with which he came in contact. The action killed the fire but also the engine; it took about $80.00 to rewire the system. Upon receiving the invoice, Bill was heard to comment that he should have "let it burn." He did have fire insurance!

Bill never cared for that car but it was all he could afford at the time. After the spacious, easy-to-drive Plymouth, the Volkswagen seemed "Mickey Mouse." When he returned from the hospital following a serious operation that summer, the small, claustrophobic interior and stiff suspension did little to change his mind. He also said it "smelled funny."

The car didn't endear itself to my brother either. Bill was to be in Bond Head early one August morning in order to catch a ride to a cattle show in Peterborough. Under a canopy of stars he settled in for the seventy-five-mile journey ... a wonderful time of day to drive with barely a soul on the road. Even the tiny four-cylinder engine seemed to share in the spirit, singing along in the darkness ... until Arthur (again) where it died. One minute the engine was running beautifully, the next as if the ignition had been switched off.

After a couple of tries on the starter button proved worthless, Bill retrieved his suitcase from the back seat, slammed the door and began walking down the shoulder of the highway in the darkness. He didn't even bother to look under the hood ... without a flashlight, what was there to see? Plus, he never had much idea what inspired these stupid little engines to run anyway.

The low traffic flow that seemed such a pleasant experience a half hour ago now presented a problem, but he must have had a lucky thumb, reaching his destination in just two steps ... and on time. Before he left Bond Head, Bill phoned Dad and told him where the car was and what he could do with it.

Richard was working at a resort in Muskoka that summer so I became "top man" to accompany Dad for retrieval service. Dad tried the starter to no avail, then opened the hood. As plain as day was the problem; the coil wire had merely jiggled loose. Once snapped back into place the car started immediately. Since I was a "little shy" on age as a licensed driver ... like three years ... we pulled the car home as planned and as I recall, only ran into the back of Dad's bumper twice.

I guess by now we figured the average farm couldn't operate without a pickup, so with some financial assistance from Dad, Bill purchased a 1959 Fargo. He constructed a wooden rack over the pickup's bed, and although designed for cattle, it was tall enough for a giraffe to travel in comfort. The Fargo proved to be a reliable vehicle for my brother and suffered no issues beyond his control such as collisions, roll-overs, fires or enthusiastic apprentice mechanics.

As it was law in those days to have your name clearly displayed, my brother hand painted BILL TURNER in neat lettering on either door of the truck. Mom questioned her son's effort, stating he should have written WILLIAM TURNER instead. It had only been a decade earlier while opening his first bank account that Mom had criticized him for signing "Billy" instead of "Bill" ... It seemed he simply couldn't win.

Looking at the issue through the power of hindsight, it would seem this transformation undertaken by my brother to evolve his Christian name to some higher level ... was a complete waste of time. Whether, "Bishop," "Holiday," "Martin," "Crystal," "Carter," "Joel," "Graham" or a dozen others ... maybe some people are just meant to be known as "Billy."

THE WORST OF TIMES

Sorting through today's mail, amongst the flyers and bills I found an invitation to my high school reunion ... "Join us for a weekend of celebration and fun. Renew acquaintances, reminisce with former classmates, relive memories and enjoy photographs from the best years of our lives ... "

As I read the lines, my mind slowly unravelled back to 1962. I guess a person is never aware of it at the time ... that juncture when childhood ends, but 1962 was undoubtedly that point for me.

Gone were the long holidays with our city cousins, as like us, they now had summer jobs to occupy their time. Gone was the intimacy of the one-room school and the protection it afforded. Gone was the freedom to just hop on our bikes and head to town when the spirit moved us. Even the spirit of Christmas dissolved that year.

What drove home the message of how I'd "grown up" was the fact I slept like a log that Christmas Eve. No more sugarplums dancing in my head. No listening for the sound of sleigh bells. No waking up a half dozen times in anticipation of the next day. No more running downstairs with my brothers in the cold, dark, early morning hours to retrieve our stockings. The magic was gone ... and childhood with it.

The least looked-forward-to event that entire year for me was the transition from elementary to secondary school. I wished nature's time clock could somehow be halted, but the summer had raced by and now it was September 4th and I was standing with my brother Richard at the entrance-way to our driveway. With the yellow bus now in full view, the pit of my stomach felt as though it were harbouring a cement block.

No single event triggered it ... no moment in time signalled a change that I can recall, but sometime during that first week or two of school, I became acutely aware of a small group of students who'd decided to dedicate a substantial portion of their school hours for the purpose of making mine miserable. I was completely unprepared as I had no experience with bullying (I don't think I was even familiar with the term). To this day some fifty years later I'm still unsure why I was singled out ... maybe the feeling of superiority that some individuals crave doesn't need a reason. I was quite shy, so perhaps therein lies the answer why I was the chosen target.

Whatever the reason, thus began an almost daily repetition of hiding and defacing books and other personal property, hiding my clothes during gym class, stacking my locker so everything would fall onto the floor when opened, stealing my lunch (squashing my sandwiches was always good for a laugh). Books knocked from under my arm and kicked the length of the hallway was a favourite, as was "hallway ricochet" ... two or three students constantly shoving me from side to side into the steel lockers while walking the halls.

"Fight back!" one of my classmates prodded me. "Individually, they're cowards." I'd never come close to a schoolyard scuffle in my lifetime, so was terrified when I heard myself tell the thugs that I would meet them "one at a time" after school. As predicted, they were cowards, as three or four were waiting at the back door for me. All I remember is being knocked to the ground several times and warned of the repercussions if I ever decided to play "hero" again.

This constant physiological battle in which I was embroiled soon became all consuming ... I'd wake in the morning with that familiar ache in my gut, imagining the upcoming day ... even the prospect of securing a seat on the crowded bus became a dreaded event. I was filled with apprehension opening my locker each morning as it had been sabotaged so many times. I actually got the nerve to ask for a new combination number from the business office, hoping that would be one less thing to worry about.

Three days later, I opened my locker to the familiar avalanche of books and supplies. This time however, the rings on all of my binders had been methodically opened, sending countless sheets soaring through the air like dandelion fluff. I'll never forget how angry and humiliated I felt, grovelling on the floor that morning for the scattered paper, face as red as a pot of boiling beets, while students passing by laughed and offered sarcastic remarks. "Turner ... you should try out for our football team" (they were known as the "redmen") ... "You could be our mascot!"

Every day drove me further into the chasm of isolation and self-doubt. I felt at a loss to contribute anything even remotely intelligent or interesting during class discussions and never offered to answer a question even if I was absolutely certain of the correct response.

Almost as a virus, this emotional trauma infected everything in its path and in effect the simplest studies became a challenge ... "shop" for instance. In grade nine the curriculum was divided between woodworking and sheet metal. In the former, we were told to construct a small bookcase. A six- by eighteen-inch base with a couple of ends to support the books ... sounds simple enough doesn't it? For a variety of reasons, my sad exhibit took forever to construct and was so flimsy when completed that it could barely support paperbacks. It did provide plenty of material for colourful comments from fellow students however.

My brother Richard made a nice bookcase when he was in grade nine. Mom probably had it for twenty years. I was too embarrassed to even bring mine home. I won't even try to explain how my "cookie cutter" attempt turned out in sheet metal class. By the way ... Rich made a nice one of those too.

In "Electronics" class, Mr. Burns did his best to instill unfamiliar terminologies such as ohms, voltage, amperage, resistance, frequency modulation and polarity into our vocabulary. Rich was a whiz at anything electrical, so I probably wasn't imagining the tone in Mr. Burns' voice when he asked if I were Richard's brother.

Agriculture, a subject available only to boys, was a piece of cake ... or so we imagined. However, when it came to the technical aspects of fertilizer analysis, soil nutrition, genetics, incubation, or even parts of an egg, we were just as stupid as the town kids. In fact it was even more embarrassing as they thought we knew this already. Other exercises found us studying rocks, taking soil samples, identifying weeds ... even knot making.

While the latter seems more associated with Boy Scouts, a special project that year instructed us to make a calf halter, where each student was furnished with a length of half-inch rope, plus a book of instructions. With some unique slip-knots and braiding and a loop or two, a halter made an attractive and useful addition to any farm.

Even with "easy" instructions, knot-making proved to be just one more exercise in which I was inept. My knots appeared as though chewed by rats. The slip-knot wouldn't, and the loop was inside out. The braided end I gave up in a fit of frustration. Mr. Logan gave me two out of ten and asked if I wished to try again. Next time witnessed a vast improvement ... a nine ... oh, did I mention that Richard made that one? I owe you one Rich.

Phys. Ed. was undoubtedly the class I hated most. Although I enjoyed watching most sports events from the sidelines, lack of confidence in my abilities demanded little or no active participation.

In volleyball I could never master the "serve," the ball frequently concluding in the steel rafters of the gymnasium, accompanied by either gales of laughter or the more common, "What an idiot!" I was extremely uncomfortable in the front row as well, where most balls I handled ended up in the net. "It's Turner ... what the hell did you expect!"

Basketball? ... One fundamental we had to continually practice dictated everyone line up on one side of the gym, then individually dribble the ball down the floor and sink a basket ... that was the way it was supposed to be. After several failed attempts, the teacher would holler ... "Hey Turner, we haven't got all day, go back to the end of the line!" A few minutes later I would get to repeat the spectacle, giving everyone another chance for mirth and merriment at my expense. As you can guess, I wasn't an active proponent of the "try try again" axiom.

Football? ... "Hey, Turner ... you're supposed to use your hands to catch the ball ... not your face!"

I recall arriving at school one day and discovering a group of kids standing around my locker laughing. Someone had taped a large message to the door. IF AT FIRST YOU DON'T SUCCEED ... QUIT ... FAILURE IS PROBABLY YOUR THING! Although it was just one more in a succession of humiliating moments, it probably contained a strong dose of truth as both self-confidence and "school spirit" were practically non-existent at that point.

Recently I was discussing the subject of high school with a friend. "You must have had *some* good times?" she asked. At that particular moment nothing came to mind, but in retrospect, two or three recollections surfaced.

Mr. Logan, my agriculture teacher was a class act. Knowledgeable, but in a down-to-earth fashion, a great sense of humour and most importantly, sensitive and caring to each pupil's varied needs.

Mr. Perrault, French teacher. Any Friday he could get away with it, he'd smuggle his guitar in through the second-storey window of his classroom and treat us to French-Canadian folk songs.

Mr. Barton was my English Literature teacher. Like Mr. Perrault, Friday afternoons were often special. "Story Time" we called it. For forty minutes we could just listen and enjoy some literary passage without having to analyze, scrutinize, decipher and dissect it to death. It was from Mr. Barton I began to appreciate literature, poetry and well-written compositions. It would be years before I'd make any attempt at writing myself, but perhaps the seeds were being sown during those Friday afternoon Literature classes.

In all fairness, my second and third year were better ... they would have to be. There's no way I could have sustained another year such as the first. If it had simply been a matter of the occasional good-natured prank, I could have handled it. There's nothing wrong with that ... but it was more than mere "pranks." Oft-times it was verbal abuse, prejudiced and mean-spirited, designed solely to inflict maximum hurt and humiliation.

Looking back half a century, I can't imagine I was the sole recipient of these bullying tactics, but being so entangled within my own emotional web, I guess I wouldn't have noticed anyway. Frustration, emptiness, humiliation, apathy and even loneliness (pick your noun and it applied) had become deeply ingrained and I felt helpless to reverse the tide.

Partly from being warned of the consequences and partly simple embarrassment, I never confided in anyone. Certainly not a guidance counsellor or my brother or parents; I could have imagined the exchange with Mom. "What did you do to them?" ... "I didn't do anything" ... "Well you must have done something ... they wouldn't pick on you for no reason!"

Phys. Ed. continued to be my biggest nemesis ... with both teacher and fellow students seldom missing a chance to point out my pathetic athletic abilities ... and by this time I'd acquired a protective emotional covering to hide my true feelings, which undoubtedly projected a "You can go to hell and everything in this school with it!" attitude.

When it came to Phys. Ed., recalling a single unpleasant memory is difficult, but choosing up sides for team competition no doubt headed the list. Can there be a more soul-wrenching experience as you stand there scuffing your running shoes against the gym floor, pretending you don't notice or care that you will be the last picked again?

One time the number came out uneven and someone complained that our side had "more guys." I recall vividly, a fellow student hollering ... "Turner's a zero ... he doesn't count anyway!" It hadn't been a good day (my gym bag had been filled with sawdust and my gym shoes thrown in the shower) so I simply replied ... "Fine ... if I don't count, you won't miss me!" and walked out. "Come back here!" I heard the teacher holler ... "It was just a joke!" I kept walking. "If you keep walking then walk right to the principal's office!" I walked to the office and right on by. Principal Gray was on the phone and I could feel his eyes on me all the way down the hall but he never stopped me.

A couple of other gym class adventures netted detention for "insubordination" but I never showed up and nobody ever bothered to check. As long as the teacher in question was convinced you'd been embarrassed or demoralized by the experience in front of your classmates ... that was all that mattered. At this point, I had long since stopped caring what anybody thought.

So there was little doubt in which direction I was headed as far as higher education was concerned. During the second semester in my third year, attendance had been erratic and intermittent. In February, I managed to let a cold hang on long enough to grant a week's holiday, and I'd missed every Monday since Christmas. I hated Mondays ... Phys. Ed. was first class. What a way to start a week! By this time, Dad was working the farm alone and offered little resistance when I volunteered to stay home and help. That year's Christmas exams had yielded four in the low "50s" and by Easter my score had progressed to an even worse state ... two failures. "These marks are deplorable!" wrote Principal Gray on my report card to my parents. "Get after him fast!!!"

On Friday, April 30, 1965, I exited the front doors of Norwell Secondary for the final time. Two years, seven months and twenty-six days. I guess the question of whether I made any kind of academic contribution during my high school internment can be answered quite simply ... Seventeen days passed before anyone in the Norwell hierarchy even realized I was missing and finally phoned Mom.

... I re-read the invitation in front of me " ... so join us for a weekend of celebration and fun. Renew old acquaintances. Reminisce with classmates. Relive memories and enjoy photographs from the best years of our lives! Please R.S.V.P by April 15" ... I decided to pass.

AS THE PAGE TURNS

The written word has been an integral measure of my family's past for ... well who knows how long? In the late 1800s the face of the world was changing as Europeans by the tens of thousands, enticed by the promise of wealth and freedom, left their famine-infested farmlands and immigrated to North America. Realism dictated otherwise as the promise came at a high price, but it was this monumental challenge to literally hack a living out of this country of wilderness ... or starve, that gave our ancestors the resolve for survival and paved the road for the generations that followed.

And it wasn't just the world landscape that was in transition ... so was the domain of pen and ink. Books to this point relied heavily on the states of romanticism and nobility, furnished in a poetic style seemingly no longer relevant. The hardships and adversities that had become simply a part of life for these new pioneers were reflected in the stories and novels of this new age. Stories of average people with genuine tribulations and struggles, presented not in a context of poetic rambling, but rather language which common people could understand and relate to.

Authors of the day such as Balzac, Shaw, Crane, Dickens, Wilde and Bovary, transported this realism onto the printed page in grittier fashion than had ever been attempted. Thus it would be these writers that would entertain and educate the past generations of our family.

As well, newspapers were a major force in bringing world-wide events to your front door. My mother's family subscribed to no less than three daily newspapers. The *Mail and Empire, Globe and Mail* and *The Daily Star.* My great-grandfather Thomas Carruthers was an avid reader and passed this virtue to his children. His son Will ... my grandfather, read everything he could obtain and in turn passed the message to his children. "Reading stimulates the mind," he said.

Grandpa also "stimulated" his brain by engaging in endless crossword and jigsaw puzzles. I don't recall anyone who could complete a crossword with more speed. Grandpa Will was also a man of little patience so if the proper word wasn't instantly available from his brain's vocabulary, he'd merely substitute something that fit. Same with jigsaws ... a little "persuasion" was often needed, despite my grand-mother's scolding ... "If the piece doesn't fit easily, Will, then it's not the right one!"

When my mother graduated from Business College in 1932, overall unemployment in Toronto was 25%. The figure was twice that for students. It was therefore signifi-cant when Mom at last found employment ... and in a form valued by everyone in her family ... the library.

The Toronto Public Library system had branches scat-tered throughout the city and Mom had a card for most of them, as she wasn't a big fan of the number restriction on books one could take home from a single library at any given time. Having to keep track which books were returned to which branch on which day was a small price to pay for the availability of extra reading material. It was the Queen and Lisgar branch of Toronto's library organization where Mom landed her job as library assistant. Just a few hours a week at twenty-five cents an hour, which even by Depression standards was low, but what better environment than one surrounded by books!

My mother had certainly been around the library structure enough to understand the fundamentals of book borrowing, returning and stamping, but the cataloguing system needed some concentration. The method, still in use today despite computerization, was the Dewey Decimal System, named for its developer Melvil Dewey, who'd generated the practice in 1878. As my mother watched and listened, the head librarian gave a detailed account of how it worked.

"This system," she began, "classifies books by dividing them into ten main groups. Each of these different groups is represented by certain figures. Now notice here," she pointed, "numbers 100–199 ... that's philosophy; 200–299 ... religion; 300–399 ... social science. Now each of these ten main classes further divide into more specialized subjects; for instance, 600-699 ... technology; but within that structure ... 630–639, agriculture is represented, which itself is divided into different categories.

Are you following me? ... good ... let's continue with agriculture. Notice we have classes for Field Crops, Garden Crops, Dairy, Beef, etc. When the classifications become very detailed, decimal points are used. For example ... books on useful insects are grouped under 638 ... beekeeping 638.1 ... silkworms ... 638.2. Do you understand a little how the system operates now?" Mom prayed her complete bewilderment didn't display too strongly.

An added bonus for a librarian's assistant meant you were at the front of the line when the weekly shipment of new books arrived. What a feeling to be the first reader of a never before opened book! The Queen and Lisgar branch was a two-storey building with the entire basement dedicated entirely to children's books. A lady by the name of Alice Kane began her career as children's librarian about the same time Mom did and remained in that capacity for forty-three years.

Part of Alice Kane's job consisted of storytelling ... and as a sidebar ... in 1973 after retiring from the library she continued her career as a professional. In March 1990, the now eighty-two-year-old lady was honoured by the Ontario Folk Arts Recognition Fellowship for her "artistic accomplishments and excellence in the art of storytelling." My mother well remembered this little red-haired, green-eyed Irish woman and how she captivated audiences with her warm style of storytelling. She wasn't at all surprised Alice was still going strong.

"Guest authors" often dropped by the Toronto libraries for signings, promotion, speeches and to simply meet with readers of their books, and during the seven years Mom spent at the Q and L branch, the best remembered was Lucy Maud Montgomery, author of the famous "Anne" series of books.

My father came to the city in 1935, working as an office clerk for a confectionary company and boarded with Mom's family. Up until this time, most of Dad's reading material had centred on poetry as that was his father's preferred genre. A nineteenth-century English poet, Charles Kingsley, was a favourite and my father recalled him reciting melancholy Kingsley rhymes from memory.

As romance bloomed between them, so did Mom's desire to elevate her beau from the narrow field of poetry to an arena of unlimited choice. When the company he worked for filed bankruptcy and with no other work in sight, Dad returned to his home in Eugenia 100 miles away. Depression dollars were scarce if they existed at all for travel, so Mom activated a "books by rail" system.

For a dime, two or three books could be sent on the morning train from Toronto for arrival at Ceylon Station by noon. From there, the mail would be picked up and taken to Eugenia post office for delivery later that day. Through this system, Mom provided a variety of reading material of which Dad had never dreamed. When finished, he'd return the books along with a personal critique on the subject matter of each book.

Mom stayed at the Q and L library branch for seven years, working right up until noon of her wedding day in May 1939. Following my parents' marriage, it was two years' farming in the wilds of northern Grey County, a couple more near Brampton in the County of Peel, then ten at a dairy operation at Bond Head in Simcoe County, before purchasing their own piece of land in nearby Bradford.

Throughout this turnover of locations Dad found little time for books, but Mom continued her favourite pastime whenever and wherever, despite raising six kids with few dollars on a farm with few amenities. If certain household chores had to be curbed for personal well-being ... so be it. I recall Mom telling someone, "There are a lot more important things in this world than housework." I also recall overhearing her tell someone decades ago that if for whatever reason she reached a stage in life that she was unable to read ... "then I don't want to be around."

For me, serious introduction to the library system came in 1957. Our family had just moved from Simcoe County to a farm in Perth County. That first Saturday after arrival, Mom carted me and a couple of my brothers to the local library situated in our new hometown of Palmerston.

I guess if one was to compare the various library buildings in the towns and villages of Ontario at the time, Palmerston stood well above its counterparts. Where some institutions were quite attractive, employing an ample supply of space, others were merely rooms hardly large enough to position a desk. Palmerston was both attractive and spacious and unique as well, its library containing a beautiful concert hall on the second floor, plus various small rooms on the library floor serving as clerk and police offices. In the basement, Boy Scouts, Cubs, AA and several other organizations utilized the area at different times.

Apparently this unique building caused quite a commotion when first built. With the aid of a $10,000 Carnegie library grant, this structure was built in 1903. A lot of money in early twentieth-century dollars! Between 1886 and 1919 when Dale Carnegie passed away, the Carnegie Foundation allocated $56 million for nearly 2,000 libraries in North America.

When the library was being considered, Palmerston's town council at the time thought it would be a good idea and good business to have one building serve a multitude of services, so chipped in an additional $2,000 for "extras." When the Carnegie representatives inspected the building they were extremely upset with these additions. "A Carnegie building must be a library only!" However the funds had already been allocated, so the structure was passed. A new clause was written into all Carnegie contracts henceforth: "All plans for future libraries must be approved before any grant money will be given."

In 1964, a notice in our local newspaper stated Palmerston Public library was looking for an assistant. It had been twenty-five years since Mom had resigned her position at the Toronto library so she was reticent about applying, but Dad persuaded her to file an application, which was accepted. The current librarian was retiring and her assistant, Caroline Cameron was moving up to fill her role, thus creating a job for Mom. At the outset the job entailed just a few hours a week at a pay scale of eighty cents an hour.

An entirely new wave of reading material inundated our household when Mom was on the front line. The first books I recall reading with any regularity were by an English writer, a series of books about five kids and a dog who went about solving simple mysteries. Thornton W. Burgess books such as "Blackie the Crow" and "Bowser the Hound" grabbed our interest for a while and of course Freddie and Flossie, the "Bobbsey Twins." The best loved of that period were Franklin W. Dixon's "Hardy Boys" series. My brothers and I joined Frank and Joe in every mystery in which they became entangled.

Mom read most anything, partly for enjoyment, partly to give library patrons an idea of what they were selecting. Like the elderly lady who one afternoon chose a book ... one of questionable reading material in Mom's mind, especially for this lady whom she knew well. Mother suggested she didn't think she would enjoy this particular book as it contained a lot of sex and profanity. "Isn't that the way," remarked the dear old soul. "So many books are like that nowadays! ... I'll take it."

Although Mom was a full-fledged assistant with more actual experience than the head librarian, Mrs. Cameron never recognized her as such. One day some executives from the county library board were visiting and Mrs. Cameron was staging a great show to impress how almost single-handedly she was running everything. When introducing her guests to Mom she simply said; "This is Mrs. Turner ... she helps dust shelves."

Mrs. Cameron retired in 1970 and Mom became head librarian. I don't know what the library board rules for retirement are nowadays, but Mom wasn't ready to call it quits at sixty-five, so worked five more years until 1982.

It's interesting to observe how anyone who grew up in the Great Depression has a different way of viewing economics. When Mom became head librarian her pay doubled to nearly $2.00 an hour and you would think she had won the lottery! When Palmerston joined the regional Wellington County Library System in the mid-1970s, her salary exploded to $3.50 an hour. Mom wondered how they could afford to pay such "extravagant wages."

There was one aspect following the regional takeover with which Mom didn't easily come to terms, especially as she grew older ... "Story Hour," a "gruelling 60 minutes" (her words) of storytelling and games for pre-school children. These Tuesday morning sessions could entertain anywhere from twenty to thirty-five kids or more. Unlike libraries in Toronto and other high population areas, small centres such as Palmerston could not justify an exclusive children's librarian. I recall one day Mom returning from one of these weekly marathons: "Such bedlam!" she exclaimed. "Why are kids so hyper these days? ... I always respected Alice Kane, but even more so now. That woman must have had the patience of the biblical Job!"

Being involved in the realm of books for so many years gave Mom a unique insight into library patrons' wants and needs, and this perception extended as well to her own family. Knowing where my interests lay, Mom would keep me intrigued with Henry Ford, Sam McLaughlin, Billy Durant, Charlie Nash, Harley Earl, John DeLorean, Cyrus McCormick, Jerome Case, the Massey family and other greats in similar fields.

As well as biographies, I was a fan also of "character studies." One of the best accounts in this venue at the time was Hugh Garner's *Cabbagetown*, depicting life in this area of Toronto during the Great Depression. Noting my high interest in that book, Mom suggested a writer I'd probably like ... John Steinbeck ... and offered *Travels with Charley*. I'm not sure if I was even aware of the American writer at that point, but was instantly hooked. Mom then dug out every Steinbeck book she could find, from his first, *Cup of Gold*, in 1927, through to *The Winter of our Discontent* and the aforementioned *Travels with Charley* in the early 1960s. Steinbeck wrote more than two dozen books in his forty-year career ... classics like *Of Mice and Men*, *The Grapes of Wrath* and *East of Eden*, and I believe I've read them all ... many of them twice.

When Mom retired, her own weekly quota of reading material continued to grow. Dad was retired by this time as well and had reinstated his love affair with the printed word. Each would sit in their respective living room chair, surrounded by a stack of books of varied subjects. Dad especially liked anything linked to Monarchy, and hockey-associated sports figures were also a favourite. Mom liked mysteries and historical fiction and both enjoyed biographies of people in the entertainment field or political arena ... with the occasional exception. Mom was a tried and true Liberal so prejudice sometimes showed its hand.

"Harold is reading Brian Mulroney's (Conservative Canadian Prime Minister) story right now. I never did trust that big grin on that big chin!" Another friction point was John Diefenbaker (another Conservative Prime Minister). "I certainly have better things to do than waste my time reading about him!"

Mom suffered a heart attack in December of 1999 and was hospitalized. Although seemingly mild at the time, complications due to heart valve malfunction and her eighty-seven years dictated there was very little health science could offer. One day I was in the hospital visiting and someone had left a magazine by her bed. She was quite weak at this point and in a quiet voice said, "I never thought I'd see the day when I didn't want to, or was unable to read."

Three days later she passed away ... fulfilling the personal promise I'd overheard those many long years before.

*Great-grandfather William Magee, my
father and Billy ... 1946*

My parents' 1939 DeSoto

Our West Gwillimbury house, Simcoe County ... 1955

*My Aunt Alma Carruthers posing on our
new Allis-Chalmers ... 1953*

Wallace Township farm, Perth County ... 1958

*My brother Donnie waiting for a ride in his
brother Bill's truck complete with dents*

*My grandparents Oliver and Janie
Turner's wedding day ... 1910*

*1959; Back row from left ... Richard, Vivien,
Donnie, Bill, Mom and Dad
Front row, David and Brian*

Our dog Scamp atop the "Chief," our 1950 Pontiac

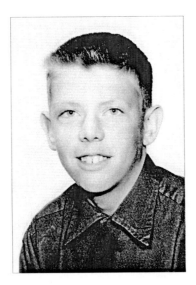

Author's grade eight graduation picture ... 1962

A MATTER OF CHOICES

"What are you going to be when you grow up?" How many times do we get asked that question throughout our adolescent years! I recall that childhood nursery rhyme ... "Tinker, tailor, soldier, sailor, doctor, lawyer, which shall it be ... ?"

Being a descendant of generations of farmers, agriculture was a natural first choice, but other options had surfaced from time to time. I wanted to be a teacher at one point, the attraction of that "little red schoolhouse" syndrome never seemingly far away. However by the time I would have been entering teachers' college in the mid-1960s the one-room school institution with which I was familiar would've disappeared down the same road as fender skirts and fly stickers.

A fire ranger garnered my attention for a while; I even showed up at high school "career day" to pursue the logistics of that idea. As I was a loner, the idea of being isolated in a smoke tower somewhere in Northern Ontario held a certain appeal. A technician for the Cattle Breeder's Association was considered ... not sure where that one came from. A used car salesman; I gave this one plenty of thought, being crazy about anything related to cars. In fact my uncle Bill Magee had been in the used car business for years in Toronto and indicated he could open some doors. A tour bus driver stimulated my imagination for a brief period ... except I didn't care all that much for crowds of people. But I really did want to drive a bus ... if I could just drive the bus empty ...

So ... an interesting cross-section of potential occupations: teaching kids, breeding cattle, watching for forest fires, selling cars and driving buses. But farming always seemed the recurring theme.

But what kind of farming ... Dairying? ... that's what I'd grown up with. A beef feedlot captured my consideration for a spell. Chickens? Yes, I even subscribed to the *Canadian Poultryman* for a year. What about raising registered Holstein heifers? There was some big money to be made in that field especially if you got into the export trade. Except I had paid little attention to cattle pedigrees and that sort of thing ... my brother Bill was the expert on that subject.

Maybe it was because we were inundated with farming magazines that agriculture would constantly be in the running as a career choice. Dad subscribed to a mailbox-full of farm magazines. *Holstein Journal, Good Farming, Country Guide, Farmer's Advocate, Hoard's Dairyman, Farm and Country* and *Family Herald* are a few that come to mind.

For some reason our family's favourite seemed to be *Family Herald,* a Montreal-published bi-weekly magazine started in 1869. When Dad began farming in 1953, a year's subscription was still just a dollar. For a century the *Family Herald* guided its readers through a myriad of topics. General themes like crop rotation, fertilizer application and feeding techniques; and more specialized subjects such as eradicating thistles from your pasture, bats from your basement, ants from your drawers, squirrels from your attic, racoons from the hayloft or bees from your woodshed. It offered free advice and plans for building construction. It would evaluate old coins, stamps and jewellery and offer sewing hints and cooking and baking suggestions for busy housewives.

An ordained minister was available for answering spiritual questions, as were doctors, veterinarians and lawyers for their respective fields. Although spiritual guidance was free, legal assistance and medical advice ... whether human or animal ... were more sophisticated as they charged a dollar plus the inclusion of a self-addressed postage-paid envelope.

Medicine was a big issue in *Family Herald.* Whether you were afflicted with bad nerves or bad kidneys, suffered from diarrhea or constipation, arthritis or sore feet, a product was available by mail order for relief. There were no liquor or tobacco ads and the magazine's conservative position was evident in its choice of photographs as well. A cow's udder was acceptable but not a bull's testicles. An airbrush-equipped artist guaranteed nothing showed between the hind legs when the photo went to press.

My favourite portion of that magazine from long ago were the machinery ads. It was those mostly black and white photos depicting successful farmers working with modern machinery that kept my dreams of a career in agriculture alive. But there was still that question ... what kind of farming? During the winter of 1968, I made a half-hearted attempt at the veal calf business, planning to run forty or fifty at a time, but even with Dad practically giving me the calves, I barely broke even and by April had called it quits.

That veal calf experiment had been the end result of a spat between Dad and me. The episode began in February of that year when I answered a newspaper ad for a truck driver/salesman for the Wittich's Bakery Co. Dad and I had gotten into an argument one day about farming practices (we had several at that point of my life) and I mentioned that if I had to farm his way perhaps I'd do something else for a living. Dad, who had grown tired of my attitude, responded that I didn't have the ambition to apply for a job let alone find one.

The Wittich's Company contacted me on a Wednesday, I drove the twenty miles to the village of Ayton in a snowstorm for an interview Friday and was told I could start work the following Monday. The look of surprise on Dad's face when I made the announcement was worth it!

I didn't really want the job as I took it for spite, so when Dad offered me a small wage to stay home and help him that winter and in return he'd supply a few calves to start my veal business ... it was probably the "out" I was looking for. As far as the Wittich's Bakery Company ... so devastated were they from the potential loss of my services, they never recovered and were soon swallowed by the Weston's conglomerate.

When the veal project bombed, I continued to milk cows as I had been doing all winter. When spring arrived, Dad began setting the stage for retiring from dairying and took a summer job at the local golf course, leaving me and my brother Brian to handle the day-to-day operation of our dairy herd. I was relatively sure milking cows would not be my vocation, as the daily grind of twice-a-day milking held little appeal and without Brian's help, I doubt if I'd have bothered at all.

Following four years of high school, Brian took a year's reprieve before beginning studies at University of Guelph. Brian was so easy-going it was irritating. I'd lose my temper when some stupid cow or calf misbehaved. Not Brian; I'd become frustrated when a machine would break down on a busy day. Not Brian; "Getting mad doesn't do any good" was his answer to every situation. Brian never asked or received a cent from me for his hard work or loyalty. No doubt that was the reason he chose to work for my brother Bill the following summer.

My youngest brother Don then became my right-hand man ... at the same pay scale, although during a weak moment I did promise a monetary reward if he'd pick some mustard for me. Before the days of drenching our grain crops with herbicide, farmers picked the yellow weed by hand. Once a year, two or three people for two or three hours could take care of the nuisance plant for the entire farm. "I'll give you a cent for every plant you pull." It was a sultry June day and I knew Don would quickly tire of the project. The mustard plants were widely scattered so a fair bit of time was involved to make much headway. Even if he picked a couple dozen plants, I figured a quarter wouldn't hurt me.

Within an hour Don had returned with a report he'd picked 100 plants. "What ... already!" ... "Yep, that'll be a dollar." ... "No way have you picked 100 plants that fast!" I answered, trying to weasel out of my bargain. Just then Brian strolled onto the scene. "What's up?" "Dave won't pay me for the mustard I picked." I turned to Brian. "He says he picked 100 plants and he's only been gone a few minutes!" Brian studied the case for a second or two. "It's simple ... we just count the plants ... if there's 100 ... then you owe him the money."

Unfortunately, and with little forethought, Don had thrown the plants in the creek. Brian studied the dilemma further. "Well with no evidence ... and anyway who picks exactly 100 plants? You might pick 90 or 95 or even 105 ... but not 100." Brian's deductions actually made little sense but if it meant I could squirm out from under my deal, so be it.

Despite Don's protest he'd engaged in this agreement with the best of intentions and had indeed picked 100 plants, Brian wasn't convinced. "I think he's lying, I wouldn't pay him." So I didn't. When discussing the incident years later, Don related it was at that point he lost faith in the free enterprise system.

Whether it was veal, beef, cash crop, chickens, pigs or exporting heifers ... no proposal we offered Farm Credit Corporation suited their "long term projections." We battled all year and it seemed as if Dad and I may as well have taken a room at their office, such was our frequency ... but if I'd consider milking cows ... Finally I relented and agreed to at least consider Farm Credit's advice about dairying. Going this route, Farm Credit would lend $10,000 for stabling improvements and an equal amount for cattle and quota purchases.

I had always been impressed with the products from Berg, a Wisconsin-based stable equipment company, so commissioned a sales agent from their London office for an estimate.

Extending a hand he introduced himself; "Ed Lammers is the name ... stabling the game!" After asking if I had anything particular or special in mind, I told him I just wanted him to draw a floor plan that would accommodate two rows of cattle and we'd go from there.

Ed retrieved a huge tape measure from his coat pocket and together we proceeded to measure the interior of the stable. "Forty-eight feet right on!" I hollered from across the stable ... "Okay ... what about the length?" ... "About sixty-seven feet." ... "Exactly?" ... "Well it's an inch over but I guess that doesn't make much difference" ... "Well I guess it depends what you're talking about!"

For about fifteen minutes, Ed scribbled, figured, added, subtracted, underlined and erased, then finally looked up from his clipboard. "Okay ... let's throw this up in the air and see if it flies ... If we made the stalls four feet wide running north and south and installed a three-foot walkway at either end, we could house two rows with 15 ¼ cows in each row ... Have you any quarter-sized cows?" I smiled as I recalled Gay, a dwarf cow that was part of our herd for years. "Not anymore," I answered. "Alright, we'll say fifteen and extend the walkways a hair."

"Do you want your cows to face in or out?" I pondered a moment as there were advantages to either option. Tail to tail was nice for milking, head to head easier for feeding. "Facing in" was my verdict. "I like that", answered Ed, scribbling some more. "If I was a cow, I'd rather stare at another cow than a stone wall." Once Ed added some calf pens, a maternity stall and feed storage area, the old barn had taken on an entirely different light.

Ed's estimate including milking stalls, pens, stable cleaner, water bowls and thermostatically controlled ventilation fans ... was $8500. He further stated he'd knock off $1000 if I personally cleared away the remains of the wooden and concrete stalls from the existing stable.

I actually found myself kind of excited after Ed left. Perhaps milking cows in a new modern environment would be alright. We were used to a stable where at any given moment a calf would jump out of its pen or a cow would wander from her stall with a chain and perhaps a two-by-four dangling from its neck.

These interruptions weren't confined to inside. There was the night we heard this dreadful racket out in the pasture field. Almost afraid to investigate, Dad and I just stared into the blackness as we tried to decipher the origin of the sound which resembled rattling chains and scraping metal. As our eyes became accustomed to the darkness, it appeared to be some sort of moose or perhaps a reindeer pacing back and forth across the pasture field. As we timidly moved closer the scene revealed what looked like a cow ... except for these huge antlers about twelve feet long hanging over its back and dragging on the ground. The "antlers" as it turned out were actually a gate. I guess the animal was reaching through a hole in the wire mesh gate when it became entangled, then literally walked off with it.

There would be no such calamities on my farm. A secure stable constructed entirely of steel and cement, and outside, every field would be secured by tight woven wire fencing and swinging iron gates.

Although this dairying proposal seemed the answer for my father who was anxious to transfer ownership of the farm to me, he didn't prove to be as enthusiastic about modernizing the stable as I presumed. After relating in general terms what the Berg salesman had suggested, Dad said; "You always said you didn't want to be tied down to milking cows seven days a week" ... "Well yeah, but ... " "In fact you stood here just a couple of weeks ago and emphatically stated you hated milking cows" ... "Well yeah, but ... " "And remember once the stable's converted to dairying there's nothing else you can do with it" ... "Well yeah, but ... "

What it boiled down to ... Dad simply didn't like being dictated by a "government run" operation like Farm Credit on what agricultural path we should embrace. Although I hated to admit it, deep down I figured he might be right. I never was enthralled with livestock, especially cows, and in short order probably would have become sick of the twice-a-day, seven-days-a week, no-days-off, zero-holiday routine. Machinery ... that was the part of farming I enjoyed, and dreaming about an endless array of modern tractors and equipment had filled countless hours throughout my adolescence.

That I actually agreed with Dad at all was a milestone in itself, as we agreed on very little. I was at the stage where I knew everything and could hardly comprehend how he had got this far with the little knowledge he possessed. I was reminded of Mark Twain who wrote he couldn't believe how ignorant his parents were when he was fourteen. By the time he was twenty-one, he couldn't believe how much they had learned in just seven years.

When the dairying decision was scrapped, it was of course back to square one. So in effect it had been a wasted year and I was no further ahead career-wise. That summer of 1969 proved to be a transitional year as most of our dwindling dairy herd was transferred to my brother Bill's farm and just the heifers and dry cows remained. By now Dad was employed full time off the farm, Brian was work-ing for Bill (with pay) and I was working steady part time at a neighbouring farm. But I'd be twenty-one in a few months and had been drifting without focus long enough. Whether I wanted to admit it or not, I'd "grown up" and that oft-asked question of my youth deserved a definite answer.

THE BEST LAID PLANS ...

On October 21, 1970, after more than a year from when first applying to Farm Credit Corporation, with my brother-in-law as witness, our home farm was transferred from my parents' to my name. At last I was ready to show the neighbourhood what I could do.

Over that time-period, many different avenues for my agricultural future had been explored, discussed, considered then discarded for whatever reason. Finally ... a decision, although I'm still not certain why I chose swine, as our family had little experience with pigs; more than likely my decision was influenced by our neighbour Doug Hamilton at whose farm I had spent many hours through the years.

Doug, who operated a beef and swine operation, also had a successful livestock trucking business. With his contacts he could supply any customer whatever they desired in the livestock field. Whether you needed 30 or 300 wiener pigs, one call was all it took. Plus he'd make sure they were shipped at optimum weight when marketing time approached. I figured my lack of experience coupled with his knowledge would be a good fit as I travelled down this new road.

Once resolved to swine, I put the wheels in motion, opting for steel mesh partitioning for construction of pens. The panelling could be manufactured any length desired and steel posts lagged to the floor supposedly held it all together. By simply removing a long steel pin, each panel could be easily opened, shut or removed altogether if a larger pen were desired. Also by "easily" installing the steel panelling myself, I was told I could save considerable expense.

I hired a contracting crew to replace the old wooden support posts with steel units and to cement the entire floor area, utilizing between forty and fifty cubic yards of concrete in the process. Removing several planks from the upstairs floor and running the wet cement down a chute to the waiting wheelbarrows saved a good deal time. But first the old stable had to be ripped out. I'd never operated a jack-hammer before but I soon learned! Those old cattle stalls with their thick concrete dividers proved to be a genuine challenge.

Since the stable cleaner I'd chosen originated from Beatty Bros. in Fergus, it made sense to order everything from them. A seemingly good idea until a strike fouled up the schedule. With only one source for materials, I was at a standstill. I'd hoped to have everything in operation by November 1, but didn't even receive any equipment until after that deadline.

It appeared a colossal undertaking when the whole works was finally dumped on the floor of my new stable. Steel mesh panels, anchor posts, a five-gallon pail of steel locking pins, the stable cleaner motor and transmission, 250 feet of gutter chain, feeders that had to be assembled, plus water bowls and fans and all their associated hardware.

Nothing however was sent to secure the posts for the steel panelling, that job apparently left to each individual. Following a couple of trial-and-error attempts, I finally settled on the proper lags and shields, although was forced to buy a heavy-duty drill to bore the more than 200 two-inch-deep holes into the concrete. I had reasoned with the relatively fresh cement, this would be easy. Ha! ... It took all of my 150 lbs. to apply enough pressure and countless replacement bits to complete the job.

I can handle general electrical work so installed the lights, receptacles, etc. and hired the more complicated issues like wiring the thermostatically controlled multi-speed fans as well as the stable cleaner. A heavier hydro service was a necessity for the stable cleaner as we'd always been "under serviced." There were certain appliances Mom was simply unable to operate while we were milking or it would trip the main switch. Countless times, I or one of my brothers would race to the house to reset the switch. It became almost a game, as arrival within thirty seconds would prevent the milking machines from losing their vacuum and disconnecting.

A full day was realized to install the stable cleaner conveyor, but what a thrill when I threw the switch for the initial start-up. I was like a kid with a new Christmas toy as I tossed a few scraps of wood into the gutter, watching with fascination as the paddles dragged them around the circumference of the stable and up the elevator to the barnyard. It would be almost fun cleaning stables with this marvel of engineering!

To keep costs in line, I built a wooden feed storage bin instead of buying a manufactured unit, and although my carpentry skills were limited, furnished air inlets by utilizing the "feed holes" where we formerly dropped hay and straw bales into the stable. My old high school shop teacher would have been proud … or perhaps amazed, at the adjustable hinged plywood shutters I constructed, which could be fully opened in warm weather, completely closed in cold weather and positioned anywhere in between for more moderate temperatures.

Dad had utilized an old belt-driven "hammer mill" as they were commonly referred, to grind rations for the cattle but that wouldn't do for a progressive farmer like me, so I purchased a brand new Gehl "Mix-All" portable grinder/mixer.

I suppose the belt-driven mill was alright in its day, saving countless trips to the local feed mill, but getting the belt aligned always seemed a major challenge. Attempting to wrestle 100 feet of stiff, wide cumbersome belting onto our Allis-Chalmers' rather inaccessible drive pulley proved to be especially trying.

Grain was carried to the mill in five-gallon pails and upon being ground was deposited into a discharge chute that held a pair of 100-lb. capacity jute bags. If you weren't watching closely, the bags could overfill quickly … which would plug the mill.

However this new mill would address all these problems. Grain was poured into the grinding chamber as in a regular mill, but instead of stopping the operation each time a bag was full, this machine had a sixty-five-bushel capacity holding tank integral with the grinder. Once the grain was ground, it was automatically transferred by auger to this tank, where another auger unloaded it into your storage bin. No interruptions, no bags, no belts, no swearing.

Friday, December 11, was a memorable day when Doug Hamilton phoned that he'd be delivering my first round of pigs later that evening. Around midnight his truck rolled in with eighty-five pigs on board. In anticipation I had two pens bedded with straw, plus a heat lamp to ward off any chills my new guests might encounter. In each self-feeder I had placed a generous helping of Co-op medicated starter pellets, another Doug Hamilton suggestion. "In my opinion, for new pigs that medicated feed is the best money you can spend."

By Christmas the barn was full ... about 320 pigs. Originally I had hoped for $15,000 gross sales and as that long winter dragged on and bills mounted, I realized I would need all of it. I continually heard myself telling my creditors ... "as soon as the pigs are shipped ... " It wasn't just snowbirds heading south that winter ... the pork price was going the same direction, which didn't boost creditor confidence either.

The pork market wasn't the only depressing item that winter ... so was the weather with storm following storm and bitterly cold. Compounding the problems of extreme wind chills were a couple of all-day hydro failures, plus frequent interruptions in our water supply as our old pressure system began to show its age. The lane had become hopelessly blocked with drifts ten feet high, forcing the plumber to continually utilize his snowmobile to carry his tools to the site.

I shipped my first pigs early in March and over the next three or four weeks until the barn was empty, the price remained mired in the depths of a surplus market. The dismal return meant a $5,000 shortfall in my monetary projections ... a lot of money in 1970 dollars. By the time I paid the bank, machinery payments, the feed mill, the mortgage, past due truck insurance ... well you get the picture.

Conditions appeared somewhat brighter as the pork market edged upwards by the time my second round of pigs was shipped. Although prices were up, input costs increased dramatically as I was forced to buy barley and corn to get me through to harvest as my own supply was exhausted. At that point, I was reminded of a neighbour's assessment of pig farming. "All I ever had was an empty wallet and an empty granary."

Meanwhile agricultural "experts" of the day were continually promoting the advantages of growing corn. I read the articles with fascination. Who would grow old-fashioned oats and barley when one could get double the yields with corn ... and a crop far superior for raising pigs anyway? I guess you could say Dad and I were on opposing sides on this subject!

"Corn takes twice as much fertilizer," Dad began, "and the seed is three times more expensive, not to mention the expensive chemicals for weed control. You'll have to buy a planter or hire someone. You'll have to get someone to harvest it at a time of year when you're up to your behind in mud. Pay to have it hauled to the dryer. Pay exorbitant drying rates so you can pay someone to haul it back home. That sounds like something someone from the Department of Agriculture would dream up ... probably someone who wouldn't recognize a pile of manure if he fell into it!"

... Well ... what did an old hayseed from the horse age know about modern farming anyway!

I did pay attention to the "old hayseed" on one point however ... instead of "exorbitant" commercial drying. I decided to allow Mother Nature to do the job, so built a corn crib ... a fairly novel idea as most farmers in our area at that time grew corn strictly for ensilage.

At over 100 feet long, that crib was probably the largest in our county. To even out the capital investment, I decided to forgo the roof and cement floor until the second season ... not a good idea as it turned out. While the blackbirds ate their way down from the top, the local rat population was doing likewise from the bottom. Not only would a concrete floor have reduced the rodent potential, it would have been so much easier to shovel cobs off a smooth surface. So although the corn crib concept appeared sound, in retrospect it would seem to have been poorly thought out ... Isn't it interesting how much easier it is to admit a bad decision forty years after the fact!

As corn pickers were almost non-existent in our area of North Perth, I bought a single row New Idea harvester ... just $500 down. Despite Dad's prediction, the weather was beautiful through late October and early November, the fields dry and most importantly the crop excellent. The only bottleneck in the procedure was unloading. I used gravity boxes designed for free-flowing grain not corn cobs, thus they would jam like a bugger. Unloading the wagons was a job I designated to Don, however, so I didn't worry too much about it. I did pay him something for his labour. Following the "mustard" episode, Don for some reason refused to help anymore unless compensated.

The following year, I rented sixty acres through a government program known as the Agricultural Rehabilitation & Development Act. This farm was far from the top of any agricultural list, its most significant drawback a lack of drainage in a wet year. It was perfectly suited to the ARDA program however, which matched "less than ideal" farms with candidates of "limited resources." I couldn't have been more qualified!

The neighbour who owned the farm wanted $16,000. ARDA appraised a more modest $12,000 figure. If I could find the difference, we had a deal. Through the terms of the agreement, only the taxes had to be paid the initial year. The second through fifth years called for taxes plus 5% of the principal. After five years I could buy the farm or lease for another five years at "regular" interest rates.

I leased the farm on the condition ARDA would provide the $12,000, and I the remaining $4,000 for an October 1st closing date. The farm had been planted to corn the previous year and because of the carry-over effects of that year's herbicide, corn would be the only option this season as well. In addition I rented an additional sixty-acre parcel to plant barley and another fifty acres at a bargain price of $5.00 an acre. As it turned out that was all it was worth but acreage-wise I was a big operator!

After all, wasn't that what the "experts" preached ... "There's no room for the small farmer in today's world." I ate it up. With my large land base I would certainly need larger equipment ... no problem! I purchased a 100 hp. Ford tractor, a five-furrow plow and added extensions to the cultivator I already owned.

The 1972 crop season consisted of a long drought-ridden spring, a severe mid-June frost, followed by a wet, cooler than normal summer. One day in early September, Leon Barker, who owned the ARDA farm I was in the process of buying, asked if I'd be interested in selling the corn crop on my (his) farm for silage. I wondered why he'd sell the farm then turn around and buy back the crop, but learned he'd run out of credit and had no other choice. I told him I was planning to keep it for "grain" corn as it would be worth more. Leon doubted it would ever mature and figured selling the crop for silage would be good business for both of us.

I remained steadfast in my decision and could tell Leon wasn't too happy with my answer. As he turned to leave he asked, "That ARDA deal is nearly ready is it?" ... "I guess so ... I haven't heard differently." He didn't seem too pleased with my report but left without further comment.

Government wheels turn at glacier-like speed and since I hadn't bothered to keep regular updates, I didn't realize the deal had become mired in red tape. Horace Wells, the real estate agent handling the sale, drove into the yard a couple of days later. Generally, Horace is pretty relaxed and it takes him awhile to get to the point ... but this day I could see was worried.

"I guess our friend Mr. Barker is none too happy about the progress of this farm deal," Horace began. "He apparently made some inquiries and discovered it to be a long way from being finalized." Horace paused, before continuing. "So ... Mr. Barker has notified his legal counsel that unless he has the money by October 1st, he's going to take the corn crop himself."

I digested this bombshell ... "Can he do that?" ... "Well," drawled Horace, "he's within his rights legally ... I'm afraid our friend Mr. Barker is in dire straits financially and probably feels this is his only avenue." "There's no way to speed up the government," I surmised, "so what can we do?" "I'll make a few calls and see what can or can't be done," said Horace upon leaving. "Don't lose too much sleep over this, David ... before I'd see that happen I'd lend you the money."

... Which is exactly what Horace did ... at least part of it. Dad lent me some. Bill had just sold a couple of high-priced cows and lent me another chunk. It was a widespread and complicated transaction but most importantly for me, the $16,000 figure was raised. It was February before the proceeds from the government arrived and everyone was paid back.

Because of the assorted problems associated with the previous year's storage, crib drying had lost much of its appeal. To be satisfactory, pig feed must be shelled, which turned out to be a time-consuming and tedious practice especially in winter. So I sold the picker (the payments were overdue anyway) and planned to have the crop custom harvested.

I hated to admit it ... but Leon had been absolutely correct in his assessment of my corn crop. With what followed, selling the corn to Leon would have been the best decision I could have made. At that period of my life, "right" decisions seemed few and far between. Due to the inclement weather the cobs simply would not "dry down." The one load I took to the elevator proved to be too wet to even flow through their dryer, forcing me to sell it to a farmer with a Harvestore silo at a fire sale price. The other option was to dump it in the nearest manure pile. A week later I tried one more sample and it was off the scale in moisture, failing to even register a figure on their test meter.

Final result, the crop remained in the field until spring. The barley ran out by Christmas and with no additional crop, my feed bills went skyward, causing me to run out of credit ... or perhaps it was credibility, with the bank.

I did manage to salvage a small percentage of corn when the spring weather arrived, although it contained a fair bit of mildew. A Listowel feed mill operator who wasn't too particular about quality took it off my hands. Needless to say he wasn't too particular about paying much either.

Early in 1973, I elected to go the "contract" route with the Drayton Co-op. Under their program they would purchase the pigs and provide the feed. All I had to furnish was shelter, bedding and water. For this arrangement, I was guaranteed a certain price per pig shipped ... I think it was about $4.00 ... plus 50% of any leftover profit. I'd incur no further debt, plus I was free to sell my grain crops for cash. With this system in place, maybe my fortunes would finally turn. At this point, they really had only one direction to go.

I would spend many hours over the next few months reflecting on where my dream of just two years before had gone wrong: In the end, the analysis was a waste of time and worthless in value as I could entertain countless reasons to justify my failures, shortcomings, explanations, defences, alibis and excuses.

Nature's elements and disappointing commodity prices had certainly contributed to the downfall, but equally to blame whether I wanted to admit it or not, were a multitude of management missteps. In the end maybe I should have simply been more attentive to the advice of leftover horse-era hayseeds!

THE WORLD ACCORDING TO WANDA

It was no doubt the last thing I needed, but in the spring of 1973 with more than a hundred acres of un-harvested corn still in the fields from the previous season ... I decided to rent more land. But this particular farm was a story in itself, beginning with a phone call the previous autumn from a man who had land and a barn to rent.

Next afternoon I stood at the doorway of a large sprawling farmhouse just a few minutes from home. A woman, probably in her late forties, with a cigarette clamped between her lips and wearing an orange, perspiration-stained T-shirt, answered my knock. "Yeah, what can I do for you?" I immediately recognized her gravelly voice as the "man" who had phoned the day before. I introduced myself and was invited in. "The name's Becker ... Wanda Becker." Over a cup of coffee she filled me in on the story of the farm.

"There's about 140 acres; at least that's what the neighbour who rented it last year figured. He doesn't want it this year ... says he's too busy. That's a laugh. The bugger hasn't worked a full day since I've known him! It's real good land," she continued, "but there's just me and my daughter as my son of a bitchin' husband ran off. All I need is enough to pay the taxes and Farm Credit."

I accompanied her out to the stable. The barn itself appeared relatively new, but the stable had an unfinished look, as though construction had been devoid of any structured plan. "I don't know what the hell he was thinking," said Wanda, reading my mind, "but the bastard left before it was done anyway!" I gathered she was talking about her husband again.

I later learned he had gone to the local elevator a couple of years earlier with a tractor-trailer load of wheat, thanked the driver for the ride, waited around for the cheque to be processed, pocketed the receipts and disappeared, never to be seen again.

I told Wanda I would take her offer and signed a two-year rental agreement … I think it was around $1000.00 a year including the barn. Recently a neighbour of mine had inquired about a place to house some heifers until spring, so I figured this location would provide the opportunity, grant me some income and at the same time help warm the stable for the upcoming winter.

The roughly two dozen cattle shared quarters with a sorrel stallion owned by Wanda's daughter. Nicki was crazy about horses, forever talking about owning her own horse farm and raising colts and how "Klondike" would someday make her a fortune in stud fees. Although she was barely seventeen, I couldn't help but notice from day one Nicki was a physical treasure, tall with shoulder-length auburn hair, dusky skin, greenish-grey eyes, all encased within a well-proportioned package.

I don't know how much coffee I drank at the Becker kitchen table that winter. From the beginning, Wanda had insisted I drop in for a cup or two after the morning chores. These coffee breaks proved to be a great way to catch up on neighbourhood gossip, for what Wanda didn't know ... simply wasn't worth knowing.

The circumstances were so gradual I missed the signals, but by Christmas, Wanda Becker for all intents and purpose had "adopted" me. A shopaholic if there ever was one, Wanda was a common fixture with her signature cigarette permanently attached to her lips, rummaging through the leftovers at every lawn sale and going-out-of-business clearance in a twenty-mile radius.

She was forever buying me clothes, often out of style, but I'd never been too conscious of the fashion trends of the day anyway. Everything Wanda purchased smelled of second-hand smoke, as did everything in her vicinity. Before I realized it, I was chauffeuring Wanda to doctor's appointments, lawyer visits or school activities, especially in poor weather. "I don't mind a little snow," she confessed, "but that goddam ice you can shove you know where!" Once I drove Wanda to visit some acquaintances near Kitchener ... a minister and his wife no less! For someone who probably held the Guinness record for number of four-letter words used in a single sentence ... this outing struck me as both unique and amusing.

Wanda had an agenda; although I didn't know it at the time, she was searching for a man to operate the farm and do all the things that husbands do, including keeping her warm at night. Roscoe Webb, a neighbour of Wanda's who also knew me well, thought it quite hilarious to give her my name, knowing full well Wanda's intentions. One night when Wanda had too much to drink, she confessed "that asshole Roscoe said you'd be perfect ... he didn't say you were twenty-five goddam years younger!"

When the first plan fizzled, Wanda thought she might be able to salvage something if Nicki and I were to "hit it off." With "Plan B," I'd still be in the picture and available to look after her and the farm and the horses and crops and run errands and ... and ... and.

Well, I was already several moves ahead on that front as Nicki and I were already "hitting it off." It began the evening Wanda was away at a meeting and Nicki invited me up to her room on the premise of helping her with her homework. A large desk with a typewriter, an office chair, a lounging chair, a stereo and a double bed were all nestled into this one room. Nicki sat in the easy chair while I sat on the office chair, not feeling comfortable sitting on her bed. "I've been struggling with some of these grammatical terms," she said, handing me a notebook.

I glanced at what she'd written. "Well ... personification," I began, "is when you use a human depiction to describe a non-human characteristic; for instance, the stars danced across the winter sky ... or ... a summer breeze skipped across the meadow." ... "It's hot in here don't you think?" Nicki interrupted. She peeled off the long-sleeved shirt she'd been wearing, leaving just a skimpy T-shirt ... and also I couldn't help notice ... no bra. Flashing one of her patented smiles, Nicki added. "I find when I'm studying, the less clothes the better."

... "Okay ... where were we?...oh yes ... alliteration ... well, that's when you use words beginning with the same consonant in a phrase ... like Peter picked pumpkins and peppers ... or it could be just a couple of words like ... baby bottle ... or black beauty". Nicki nodded, "you mean like bouncing breasts?" ... "Well ... yes ... that's an example ... you're right, it is hot in here!" I removed my jacket and I believe to my credit, resumed the grammar lesson.

... "Let's see ... similes? ... well that's ... " At this point Nicki got off the office chair and sat on the edge of the bed, looking straight at me. "I'm still not quite sure about alliteration ... correct me if I'm wrong but how about these examples?" She took the notebook from my hand, wrote something and handed it back. I guess it would be understatement to say I was surprised to read "pulsating penis" and "pounding penis" and a few other references I've forgotten. If there had been any question how this evening might conclude, Nicki had clearly erased all doubt!

To augment her welfare and farm rental income, Wanda Becker was part of a local book publishing company. Cooking, gardening, sewing and food preservation all fell under the topic of "Homemaking," the association's prime focus. She had some job in the editing department I believe, a task she worked at from home.

One snowy night in mid-December, I chauffeured Wanda and Nicki to the company's Christmas party (I never minded running errands quite so much when Nicki was involved). Wanda was all dressed up, complete with auburn wig. I guess she noticed me looking at her when she got into the car. "I got it for $7.00 at a sale!" she boasted. "Not a goddam thing wrong with it!"

The party was held at the Hanover Legion, about a twenty-mile drive. We were hardly underway when Wanda procured a bottle from her purse. "Need a little something to up your courage for this bitchin' weather?" ... "No thanks." She downed a couple of healthy swallows. "Sure you don't want a gulp?" ... "I'm fine, thanks." Wanda took one more pull just before we disembarked. "I sure need something if I have to spend the evening with those prissy assholes!" She offered the bottle again ... "Last chance!" ... "What is it anyway?" I asked. "Cherry brandy." I took a swallow which sort of reminded me of Vicks Formula 44, Nicki fortified herself with a slug and into the hall we went.

A Christmas tree was set up in one corner under which Nicki dumped some gifts. Wanda introduced me to a couple of co-workers while sipping on fruit punch. "I wonder where they dredged this slop from?"

... "You know," said Wanda to no one in particular and anyone within hearing range, "this stuff reminds me of the story of the two old farmers who were always arguing over whose homemade beer was the best. Someone suggested they send a sample away to the local brewery to be tested, but it got mixed up somehow and ended up at the Guelph Veterinary College. A few days later the results came back from the College stating that neither horse should be worked for two weeks!" Wanda convulsed into a fit of laughter, while her associates merely stood around looking embarrassed.

The most entertaining part of the evening was when a guy about Nicki's age came over to our table. Nodding towards me, he said to Nicki. "Is this old fart your date? ... if you want some real action from someone who can actually do the job, I'm available." I was wondering how to react to this stranger's crude remark and still keep the evening civil when Nicki, who had no issues about civility or political correctness, plowed a fist into his stomach. As he doubled over, Nicki reminded him if he opened his mouth again that ... "the next fist will be in the nuts!" Consequently, we heard no more from him. I delivered the "ladies" back home around midnight, where Wanda invited me to "finish off the party," but I figured I'd had enough excitement for one evening.

Until I met Wanda Becker, I don't think I'd even tasted liquor. Although I was nearing my mid- twenties, the occasional beer was as close as I cared to be to alcohol. Wanda sure changed my lifestyle for a while!

Wanda entertained a lot of company; the rural mail carrier was a frequent visitor as was the furnace repairman. I remember thinking … how many times can a furnace malfunction? Others showed up on a more irregular basis … but strangely few couples. Some of Wanda's guests stayed a few hours, others until they passed out, leaving in the morning or whenever they could stand. I recall myself half crawling across the Becker kitchen one morning, never feeling more ill in my life and with only the vaguest image of the night before, looking for my clothes (don't ask) then heading home to hopefully die in peace and the sooner the better.

One party regular in those days was a guy by the name of Newman, who worked at Goodyear in Kitchener. I don't remember his connection to Wanda but he was a likeable sort and great storyteller. One evening he held his audience spellbound (more than likely they were drunk) discussing the origin of Malaysian rubber, including regional climate, plus environmental and soil information that the trees needed to thrive. Another visit had him conversing at length how the synthetic rubber industry in North America had evolved to blend its characteristics with the natural variety, and how the raw product was actually moulded into tires at the Kitchener plant.

Newman showed up one Sunday afternoon just as I was finishing the chores and I was invited in to share in a glass of wine. That sounded innocent enough, except we're talking "homemade" here. Newman thought it was good, but then he could drink most anything with seemingly little effect. As for me, that so-called wine had to be the worst looking liquid I'd ever seen in a bottle. "It's a little cloudy this year," remarked Wanda, pouring me a tumbler full, "but there's not a goddam thing wrong with the taste."

All this sludge in the bottom of the glass and the rest a floating murky mixture of ... well I couldn't guess what. I figured it couldn't taste worse than it looked. Wrong! I swallowed half the glass's contents then apologized to Wanda for being in such a hurry, but had suddenly remembered supper was waiting. I managed to get outside the door before vomiting into a snow bank. I recall thinking it didn't look much different coming up as it did going down.

Meanwhile back at the ranch, the months passed with Nicki and I still "hitting it off." Nicki often came out to the barn when I was doing chores. She'd arrive wearing coveralls, removing them as soon as she got there, often working in shorts that barely covered her behind, a T-shirt and of course, no bra. Flirtation and sexual innuendos were second nature to Nicki but she needn't have tried so hard ... the minute she entered the stable she had my temperature gauge rising.

Although I couldn't see it at the time ... or ignored it, Nicki knew how to utilize what she had. She read me like a book and never missed a page, so whether it was riding boots, a horse blanket, a leather jacket or a dozen other things she wanted ... Nicki knew what was required to get it!

Motives aside, recalling those intoxicating and reckless days inspires a vignette of sight, sound and smell. Burlap bags spread out on bales of straw; cattle bawling in unison with CKNX radio, while a lustful scented mixture of perfume, alfalfa, molasses and manure filled the air.

If Nicki locked the stable door when she entered, it was a fair indication of what lay in store. One night Wanda came down to the barn to relay a phone message and discovered the door locked. Nicki may have been hot in a lot of ways but proved cool in a crisis. "Just a minute!" she hollered. Throwing her shorts and shirt out of sight, she donned her coveralls over her naked body, stepped into her boots, glanced back at me then casually walked towards the door.

"Why in the hell is the f...ing door locked!?" Wanda shouted. "What are you bastards doing in here anyway? ... "Oh, for God's sake Mom ... why do you always have to be so dramatic? ... the goddam latch sticks sometimes, that's all."

Wanda Becker may have been a lot of things ... but stupid she wasn't, so I can't imagine she didn't suspect something. If she did, perhaps she just figured "Plan B" was falling into place.

For me, Nicki was much too unpredictable for any kind of long-term relationship that Wanda might have desired. You never knew what Nicki's mood of the minute might be ... she could be incredibly hot and sweet and sexy ... or just the opposite, when you'd receive a look that would make the interior of a refrigerator seem warm in comparison.

Despite Nicki's entertaining qualities, I was feeling the strain of the Becker relationship. The two years had seemed like ten; Wanda was forever in want of something ... the water pump had quit ... or the litter carrier had come off the track ... or Klondike had gotten out of his stall, or the water was frozen ... or the car wouldn't start ... or ... or ... or

Other events had me questioning if it wasn't time to move on, like the evening Roscoe Webb and his brother Rupert hauled Rupert's mare over to get bred. While the four of us stood watching Klondike get his workout, Nicki laughed and turned to the brothers ... "Well I guess the two of you feel pretty insignificant!" I don't know if she was merely generalizing or was speaking from experience. The way she carried on I was probably naïve to think I was her "only one." What I do recall was the painfully lengthy interval of silence following her declaration.

An issue that didn't help matters between Nicki and me started when Klondike began warranting a poor report card when it came to getting mares in foal and earning the moniker of "dud" versus "stud." Nicki had big plans for that stallion and when he didn't live up to expectations, she took out her frustrations on whoever was handy. I well remember her cutting remark one evening when events came to a disappointing conclusion between us ... "Well that's characteristic of the male species isn't it? What appears promising typically ends up useless!"

Even if the temperature was dropping between Nicki and me, Wanda was still in the game and had adopted a new man to fetch, carry and whatever. How they met is anyone's guess, but Leonard was a truck driver from somewhere who Wanda enticed with who knows what story, and to his credit he managed to hang around the Becker place almost as long as I did.

I ran into Leonard in a coffee shop in London many years later, long after he'd progressed to other adventures and talk naturally got around to the Beckers. By this time Nicki had long since graduated from college and left home, determined to find her father whom she'd heard through the grapevine was in Alberta. If indeed her father was ever there, he apparently didn't want to be found, and last heard, Nicki was living in Edmonton where rumour had it second-hand she was teaching horse husbandry at an equine training centre.

Shortly after Nicki left, Wanda sold the farm and moved to an apartment in town. Unfortunately, retirement was short lived. For the first time in her life Wanda was financially secure; however the years of financial and social stress in conjunction with increased tobacco and alcohol abuse eventually took their toll, and she died before reaching sixty.

... "You know Dave," said Leonard as we continued our re-visit of the past ... "Wanda and Nicki ... they'd ask me a 100 things and I'd do it ... they'd ask 101 and I'd refuse and they'd call me every four-letter word in the book. Well I know a few of those words myself, so one night I just told both of them where they could go and what they could bloody well do when they got there! ... that's when Wanda kicked me out. The week I spent at the local hotel gave me a chance to re-evaluate my life and that's when I decided it was time to move on."

As we stared into our coffee cups, each lost in our own thoughts, Leonard broke the silence ... "I wish I could have left on better terms ... I certainly take no pride in using language like that, especially to women ... but goddam it Dave ... it seemed the only language they understood!"

NOTHING IN COMMON

It was August 1973, and at the time I was in the midst of a seemingly never-ending stream of farming challenges. Dismal market prices for pork, a disastrous frost ruining the corn crop, no end to "past due" mail notices and phone calls from bill collectors. A diversion was sorely needed and it was my best friend Doug Watt who came to the rescue.

He and his wife Judy had been living in an apartment in Toronto since their marriage two years earlier, but had now purchased a new house in the town of Orangeville, some thirty miles north of the city. The plan was professional movers would handle the large items, while I would haul many of the smaller articles in my pickup. A few friends of theirs would also be helping out with whatever they could.

The movers were supposed to be at the apartment at eight AM, but a half hour later with no sign, we went ahead and began filling the other vehicles. There were eight of us for this chore; Doug and Judy; Scott and his fiancée Mavis; Trish ... a pretty girl with the most gorgeous blue eyes ... and Ed and Gina. Ed was the so-called electrician, although I'm not sure of his qualifications. When he pulled the switch after wiring the stove at the new house, a ball of flame blazed across the kitchen floor. I never did know Ed's last name. I always referred to him simply as "Ed who wired the stove."

At 9:30, a tired-looking, ten-year-old Chevrolet moving van lumbered onto the scene. Apparently someone had vandalized the truck overnight, busted a few lights or something ... and that supposedly was the reason for their delay. The two operators at first glance didn't seem overly bright, but appeared conscientious enough and methodically went about their business.

Things went smoothly throughout the morning; the only altercation was when Ed who wired the stove wanted to stop the proceedings for a drink. Doug made it clear. "No drinking until the job's done!" A mild argument ensued, but Doug held firm and Ed who wired the stove returned to the job at hand. By one o'clock the apartment was bare and everything set for the run to Orangeville. Doug rode with me and everyone else took their own cars. We departed convoy style, the moving van limping along in the rear. It soon fell behind well out of sight, its shaky steering relegating it to a 40 mph pace.

Doug and Judy's new home was in an equally new subdivision in the southwest corner of Orangeville, hidden among a labyrinth of avenues, crescents and dead-end streets. Somehow, everyone found their way ... even our trusty moving duo, and by five o'clock everything was settled in the appropriate rooms in nearly the same condition it left Toronto. We may have had some doubts about the chosen movers at the outset, but in all fairness they did a good job, were polite and steady and didn't break anything important.

Pizza and beer proved to be supper for those left over. Gina and Ed who wired the stove had a prior engagement and left immediately following the meal. Trish had purchased champagne, and the six remaining sat on the lawn, which more accurately was a pile of dirt, and from Styrofoam cups toasted the new house. It was a beautiful warm evening and we sat out there for hours talking and enjoying what the night had to offer.

In that many of the houses on Avonmore Crescent were still vacant, there wasn't a lot to see. The major attraction was the regular twenty-minute patrol by the neighbourhood security guard. Doug and Judy had seen him around on the frequent trips to inspect the house during the summer. Apparently, he'd lost his license for some liquor infraction and now had to depend on a chauffeur to carry out his duties. He was a small, squatty little guy with white hair and beady eyes. He'd sit hunkered down in the back seat of this old Ford, his head darting from side to side as he rolled by, glaring at us more intently with each circuit.

I spent a great deal of time in Orangeville over the next few weeks. Trish would often be there and she and Judy would cook up these huge meals of spaghetti, lasagna, panzerotti, or a specialty of Trish's … cabbage rolls. Most of these dishes I'd never seen, let alone tasted. At home we were more accustomed to pork chops, mashed potatoes and creamed corn. It was my belief that was all a person needed. Mom would occasionally experiment with something different, but we kids never offered much support. More often than not we'd merely look at it and make a gagging noise. One didn't have to be polite at home.

One weekend Doug, Judy, Trish and I headed off for Lockport, New York, just to have supper … or dinner as city people referred to it ... at some restaurant called "Garloc's" that was apparently a big deal. That trip down the highway from Toronto to the American border on a Saturday afternoon with three lanes of traffic whizzing by at 80 mph was an education for a farm boy! As we neared the border, I asked Trish, who was sitting in the passenger seat, what the name of the town was where we were going. "Lockport ... but just mention Garloc's ... they'll know."

"Where are you headed?" the customs agent asked.

"Garloc's" ... "Where?" ... "Garloc's" ... "Where's that?" ... "in Lockport" ... "What's your business there?" ... "supper ... I mean dinner." He sort of shrugged and motioned us through. I'm not sure what I expected, but the exterior of this supposedly famous restaurant was certainly a letdown. Greeting us was a grey washed-out building in the middle of a dirty street. Its charm, according to my companions, lay within.

As we were a half hour early for our reservation, Doug suggested a drink. Behind a large oak counter, a bartender was mixing drinks with names I'd never heard. Trish ordered something called a "banana daiquiri." I guess she had lots of experience with these "big city" drinks, for when the bartender was mixing up this concoction, Trish informed him that ... "in Canada, they use real bananas." He gave her a sort of "well, why don't you go back to Canada" look. Doug ordered a "Scotch on the Rocks." What I wouldn't have given for a good old-fashioned Pepsi! I was so far out of my element I naively figured I had to order liquor, so ordered the same. "So, you like Scotch on the Rocks too, David!" ... "Oh sure," conveying an air of authority. What I wanted to tell Trish was ... "How can anyone drink this stuff!"

The menu was foreign as well, with endless questions about appetizers, entrées and dressing choices; nothing normal like pork chops or fried chicken … and no mashed potatoes … just a baked version the size of a small watermelon. "Prime rib" sounded like a safe bet once informed what it was. I had no idea what the waiter meant when he asked "How do you want it sir?" My first reaction … "on my plate would be nice." So … a giant slice of beef too well done to suit me, an oversized over-baked potato, plus a couple of unrecognizable vegetables were apparently what I'd driven a hundred miles for. Ah yes, but the experience!

Through the months of September and October I spent most weekends in Orangeville. Occasionally the four of us would head off to a Toronto nightclub to pay outlandish prices to drink in a room so crowded and noisy one had to yell to be heard. I experimented with some of the drinks Trish enjoyed, figuring that's what it took to impress her. Rye and water … rye and ginger, something called a "rusty nail," different flavoured daiquiris and punches, an assortment of liqueurs … I never found one I particularly cared for, so opted for regular beer. Trish consumed only imported beer. I couldn't tell the difference except for price.

Weekends at Avonmore Crescent consisted of eating, drinking, playing pool, listening to records, playing board games, watching television … sometimes even working. But whether it was hanging drapes or building a few storage shelves, nothing was too simple for Doug and me to mess up. Judy would become so frustrated, as our ineptness turned the project into a disaster every time.

At this point in time, everything was gearing up for the "open house" first Saturday in October. Doug and I spent two hours, which should have taken twenty minutes, installing a basement speaker system for the stereo. "So David," Trish inquired at supper time, "you're ready to dance are you?" I don't dance," I answered simply. She just laughed.

Probably thirty people swarmed in that evening. I knew a few like Scott and Mavis and Ed who wired the stove. I passed the initial part of the evening on the opposite side of the room from Trish, drinking beer with Scott. I figured this eliminated any chance of having to dance. This plan worked only so long. Surmising I was never going to make a move, Trish walked over to my side and gently took me by the arm. "I don't dance!" I repeated, stiffening up like a pretzel. Trish returned to her seat embarrassed, while I retired to the bathroom and threw up.

Trish never mentioned the "d" word again that evening, but next day at lunch, stated. "Next week, we are going to Oktoberfest in Kitchener ... and you're going to dance!" "I don't dance!" I repeated once more. Trish just looked at me. "What do you mean you don't dance?" ... "Well ... like when everyone else is out on the dance floor ... I'm not there!"

That statement didn't compute with Trish, so next thing I realize I'm down in the basement and she's counting out some basic steps to the tune of some scratchy polka record she scrounged from Doug's musical library. "One ... two three, one ... two three," taking me in her arms. "I'll lead," she said, slowly counting out the beat. "Relax! ... one ... two ... three ... relax! ...one ... two, three ... for Heaven's sake ... relax! ... this is supposed to be fun!" Trish then took a turn with Doug while I went to the bathroom and threw up.

I prayed I'd die or at least break my leg before the next weekend, although I did make a half-hearted attempt at some practice the night before we were to go. Under cover of darkness, with only the stars to witness my clumsy movements, I practiced my dance steps. I realized I was only kidding myself. To think I would actually be able to stroll out onto the dance floor and display any semblance of a polka ... or anything else for that matter ... was ludicrous.

Someone was looking out for me. When Doug wheeled into the parking lot of the Concordia Club, one of the major Bavarian establishments catering to Oktoberfest crowds, the attendant announced they were full up. "What others do you recommend?" asked Doug. "Sorry ... everything is booked solid." I wanted to do cartwheels on the roof of Doug's Volkswagen; instead we ate supper at the Breslau Hotel a few miles away, Trish had her imported beer and I wasn't asked to dance.

I can think of only a couple of possible explanations for my anxiety on the dance floor. In another life, I must have suffered some catastrophe. Perhaps a giant chandelier came crashing down on my head. Maybe I merely slipped on the waxed surface of the ballroom floor and was trampled to death. There's got to be some reason!

Trish visited our place once, but I'm certain she considered it once too often. Dad was friendly as he was with almost anyone, but Mom was very cold. As I recall, however, Mom never actually laid out the red carpet for any of her children's choices of friends. Once these "outsiders" were legally part of the fold it was different, but it seemed they had to endure a lengthy period of chill and distrust before that goal was achieved.

Trish didn't come close to passing inspection. It couldn't have been because she was a "city girl" as Mom could certainly relate on that point, being Toronto raised herself. I don't think it was because she was Catholic. I had never known religious prejudice to be a factor in our family. I believe it had more to do with circumstances that might arise if Trish and I were to become "serious" and Mom and Dad would have to move out. Because they had financed my farming operation to a large extent and very little if any had been paid back ... money was rather scarce at that point. And my parents simply weren't ready to retire to town yet. Another option that probably scared the hell out of Mom ... all of us living together under one roof like the Waltons! ... Whatever the reason, Trish became an innocent victim of a chilly reception.

Mom mentioned one day, how if I were to marry Trish, we would be expected to raise children. I'd always blathered on about how I was never going to be tied down with kids. "Having children is part of the Catholic creed you know!" No ... I didn't know, nor did I care ... as marriage was the last thing on my mind at this point. Although we seemed planets apart in just about everything, I was definitely swept away by Trish's charms and simply wanted to enjoy the ride however far it went ... and it went all the way to Florida! ... But that story is to be continued ...

RUNNING ON EMPTY

Few would argue the fact that the 1960s weren't particularly kind to the United States. Race riots, political assassinations, the escalation of the Vietnam War and all its inherent protests, the nuclear threat ... If the country hoped for better things in the 1970s it was deeply disappointed, as the decade dawned with war still raging, and then came a small-time, botched burglary at an office complex in Washington known as Watergate.

Because one of the burglars caught was the security co-ordinator of the committee who helped re-elect President Nixon, a full investigation was launched. This scandal turned into a news reporter's dream as countless politicians were indicted for wiretapping, blackmail, bribery etc. ... a trail that eventually led all the way to the White House.

While the corruption and cover-up scandal dragged on, the war in Vietnam finally ended. But there was no joy in this matter either, as for the first time in history the U.S. was declared the loser. A ceasefire "agreement" had been signed in January 1973, a more palatable word than "surrender." As it was, more than 56,000 servicemen died. More than 300,000 came home armless, legless, sightless or mindless, and the ones who made it back relatively intact were largely greeted with indifference and coldness among the populace. The best way to forget was to ignore. No ceremonies, banners or parades would welcome home these fighters ... they were from "that" war called Vietnam.

Amongst the depression of a scandalized government and an unwinnable jungle war, another soul-destroyer was forced upon the American people ... something they never thought they would witness ... a fuel crisis.

Over the years, many reasons have been given as to the cause. The U.S. at that time, with only 6% of the world population, consumed 33% of its energy. The number of cars had tripled in the past thirty years, hydro demands were doubling every decade. Coal-burning industries were switching to fuel oil to satisfy new environmental standards; unusually cold winters were causing a major shift to home heating oil, leaving gasoline and diesel supplies low.

All these issues had merit, but as so often the case ... political instability was the main culprit. On October 6, 1973, Egypt and Syria with help from other Arab nations had attacked Israeli-occupied territory. Because they were severely outnumbered, United States chose to back Israel, a decision that angered the Arab countries.

Things had changed over the years; now many of these Middle East countries, particularly Iran, Kuwait and Saudi Arabia, were major players in the world's supply of oil reserves and understood perfectly the game of supply and demand. What better way of getting even with a petroleum-hungry country's interference? By curtailing shipments of crude oil and thus raising demand, the oil-producing Arab countries were able to double and even triple the world price per barrel.

Almost overnight, prices soared at the pumps as gas and diesel reserves dwindled. In some of the bigger cities an "odd even" arrangement, depending on your license number, was instigated. "Gas guzzling" penalties were slapped on big V-8 cars and General Motors and Ford sold record numbers of Vegas and Pintos. The Japanese market cashed in as well, and manufacturers such as Chrysler that had no small car nearly expired.

The U.S. government in a near state of panic, legislated a speed limit of 55 mph on every road in the country, interstates included. Truckers were the most vocal, complaining a 55 mph limit was utterly inefficient for their huge rigs. To get their point across, they staged mile-long convoys to snarl traffic but it did no good. On December 1, 1973, the new limit became law.

In Canada, being much less dependent on foreign oil, no such encumbrances as line-ups or rationing surfaced. Our government did follow the U.S. lead and lower our speed limit to 50 mph (80 kph) ... and of course prices ballooned as our petroleum companies cashed in on the inflated world market price controlled by OPEC.

This gives you some idea of the environment I was heading into as I planned my Florida getaway with my new-found friend Trish. That Florida idea had been hatched so innocently ... One evening Judy was talking about the regular winter vacations she took with her parents to the Sunshine State when she was a teenager.

To this day I know not why I said it ... because I don't recall the notion ever crossing my mind ... but out of the blue I announced, "I think I'll go down to Florida this winter for a few days."

"Oh when?" asked Trish.

"Uh ... well ... I hadn't actually set a date ... "

"I'm going to Disney World in December," interrupted Trish. "I'm flying down. I've got a room booked for two nights at the Polynesian Village Resort."

"How were you planning to go?"

"Uh ... drive I guess."

"Perhaps we could meet there!" added Trish ...

"Uh ... well ... I'll have to think about it ... "

Next visit, Trish reopened the subject. "You know David ... I was thinking. If you were driving down you could bring my luggage. It would save me carrying so much on the plane." A few more suggestions and alternatives were bounced around until finally Trish said. "Why don't I just ride down with you and save the plane fare? I'll pay half the costs for gas, motels and whatever. And just like that it was settled. My brain had disengaged for a mere moment and suddenly I was on my way to Florida? What in hell had I gotten into!

I hadn't mentioned a word to Mom and Dad as the trip was more than a month away. No sense stirring up a hornet's nest until I had to. That "had to" appeared earlier than anticipated. Circumstances were set in motion when Dad responded to an advertisement in the *Palmerston Observer*, requesting a courier for a daily route to Owen Sound.

At this point my agriculture career was on life support as no financial institution would lend me any more capital to buy pigs. With my record, who could blame them? I was basically living in a vacuum and I suppose Dad figured this would be a good job at least for the winter while I contemplated my future. My only income over the past month or so had been some custom tillage work and I argued weakly that I still had a lot of acres to cover. According to Dad, the man who was offering the position didn't mind waiting a couple of weeks. Two weeks was no good for me, so I had no choice but to relate my real reason for passing on this opportunity.

This probably would have been an excellent time for a personal brain scan. I had basically no job, therefore no income, a stack of bills growing each day with interest, plus countless letters and phone calls from creditors about overdue accounts ... yet I was willing to throw it away for ... who knows what!

I was unsure what Dad's reaction would be, but had no such doubts as to Mom's! I purposely waited until one evening when my brother and his wife were present to muffle the explosion that was certain to erupt from her corner.

... "Well that seems like a stupid idea going down to Florida," Mom began. "Harold went to a lot of trouble to get you this job, and now to just go traipsing off to Florida! ... You can't afford it anyway."

"It won't cost much," I interrupted. "We're going to split the costs."

"I'm surprised," said Mom, shifting to another gear, "that Doug and Judy would even consider going down there now with all this talk about fuel shortages."

"That's probably all it is ... talk," I broke in ... "but Doug and Judy aren't going."

Mom looked at me for a moment. "You mean you're going by yourself? ... well that's even more ridiculous!"

"No ... Trish and I are going."

There was a long, long silence. It was for this moment that Richard and Peggy proved invaluable. Neither had to utter a word, but it kept Mother from blowing right through the ceiling.

Now it wasn't like I was sixteen … but to Mom I may as well have been. The thought of one of her little boys running off to Florida … with a woman! … However, she wouldn't create a scene in front of her son and daughter-in law … there would be plenty of time for that later.

To this point, Dad had said nothing. Finally he spoke. "I guess I could learn the route and drive it when you're away."

"How are you going to do that!" spluttered Mom, offering one of her signature gestures by slamming a fist down on the arm of her chair.

"It's only from nine until two … and I don't have to be at work until four … "

I am forever indebted to my father for standing by me that day. Even if my brain cells had temporarily shrivelled up … Dad obviously hadn't forgotten what it was like to be young.

This job was actually a Ministry of Health contract, originating from Palmerston. The route covered Bruce and Grey Counties, servicing hospitals, clinics and health units. Delivering lab and x-ray reports, picking up medical, food, water and milk samples, were all part of the daily route. I never considered the job as a career, but agreed with Dad that it would at least bring in a few much needed dollars throughout the winter.

Mom never let up on me over the next month, shoving all kinds of articles pertaining to the gas crisis at me. According to these articles, Canadians were having some difficulties getting enough fuel. Americans apparently resented the fact we had lots of gas and were driving down to Florida or whatever and burning up theirs. "Why don't you just tell Trish this is a bad time to go? Surely she must read the newspapers! She's supposed to be so worldly and all!"

I hated to admit Mom was right but was a little nervous myself. Perhaps this would be the perfect "out" without losing face. So I relented and promised to give Trish a call that night and discuss the matter. She had been spending the last few days with some friends in New York. Although plans changed like the barometer, the latest proposal was to pick her up on the following Sunday in New York and then head to Florida from there.

I dialled the ten digit number to New Rochelle Trish had given me. After I explained who I was, Trish came on the line. "Hi David ... How are you?" ... "Oh pretty good" ... "Great to hear your voice!" said Trish. "I've been thinking about you all week! Are you ready for the trip down?" ... "Well ... I was just wondering how the situation was down there?" ... There was a pause ... "What situation?" ... "Well, the gas situation?"..."Oh, I guess it's alright ... they're not selling any gas on Sundays so you'd better fill up Saturday night." ...

"So, you still want me to come do you?" I asked lightly. "Of course, I need you!" I wasn't exactly sure what she meant by that. The premise in phoning was to glean some information on the gas crisis, but once again Trish's charm had sidetracked me, and before I knew it, was promising to meet her Sunday.

Needless to say, Mom wasn't happy when learning the trip was still on. "Well, didn't you tell her about your concerns?"

"She said everything was normal."

"Do you call line-ups and rationing, normal? ... She probably doesn't have a clue what's going on. She just wants a free ride to Florida!" I had become very familiar with this recording over the past weeks, so said nothing as any comment would've simply ended in yet another battle of words.

At seven AM, Saturday, December 8, the Pontiac was fuelled and ready to roll. In the trunk I'd stashed a five-gallon container of gas, my combination stereo/8 track player, a whole stack of tapes, a suitcase, an overnight bag, plus two snow tires. "I'm going to worry about you every second you're gone," Mom called from the kitchen door. With that cheery salutation, I was off.

My plan was to remain in Canada as long as possible, then fill up just before crossing the border at Gananoque. The roads were dry as summer and the Pontiac put a lot of miles behind it in short order. Of all the cars I've owned, that '70 Pontiac was my favourite. It rode like a dream and the big V-8 would just whisper no matter the speed.

Once satisfied where I was going and where I was from, the U.S. border guard made a sweeping check of my trunk contents. "What's that?" ... " A radio." ... "What's in that box?" ... "Tapes." I wondered if he might raise some static about the gas container, as I heard it was illegal to carry a full container in some states. He made no mention of it and in minutes I was on my way.

Just inside the New York border at a little place called Fishers Landing, I bought some snacks to munch on while driving. I also bought a six-pack of Schlitz beer. I thought that was real cool, buying beer in a grocery store, as that was unheard of in Canada.

I followed the interstate south to the New York Thru-
way then turned east. The drive between Utica and Sche-
nectady and on down to Albany is apparently quite beautiful, but in those short, dark days of December, all I saw was
blackness, broken only by the occasional glow of another
town's neon lights in the distance.

It had been my intention to fill the car somewhere near
Albany, crash for the night and take the last 100 miles into
the city in the morning. However when I realized I'd gained
an hour passing into the Atlantic zone, I figured I could be
in New York by nine, so just kept driving ... and driving. At
9:15 I crossed the Hudson River. In White Plains, a suburb
just north of greater New York City, and with my gas supply
nearly exhausted, I pulled into a Texaco service centre with
three islands of pumps.

Four black youths were tending to customer needs,
and I felt slightly apprehensive. What if these black guys
wouldn't serve white guys? Especially from Canada ... or
would they only give me a few gallons? I recalled all Mom's
horror stories over the last two or three weeks.

My apprehension proved groundless and five minutes
later the Pontiac's tank was filled with Texaco "Fire Chief."
Directly across the street was a Howard Johnson hotel.
"$22.00," said the desk clerk ... expensive I thought ... but
I really didn't care at this point. After 700 miles I was
beat ... but I'd made it to the "Big Apple." Tomorrow, the
real adventure would begin.

A ROAD HEADING SOUTH

I awoke to the sound of voices in the hallway outside my room and it took a few seconds to recall where I was. I couldn't believe it was a quarter to nine. As I lay in bed, gathering my thoughts, the first item that came to mind ... a decent breakfast. Except for snacks, I hadn't eaten a substantial meal since the previous morning. The restaurant dining room was closed by the time I checked in the night before, so I just had a sandwich and a Coke in the cafeteria. As I looked out my window, a grey drizzly morning greeted me. I'd been fortunate the day before with clear skies and dry roads all the way.

Following breakfast, I checked out of the motel into rain that was now falling steadily. With the directions Trish had given me, I headed east to the waterfront and turned south on the two-lane highway that wound mile after mile past old but well-kept homes into New Rochelle. At that time, New Rochelle was one of the richest cities in the United States in wealth per person.

I was forced to park the car twice and ask directions, receiving a soaking in the cold rain each time. I must have looked a sight when I knocked on the door of the apartment where Trish was staying. Drenched and wrinkled clothes; hair soaked and matted flat against my scalp. Trish mixed me up a rye and water. It tasted horrible.

After about an hour, and with the car re-packed with Trish's belongings, we headed hopefully out of New York City. If I'd been driving alone, I'd probably never got out. Trish proved to be a super navigator, as we never missed an exit, or a merge. The rain had turned to wet snow by now so I was glad I could just concentrate on driving.

Down Interstate 95 we went, through New Jersey, Pennsylvania, Delaware and Maryland. The states seem so close together in this area. A gigantic interstate loop known as the Capital Beltway completely surrounded Washington D.C., with dozens of exits heading into the centre of the city. Trish chose one that eventually became New York Ave. A large number of motels and hotels were in evidence and we chose a Quality Inn ... but not before Trish had checked out the room ... particularly the bed. Like Goldilocks, she made sure it wasn't too soft or too hard. She never failed to make this inspection throughout our entire trip.

Monday morning dawned clear and bright and we drove down to the centre of the city to view the government landmarks as all tourists do. Trish also wanted to visit Arlington Cemetery just across the Potomac River before we left. It's monstrous ... 420 acres. The tenth anniversary of John Kennedy's death had just passed, probably explaining the added interest in his gravesite.

Soon we were back on Interstate 95 heading down through Virginia. There was little traffic; speed limits, despite the new government laws, were still in the 70 mph range and the weather was beautiful. It was late afternoon as we made our way through the rugged country of North

Carolina and by the time we stopped at Lumberton for the night, we were just a few miles from the South Carolina border.

Earlier in the afternoon I had a chat with a friendly old southerner who ran a Texaco station just off the interstate. It was one of those old garages where time seemingly had come to a halt. A place where the owner checked your oil, tire pressure and cleaned your windshield. As well, tobacco and a few groceries were sold, while cold drinks were kept in a galvanized tub of ice water by the cash register. In the middle of the room a couple of elderly gents sat at a tiny table, engrossed in a game of checkers.

The owner was quite interested in Canada, Canadian cars, Canadian weather, Canadian money, and anything else that crossed his mind. The guy would have talked all day I believe ... but then he hadn't much else to do. The entire time I was there, not another car made an appearance. It was easy to see how his little one-pump, regular-gas-only station, was no match for the inter-state gas-bar giants with their 200-seat fast food chains.

The only hint of trouble obtaining gasoline surfaced at a highway service centre on the South Carolina-Georgia border. "Gas Limit $10.00" read the sign on the pump. The attendant, a youth probably still in his teens, studied my Canadian license plate while the pump hummed away. "Y'all shouldn't have come down." His comment was sort of unexpected, so I said nothing. "Yep ... bad time to come down!"

Realizing by now he was expecting a reply, I explained how this trip had been planned for a while and being that I farmed, it was the only time I could get away. "So y'all farm?" he said, brightening. He then went on to ask me about the crops we grew, how many heat units we had, what kind of tractors we used, how many acres did we farm ... I answered his questions (not too honestly as I don't imagine he wanted to hear my actual farming experiences) and by this time the gas pump had clicked past the $10.00 limit by several dollars. "Oh, I'm over my limit!" I said quickly. He turned his attention back to the pump. "Ah ... never no mind," and proceeded to fill the tank to the brim.

Only eighty miles of Georgia coastline separates the states of South Carolina and Florida, so when Trish and I stopped at Brunswick, Georgia, our third night together, we were less than thirty miles from the Florida border. At that time at least, the U.S.A. was notorious for billboards ... that was one of the biggest differences I discovered between our two countries. Trish and I had observed countless signs on our trip south, but in northeast Florida from Jacksonville to St. Augustine, it seemed a display every hundred feet advertised someone's alligator farm or rattlesnake ranch.

I promised Mom I'd phone upon reaching Florida, so called Wednesday night. During our conversation, I mentioned the lovely weather. "What's it like at home?" ... "It's miserable! The last two days have been a mixture of rain and snow." ... "So how's Dad getting along with the route?" trying to change the subject. "We're both doing it. Harold seems to want me along with him. This miserable weather doesn't help either ... He gets so upset when he gets behind schedule."

I'd been hoping for a more positive report, but all the call achieved was to make me feel guilty. I guess Dad nearly drove Mom crazy that week. Every time he got slowed down, he'd remind Mom how much time they'd lost over that particular incident, then would drive like hell to get back on schedule.

Trish phoned her mother that night too. Her parents were even more "old school" than Mom. Trish never mentioned we were driving down together. As far as her mother was concerned, she had flown to Orlando and was merely meeting me there. I'm not sure how she explained the return trip, but that was her problem.

Disney World ... It was just two years old when Trish and I visited. I wouldn't even recognize it now I suppose, but at the time it was everything I'd ever dreamed or envisioned.

When I was about six years old, my parents gave me a book for Christmas about Disneyland (there was of course no Disney World then). It was a large book ... probably 11 x 14, and every page told a story of some different aspect of this magical place. As well there were cut-outs to stick on and pictures to colour, a simply amazing book. I had it for years. Now ... here it was ... Cinderella's Castle; Adventureland; Frontierland; Tomorrowland; Fantasyland ... all those mystical places I'd read about. The moment I walked through those gates ... debts, overdue bills, phone calls, collection letters, failed crops and depressed prices were immediately swept away.

One of the best features of our entire stay was Trish's foresight to book an "on site" hotel. There were just two when we were there. The "Polynesian Village" where we stayed, and the "Contemporary." No parking lot or shuttle bus hassles, no stop and go traffic heading back to the hotel. Simply step onto the monorail that operated between the park and the two hotels, and in three minutes you were there.

Our room cost $80.00 a night ... exorbitant to a farm boy! Even by 1973 standards it was pretty pricey I suppose. The Polynesian theme was carried throughout the hotel. From the lobby with its vast array of native trees and flowers, to the "Papeete Bay Verandah," a dining room on the top floor, featuring Polynesian cuisine, it was first class all the way. The rooms were larger than some apartments. The bathroom was larger than some hotel rooms. King-size vibrating bed, colour TV, sofa, whirlpool bath, a shower large enough for two, lounging chairs, writing desk, broadloom one could almost disappear into ... the towels were so thick, Trish could hardly get her suitcase closed when it was time to check out.

Originally we had planned on going on down to Miami Beach, but sometime over the past day or two we changed our minds ... after all it was Disney World we came to see. Maybe we were just ready to head home. I know I was. Since I'd only been at my job for two weeks, I looked forward to familiarizing myself with this new routine again. I knew Dad and Mom wouldn't be upset if our vacation was shortened.

Saturday afternoon we began heading northwest through the citrus belt to meet up with Interstate 75. Sunday morning found us right in the midst of the Appalachian Mountain range angling up the eastern section of Tennessee, enjoying some spectacular views of mountain peaks 2,000 feet high on one side, and valleys dropping to ... who knows how far on the other. Tennessee's speed limits were still at pre-fuel crisis level, which was 80 mph, but everyone drove 90, so it didn't take long to cover that state.

Up through the Cumberland Mountain area of southern Kentucky; cutting through endless miles of forest to Lexington and Kentucky's famous "bluegrass" area. The only grass we saw was brown. By the time we reached Ohio, all service stations seemed to be obeying the "No Sunday Sales" gas law, so north of Cincinnati with the gas gauge needle registering empty, we pulled into a rest area. After 2800 miles, my five-gallon gas container, instead of merely taking up trunk space, was finally made use of.

Monday morning in Dayton, we were treated to a surprise as far as weather, with a skiff of snow on the ground, clarifying the fact we were on the home stretch. I didn't care for the drive up I-75 through northern Ohio. For one thing it was painfully slow, this part of Ohio administering the 55 mph limit, the first we'd seen our entire trip. Also, I suppose mid-December is not the ideal time to promote a northern state, as everything had a grey and desolate tone. This was also the industrial centre of the state, the numerous smokestacks from countless cities and towns fortifying this fact vividly. Trish had also been worried that we would be "ambushed" by truckers. There had been stories of a few Ohio radicals tossing cement blocks off overpasses, to emphasize their disagreement with the 55 mph limit.

When the trucker threat failed to materialize, Trish turned her attention to the border crossing. She'd apparently bought a few gifts for friends and family, some clothes for herself, as well as a toaster-oven of all things ... and had no intention of declaring anything. The closer to the border we drew, the more convinced Trish became we were going to be searched. All I'd bought were a few records, a couple of books and some souvenirs. My camera and radio were registered, therefore I wasn't concerned.

As we approached customs, Trish was white as a sheet. "If you're so nervous, why don't you just declare your damn junk and pay the duty?" I inquired.

"I'm not paying duty!" she snapped.

"It beats going to jail!" I countered. I pulled up to the booth.

"What's your citizenship?"

"Canadian"

"How long have you been away?"

"Nine days."

"Anything to declare?"

This was zero hour as far as Trish was concerned. "Just a few souvenirs," she answered bravely.

"I bought a few records and books," I added.

"Okay ... carry on."

"Well, that was easy," I said, following the signs to the 401.

"I nearly died when you mentioned the records and books!" Trish interjected. "Suppose they'd asked to see them and found the other stuff!"

"That's probably why they didn't." I argued. "After all, he'd hardly expect two people to be away nine days and not buy something!"

Looking back on that event with the perspective of forty years, maybe Trish was smuggling something across the border of which I was completely unaware! It might explain her "uneasiness" at the time. I remember Mom harping away at me ... "You are so naive you can't see it. But think about it ... what single woman just decides to go down to Florida by herself and check into a luxury hotel? Then you just happen to come along? ... Give me a break! She saw you coming miles away." I just ignored her rants.

At that point when it came to Trish, my world had a strong rose-coloured tint to it.

The roads were dry, so the Pontiac wasn't long in eating up the hours and miles between Windsor and Toronto. Although we'd experienced no problems whatsoever in the U.S., it was still nice to get back into good old Ontario ... except for the temperature. When we stopped for gas near Kitchener, the attendant took great pride in serenading us with his rendition of Gordon Lightfoot's "10 Degrees and Getting Colder."

No one was home at Trish's place, therefore no need for explanation. We unpacked the car and thirty minutes later I was heading for Palmerston. Dusk was settling as I pulled up to the kitchen door from where I left nine days and 3300 miles ago.

Everyone seemed relieved to see me ... especially Mom. After about ten minutes of talking about me, the conversation switched back to reality. The water was frozen I was told ... had been for twenty-four hours. In the interim, my brother Bill had brought a supply from his place in a couple of milk cans. With two jobs, Dad simply hadn't time to rectify the problem.

While brewing a cup of tea I noticed several envelopes on the counter that I had no doubt were overdue bills, but I'd address that challenge tomorrow. While continuing to discuss the water dilemma, the phone rang. "This is GMAC ... We didn't receive your December 1st car payment and were wondering when we could expect it." ... Yes ... I was definitely home.

The frequency of seeing Trish dwindled over the next few months. Winter definitely made travelling less popular, and as spring emerged many crucial decisions lay ahead concerning my farming career. With the courier job, more farming duties had to be done evenings and weekends. And let's be brutally honest ... Trish simply discovered there were more interesting guys around ... because with the exception of being physically attracted to each other, we had absolutely nothing in common.

I was raised on Ontario's back concessions ... Trish the largest city in Canada. Trish was inspired by elaborate cuisine and restaurants with "atmosphere." I liked pork chops and mashed potatoes at our kitchen table. Trish dreamed of dancing the night away in a chandelier-lit ballroom, or spending her evenings in a downtown nightclub surrounded by people. I preferred reading a book or an automotive magazine on our front porch on a summer morning, or taking a walk along the creek that meandered lazily through our farm. Trish spent hours poring over the latest issue of *Better Homes and Gardens,* dreaming of that chalet tucked into a hillside somewhere in the Catskills, while I pondered the advantages of liquid manure storage in *Country Guide.*

Trish married a couple of years later, and although I lost touch personally, she remained close to Doug and Judy, so I was able to keep track of her through them. Trish was someone I thought of often, but never really expected to see again. However, life has a way of setting its own pattern ... and many years later down the road, our paths would cross under circumstances neither of us could have imagined at the time.

STEEL RAIL GHOSTS

It was Thanksgiving weekend ... 1998. I was in a nostalgic mood and decided to take a stroll through the local railway yard. As kids in the 1950s, whenever we cycled the three-mile distance to town for a haircut or a visit to the library, more often than not our adventure concluded at this station. Once a mecca of rail activity, it was almost beyond my comprehension how this station could have been reduced to this ...

Knee-high crops of grass, wild carrot and goldenrod threatened to strangle the ties between the rusted rails. Pushed unceremoniously onto a siding at some earlier date, the barely recognizable remains of a freight car chassis was slowly dissolving with the passing seasons. Piled haphazardly among other yard relics lay a portion of the signal lights that controlled traffic for decades on the Main Street crossing.

Despite a new roof recently installed in a valiant effort to slow nature's wrath, the old stationhouse, once the nucleus of this great yard, had in my opinion passed the point of restoration. Decades of steam heating had completely rotted the wooden foundation and the north vestibule wall was in a state of near collapse. Any window not boarded shut was but a shattered pane, a home for pigeon and squirrel tenants. Through the broken glass I could just make out a pot-bellied stove that probably hadn't accepted a shovelful of coal in more than thirty winters.

Outside the stationhouse, the concrete walkway, once the centre of all freight activity, was cracked, pitted, shattered and heaved by years of frost and neglect. Broken glass, cigarette butts, food wrappers and paper cups littered the already scarred surface.

... Then there was engine "81," once a regular contributor to the Owen Sound–Palmerston route, quietly protecting its tiny northeastern corner of the yard. After decades as serving as a playground for children and a victim of vandalism, the old locomotive was secured behind a padlocked fence to protect it from further degradation. The floor of the coal tender that at one time supported ten tons of the black fuel had gradually succumbed to a state of rot and decay. As well, the 5,000-gallon boiler whose heated water supplied enough pressurized steam to pull a dozen coaches or freight cars had suffered equally.

As my eyes slowly panned the ancient locomotive, I pondered when it was the railroads lost their glamour? I suppose it was the coming of the diesels ... but I guess their arrival was inevitable. Diesels were definitely cheaper to operate and cleaner by far, but they certainly lacked that awesome, fire-breathing presence that endeared the steamers to so many.

Nine decades had passed since this six-wheel driver was built in the locomotive works in Kingston, Ontario. On a January day in 1957 after forty-seven years of faithful service, "81" pulled her mixed load into the station from

Owen Sound for the last time and without ceremony or formality was retired to an isolated siding for a couple of years before being donated to the town and relocated to its present site.

I climbed the forty-odd steps to the main platform of what probably is the most famous railway landmark in any town in Ontario ... perhaps Canada ... and slowly made my way along its corridor. Although its paint was fighting a losing battle with the elements, the bridge still projected an atmosphere of strength as it kept vigil on the decaying rail yard and most of the town itself ... but for how long? Structural engineers at that time claimed the railroad monument was in need of major repairs and soon after I visited, the bridge was closed to pedestrian traffic.

As I stood gazing out at the silent yard, my mind returned once again to when we were kids and had so often stood on this very spot. In those days it wasn't uncommon to observe three or four steam locomotives heading in one direction or another transporting a variety of commodities. Discharging passengers and mail; hauling heavily loaded boxcars of gravel or coal and flat cars stacked high with lumber. Condensation forming puddles of water beneath refrigerated cars was a refreshing vision on a hot summer day.

I was reminded of the water tank where thirsty steamers lined up, or the coal tower where a worker would pull a couple of ropes, sending tons of coal hurtling from the elevated storage bin into the coal tender parked below. The roundhouse that was large enough to contain four locomotives and the huge boiler that provided heat to it as well as the station and baggage room via an underground pipeline.

The Queen's Hotel, built in 1903, was still standing in that era, although it had been empty for years and was awaiting the wrecking ball. Owned by Canadian National, "The Queen's" was an impressive building in its day. The triple-storied structure sat adjacent the stationhouse separated only by a covered walkway. When the demolition finally did come to pass, I remember Dad purchasing some lumber from the remains.

I recalled other memories of Palmerston's past ... crisp winter mornings when a combination of steam and frigid temperatures bathed everything in white frost, or humid summer afternoons when the pungent odour of coal smoke hung like a blanket over the entire town. "Wash day" in our home town was necessitated by wind direction rather than a certain day of the week.

I recall that late March day in 1957 when our family moved to Palmerston. I was eight years old and remember sitting in the passenger seat of the truck beside Dad, waiting ten minutes or so while a long freight shunted back and forth across the main intersection. At that point we had no idea what a common occurrence these delays were in this railway town, and although frustrating at times everyone realized trains were the area's bread and butter. Although the numbers had been in a gradual state of reduction since its peak years, two dozen trains still departed from that station every day except Sunday.

Spreading out of the Palmerston yard like giant steel spokes, a number of rail lines and spurs formed a network of track connecting scores of communities in Western Ontario. One of these, the main line to Stratford, passed less than 1000 feet from our front yard when it navigated the 8th Line crossing south of Palmerston. Originally operated by the Great Western Railway, this particular stretch of track had been built in 1872. There was plenty of competition in the railroad industry in the late 1800s and Great Western's chief adversary at the time, Grand Trunk, installed a parallel track in 1880 between Listowel and Palmerston to link with existing track the company owned in other areas of southwestern Ontario.

An economic downturn in the late 1890s dictated insufficient business to satisfy two rail lines, thus Great Western and Grand Trunk amalgamated, leaving the Grand Trunk line abandoned. It sat idle forty years until the 1930s when the rails were removed as part of a government Depression make-work project. Eighty years later and although overgrown with trees, one can still see signs of the raised rail bed constructed a century and a quarter before.

Following the amalgamation, all Grand Trunk passenger and freight offices and sheds were transferred from Listowel to Palmerston and GW and GT were integrated into what became known as Canadian National. At this point the Palmerston yard underwent a major expansion, now encompassing twenty-three acres with no less than twelve sets of tracks. Due to the increased danger to pedestrians, the multi-tracked Queen Street level crossing was removed and replaced by the aforementioned overhead bridge.

As kids, the railroad became just a part of everyday life. If a train was approaching our farm from the south you could easily hear the whistle at Gowanstown Station two concessions away. One concession away, the black plume from the smokestack would be clearly evident as the locomotive climbed the gentle grade toward our crossing. During winter nights when trees were bare, the intense beam of the locomotive's headlight stabbing the darkness displayed weird shadows on the walls of the bedroom I shared with my brothers. Barometric pressure, air temperature, wind velocity and direction were all factors that provided different sounds to a steam engine's whistle. When I was lying in bed on a rainy night with the wind blowing strongly from the east, that low moaning warning signal had to be the most lonesome sound I ever heard.

Our railroad passion meant a great deal of time was actually spent right at the tracks. To meet a train was simply an exercise in watching for the black smoke billowing above the trees from whatever direction, then racing to the scene on our bikes. And as long as I live I'll never forget the train's approach ... the puffing sound of those giant steam-powered pistons getting louder by the quarter minute. The stab of the headlight that seemed so intense even in midday sun and that wonderful whistle! That shrill, screaming, lonesome sounding whistle; there was nothing like it ... two long blasts, followed by one short, then one long, long scream that didn't cease until the huge locomotive cleared the crossing. That mix of whistle, escaping steam, the metallic screech of the drivers on the polished rails and the staccato-like clatter of a multitude of steel wheels thundering by ... is absolutely unforgettable! As the train rolled past, we'd all wave at the engineer and it was very important he wave back. And he always did.

Then suddenly those giant coal burners were gone: As the steam engines were methodically torched in various scrap yards around the province, it also signalled the demise for the rest of Palmerston's railway heritage. Where once two dozen trains exited and entered the station on any given day, service was gradually but steadily reduced over the following decade until all that remained was an insignificant passenger aluminum street car known as the "Dayliner."

The last time I saw a steam engine on the tracks that passed our farm was 1964, when the Michigan Railway Club organized an excursion sponsored by Canadian National. Pulling a dozen passenger coaches, the trip began in London, Ontario, journeyed to Guelph and Palmerston stations, then back to London. It was during the train's return to London that we were once again thrilled by the memorable whistle of a steam locomotive as it passed our crossing.

The final vestige of that great railway era we knew disappeared in the mid-1980s, when the track that had lain for a hundred years and carried thousands of locomotives past our farm was removed. Now each passing season accelerates the departure of the old rail bed as Mother Nature slowly but methodically reclaims her legacy.

Last autumn, some fourteen Thanksgivings later ... I returned to the Palmerston rail yard to discover what planning, determination, willpower and sheer muscle ... not to mention hours of lobbying local councils and politicians for grants, etc. ... can accomplish. I was reminded how completely wrong I'd been in my negative assumption made many years earlier. In the interim, an ambitious heritage society had completely remodelled the old stationhouse and turned the decaying building into a museum that portrays a glimpse of the vibrant railroad legacy this town once knew.

This society, in conjunction with the Lions Club of Palmerston, has been unrelenting in their quest to preserve the rail yard itself for future generations. The three sets of track closest to the old station remained intact while the balance of the yard's steel rails were removed in the restoration process. By spraying and disposing of weeds, cutting the old grass and seeding anew, a beautiful park area has resulted. The famous bridge, which years ago appeared to be heading in the same direction as the stationhouse, has now been certified to once again allow pedestrian traffic. In addition, a glossy coat of black paint has visually returned the Palmerston landmark to its days of grandeur. And "old 81," completely restored and painted ... and now fully accessible to the public ... probably looks better than when it departed the Kingston locomotive factory in 1910.

It was a beautiful sunny morning as I stood and stared down at the newly refurbished rail yard. Lush grass, winding walkways, basketball court, a covered picnic pavilion, park benches, all surrounded by splashes of autumn colour created a rewarding experience ... yet there was something almost eerie about it: a strange quietness that I couldn't describe.

Ghostly shadows from more than a century of Palmerston's railroad inheritance seemed to haunt each square foot of the old rail yard despite the "new look." I had the sensation I'd been immersed into a James Lumbers "moment in time" portrait of Palmerston's heritage, and it took little imagination to roll back through the years and visualize a time when steam trains lined every steel artery of this station. My mind's image of a steam train waiting impatiently in front of the stationhouse platform where passengers congregated and baggage was being transferred ... was as clear as glass.

This vignette was filled with automobiles with names long gone ... Studebaker, Monarch, Rambler and DeSoto ... an era of fedoras, fins and fender skirts, and when $7.00 would fill the gas tank of most any car. It was a time when the soft drink machine on the stationhouse platform dispensed five-cent bottles of Coca Cola ... nickel chocolate bars were available in the stationhouse lobby and OPEC, GST, SUV and GPS were merely letters of the alphabet.

As the scene played out before me, I heard the conductor announce the final "All aboard!" then watched as he signalled the engineer and disappeared inside the coach. Instantly the engine delivered a mighty shudder as pressurized steam rushed to its cylinders. As the huge locomotive merged its mixed load of freight and passenger coaches onto the Stratford mainline, a thick billowy plume of black smoke forced its way upward into the clear blue October sky. Crossing the King Street intersection, the engine's steadily increasing chant reverberated throughout the still morning air. Two miles south of the Palmerston station, the engineer extended his arm from the open window of the locomotive's cab to return a wave to the little boy waiting on his bicycle at the 8th Line crossing.

WHEELS OF TIME

Few things characterize both rural and urban culture more than bicycles. In North America during the last decade of the nineteenth century, the noisy contraptions known as automobiles were little more than a curiosity. For single passenger transportation in this era, the bicycle was clearly king. The first modern bicycle (equal size wheels) was developed in England around 1880, but it wasn't until the advent of Scottish veterinarian John Dunlop's pneumatic tire a decade later that the phenomenon really gained steam.

In Canada alone at least twenty-five bicycle manufacturers existed at the close of the nineteenth century, and five of the most prolific operated in the heartland of Ontario. Brands by the name of Gendron, Welland Vale, Lozier, Goold and Massey-Harris were the consistent sales leaders, accounting for nearly eighty percent of total production.

Such was the optimism for bicycle sales in this period, in 1895 Massey-Harris erected a special building alongside its Toronto machinery plant for the sole manufacture of their top selling "Silver Ribbon" model, which featured Dunlop tires with wooden rims and fenders.

In 1899, facing stiff competition from rival manufacturers both in Canada and the United States, together with increasing sales of its agricultural products, Massey-Harris along with the aforementioned companies sold their interests to the newly formed Canada Cycle and Motor Company. This organization, which would become familiarly known as CCM, utilized the M-H plant and continued to sell the acquired brands under their own names.

Incidentally, "Motor" referred to CCM's automotive interests as the company was sales agent for Winton, Locomobile and Waverley cars. Beginning in 1905, CCM began manufacturing its own automobile, the Russell, the first automobile to be built in Canada and named after vice-president and general manager T.A. (Tommy) Russell.

By this time in order to keep pace with its expanding market, CCM moved out of downtown Toronto to the western suburb of Weston and erected a larger factory. Although the auto manufacturing division never ignited as hoped, CCM turned the bicycle into a multi-million-dollar enterprise. CCM continued to manufacture the Massey-Harris bicycle line well into the twentieth century, still equipped with wooden rims and fenders on some models as late as the mid-1920s. Sources report M-H bicycles still being produced into the early 1930s.

When I recall my years as a kid in rural Ontario, it's interesting how often that memory involves a bike in some way. Whether it was to school, to town, the swimming hole on a hot August day, fishing, bringing the cows for milking or merely going for a ride down the back concessions of our township ... a bicycle provided that freedom.

"It's expensive buying bikes," I once overheard my father tell someone, "but wait until they all want cars!"

Since there were five of us covering a ten-year span, that observation did put the scenario into perspective.

The first bicycle in our family ... actually a tricycle, was a Massey-Harris ... sort of. It was my brother Bill's (or Billy as he was known then) bike, consisting of a collection of parts cobbled together in the mid-1940s by my grandfather ... mostly odds and ends scrounged from the reject bin at the Massey-Harris Toronto factory where he worked. Onto this homemade riding toy my grandfather had furnished a wooden maple seat cut from an empty packing crate. Various pieces of scrap tubing formed the handlebars and frame and a couple of brass wheels were courtesy of a discarded feed cart.

Although crude by today's standards, it served my brother well for two or three years. By the time Bill was ready for more advanced transportation the tricycle had run its course and was cannibalized for any worthwhile parts. Dad discovered one of the rear wheels to be a perfect-sized drain cover in the cement floor of the milk house of the dairy operation where he worked.

Next bicycle to enter the picture was a two-wheeled model from the Sunshine Waterloo Company, a derivative of Massey-Harris; a bicycle born from a union of H.V. McKay of Sunshine Harvester Works in Australia, Waterloo Manufacturing Co. of Waterloo Ontario and Massey-Harris Canada.

M-H's plan in this merger was to adapt McKay's self-propelled combine design to sell in the promising agriculture market of the 1920s. Waterloo Mfg's long and successful record supplying agricultural products to North America, together with their manufacturing capacity, would make it ideal to bring this dream to fruition.

But many obstacles prevailed, not the least being the Australian designed combine just seemed hopelessly unable to adapt to the ideals of the North American farmer. Factor in the 1929 stock market crash and resulting Great Depression and you get the idea.

With all these negative factors in force and in order to keep the Waterloo factory operating, this trilogy of companies was forced to diversify, and as a result the Sunshine Waterloo Company was formed. In order to survive in the brutal economic conditions of the 1930s, Sunshine manufactured anything that could capture a market: baby carriages, doll carriages, roller skates, office equipment, steel shelving, stoves and of course bicycles, which they manufactured until 1954.

So, two of the results of this long legacy of merger, invention and development culminated in the pair of Sunshine bicycles that my brother and sister proudly took possession of in the spring of 1948.

These rather unique bikes rode on thirteen-inch diameter solid rubber tires and were fitted with a stamped metal seat so comfort wasn't their strongest suit. There was no "coast" feature as in modern bicycles, just a "full-time" half-inch-wide rubber belt-driven mechanism in lieu of a steel roller chain ... meaning the pedals revolved continuously. One quickly learned to keep their feet well spread apart on downhill grades, thus avoiding a painful reminder on the back of your legs from the whirling pedals.

This direct-drive system also meant there was no brake availability. For deceleration, the soles of your running shoes were as good as it got. Another shortcoming ... and this was a chronic one, slipping drive belts, aggravated by the never-ending succession of hills that dominated Simcoe

County. This problem constantly required their father to regularly apply liberal amounts of belt dressing to provide adequate friction.

I received my first two-wheeled bike in 1959, a reconditioned CCM for which Dad paid $30.00. In that era, CCM was the name in bicycles and their tagline "Can't Catch Me" was the phrase of the day. I spent a lot of time on the seat of that CCM over the next few years, my imagination taking me around the world in a limitless array of vehicles, hauling gravel, grain, fuel, lumber, milk, groceries, soft drinks ... even beer.

Other times, the pendulum of my imagination swung from tearing up race tracks at the wheel of a Saturday night stock car, to driving a Grey Coach tour bus across the country, to a Highway Patrol officer aiding Broderick Crawford as he chased traffic offenders across California. Clipping a piece of cardboard to my spokes transformed my CCM into instant motorcycle; the snap of stiff cardboard reverberating on the steel spokes every bit as convincing as the exhaust note on a Harley D.

There were the inevitable scrapes and bruises, but otherwise that old CCM and I survived hundreds and hundreds of miles of gravel side roads. But as predicted, when cars began to dominate our interest, bicycles became less important. I don't recall the fate of that old bike, whether it was given away or merely junked, but it's long gone ... replaced by a unit with all the features we expect today. However this modern bike seems to lack the spirit ... or perhaps it's the heart ... of the one I knew in my youth. Perhaps American author Thomas Wolfe was correct when he penned the line "You can't go home again."

Well a few summers ago my brothers and I took a memory trip back to the Simcoe County farm where we spent the early years of our lives. The 150-year-old barn, such an important chapter of our younger years, appeared unchanged, an enduring monument to its construction as well as its caretakers through the decades. A varied assortment of memories, depending upon our age, flooded through our minds as we stood within its weathered walls.

However where the elements of past and present converged that day for me was in the milk house. Embedded in the concrete floor, still substituting as a drain cover, was the wheel from my brother's tricycle ... the one our grandfather had built from scrap Massey-Harris parts. That brass wheel was as solid as the day Dad placed it there ... more than fifty years earlier ... Maybe Mr. Wolfe was wrong ... perhaps you can.

Palmerston Public Library where my mother worked for eighteen years

I was full of optimism when I purchased my new Ford tractor in 1972

*Palmerston's century-old railroad pedestrian
bridge still strikes an imposing presence*

The author's first set of wheels … 1951

RESTLESS WANDERER

In December 1973 while speeding through Kentucky on Interstate 75 on my way home from Florida, I'd promised myself that someday I would return to explore this beautiful segment of the country within its summer glory, so in July 1976, I turned this promise into reality.

My plan was to see the "real" Kentucky, by sticking to the state and secondary roads and camping in the back of my pickup truck. Mom didn't like the thought of me traipsing about the country camping alone, and it certainly didn't help her reservations when my brother Don commented that Kentucky had one of the highest ratios per capita of rattlesnakes. He then recounted a story he'd read in *Reader's Digest* where a huge snake had crawled into someone's sleeping bag during the night!

Although I made little comment at the time to Don's "snake story," it certainly remained embedded in my mind, as just the sight of a garter snake can send my heart rate soaring. Maybe it's just me … but there's something about a land creature moving without legs that's completely abnormal!

So I'd already chickened out on the "rough camping" idea by the time I came upon a "real" campground just south of London, Kentucky, late in the afternoon of my second day on the road. "Levi Jackson State Park ... Year Round Camping," read the sign, where I followed a string of camper vehicles along a winding gravel driveway.

"Do you have any other passengers or pets in the back?" asked the attendant at the gate.

"No."

"How long will you be staying?"

"Just overnight."

"Okay ... that'll be six dollars." He then pointed out my campsite on a tiny map containing a hopeless maze of arteries. After driving around investigating all the little crescents and loops, I finally stumbled upon my station and backed the Chevy into the narrow slot beneath two pine trees.

All around me campers were busily unloading vehicles and the odour of charcoal-broiled food filled the humid evening air. Children and dogs ran freely up and down the corridor between the parked cars with seemingly little supervision. A black Lab lumbered over to where I sat, tail wagging expectantly. After being stared at for a few moments I gave him a pat on the head. He continued to stare so I scratched his ears and offered a piece of my ham sandwich.

"Is Morty bothering you?" a heavy-set man hollered from next door.

"Not really," I answered. "Come on Morty ... here Morty!" The dog hung around for one more bite then left when he figured the picnic was over.

Later, I noticed Morty several stalls down.

"Is Morty bothering you?" ... "No," was the reply "but I don't think Freeman likes him." Freeman, a little Schnauzer, had been yapping his head off continually since I'd arrived. "Come on Morty ... here Morty!" Finally Morty galloped off "home."

Directly across the driveway, Daniel was having some issues. Daniel wasn't of the canine breed but rather a red-haired kid seven or eight years old. All I heard throughout the evening was "Daniel, smarten up! ... Daniel, if you do that one more time! ... Daniel I'm warning you! ... Daniel if you don't behave we're leaving this minute!" Daniel obviously had learned long ago the idleness of his parent's threats.

I read until it became too dark then retired to my "apartment." Without a hint of breeze, the humid air was oppressive even with the truck's screen windows open wide. I stripped down to my underwear and by flashlight retrieved my radio from its Styrofoam travelling container and began scanning for a clear country music station. Through the window I could hear both Freeman and Morty barking and Daniel being threatened yet again. "Daniel, if I have to come over there!"

A Lexington station proved clear and powerful so I lay in the darkness and listened to a string of old songs I hadn't heard in years. This country music format was occasionally broken by ... "Here Morty ... here Morty!" ... or ... "Daniel, this is your last chance!" I thought to myself; how long does an eight-year-old get to stay up? Just as I switched off the radio following the eleven o'clock news, I heard ... "Daniel, I've had about enough of you!" ... Well I know I had.

Next morning, just after sunrise I eased the truck out onto the road. It seemed as if Morty, Freeman, Daniel and everyone else was still asleep. I hadn't slept well because of the heat and humidity but it was a beautiful morning and I was glad to be back on the road.

Just a few miles into my drive I passed through Corbin, Kentucky. On the main street of this little town one of America's best kept secrets was launched. Although he didn't begin franchising his idea until 1952 (he carried the recipe around with him in the glove compartment of his car for years), it was here in 1931 that Colonel Harland Sanders opened his first restaurant and began serving his mysteriously made fried chicken. Although vacant, the original restaurant was still standing at that time and undergoing legal proceedings to be placed on the U.S. National Register of Historic Places. Whether it ever happened, I don't know.

An interesting stop was Cumberland Gap at Middlesboro, where the states of Kentucky, Tennessee and Virginia meet. An exploration party led by Thomas Walker discovered this cleft in the Cumberland Mountains in 1750. Twenty-five years later, a North Carolina company hired Daniel Boone to head a group of woodsmen to improve and connect the existing trails to Kentucky. These trails ran haphazardly throughout the region and were known by such descriptive names as the "Dug Road," "Old Reedy Creek Road," "Troublesome Road" and "Wilderness Road."

A drive up a steep spiralling road followed by a short walk to a stone wall-encased platform, afforded a breathtaking picture of the surrounding countryside and a clear view of the "Gap."

It appeared as if someone had taken a giant chainsaw and notched an equally giant "V" into this section of the Cumberland range. Below my observation point, Highway 58 and a spur of the Louisville & Nashville Railroad line threaded its way through the break in the mountains into Tennessee and Virginia.

It's difficult to comprehend that men actually cut a passable road through this area with nothing more than a broad axe. A footpath lined with colourful bushes of mountain laurel and rhododendron emptied into a tiny clearing overlooking another section of the Gap. At the crest of this clearing a cannon kept silent vigil, a reminder of Civil War days when the Union army utilized the Cumberland Gap on their march southward into Tennessee.

Northeast of Middlesboro I drove through miles of what was ... or had been ... Kentucky's main coal producing area, a part of the state that gained little acclaim in the vacation brochures. Over the years it seemed a variety of circumstance had conspired against this region. The declining role of coal itself was a major one. As well, environmental and safety concerns played a large part in the shift to other fuels, where many mining companies simply closed down rather than spend the money to meet the new standards. Classic Merle Travis songs like "Nine Pound Hammer," "Dark as a Dungeon" and "Sixteen Tons" were written about this area when the mining industry was vibrant ... but that seemed far away even in 1976. Boarded-up factories, neglected homes and rusting railway track all mirrored the downturn in this once proud part of Kentucky.

From "Coal Country" I headed west through the Daniel Boone National Forest, across the Cumberland River and into "Cave Country." I stopped at "Mammoth Cave National Park," northeast of Bowling Green, where miles of underground corridors had been developed, giving tourists a chance to view a superior example of nature's ever changing work.

Our guide Wendy was a beautiful Kentucky native. Her copper-toned tan, nut brown hair, eyes the colour of chocolate, short yellow mini-skirt and ample breasts all joined forces for an attractive package. She presented a fascinating account of the origins of these caves beginning with the one we were in, apparently discovered in 1799 by someone chasing a wounded bear.

Through her infectious southern drawl, I learned everything there was to know about stalactite and stalagmite. Because of her accent, those two words were forever pronounced with heavy emphasis on the last syllable. Stallag ... *mites* ... we were told, were stone formations rising from the cave floor, formed when water dripping from the walls and roof carried with it deposits of calcium carbonate ... or calcite. As the water evaporated, this calcite built into colourful functions which looked like upside down icicles.

Stalac ... *tites* ... the direct opposite, formed on the cave's roof and hung down like proper icicles. The stalac ... *tites* ... were especially interesting as every time our hostess reached to describe a certain formation, her skimpy skirt rode ever higher. So amazed was I of this underground wilderness, I remained for the second tour. It was so pleasantly cool down there and ... well ... that Kentucky scenery can really get to you!

Northwards from "Cave Country" is "Lincoln Country." Both Abraham Lincoln's birthplace and boyhood home are historic sites. A marble and granite building had been erected on the grounds of the old Lincoln farm through generous donations from millions of American school children. Inside the memorial building resides the original log house in which Lincoln was born. Most fascinating to me was a huge oak tree in a corner of the lot, all trussed with wire to protect it from nature's wrath ... a tree so ancient it was already providing shade at the time of Lincoln's birth in 1809! When a state has raised a person of fame it has to make the most of it I guess. Over in Springfield, twenty miles west, one can visit Abraham Lincoln's maternal grandparents' log house ... I didn't bother.

I stopped at a gas station near Elizabethtown and while filling the tank and checking my "awl," the attendant chatted away on a variety of subjects. Noting my Canadian license plate, he volunteered how he'd been up in my area just the year before. "I was fishin' ... beautiful country!" I agreed and asked what part of Ontario he'd visited. He thought for a few seconds ... "Manitoba."

Further up the road in a Georgian-styled home in Bardstown is the setting supposedly of Stephen Foster's composition, "My Old Kentucky Home." As the story goes, in 1852 while visiting cousins in this very house, Foster penned what was to become the state song. Bardstown built an amphitheatre where each summer visitors could enjoy his songs in "The Stephen Foster Story." It was supper time when I arrived, so after checking into a motel I figured this presentation would be an ideal way to pass the evening, but I guess it's a popular attraction as the show was sold out.

After the hassle of that first evening I had given up on the camping idea. It seemed ridiculous to spend $6.00 in an overnight campground, when for $10.00 one could have a clean air-conditioned room with all the comforts of home ... and no barking dogs or "Daniels."

Kentucky's capital, Frankfort, roughly halfway between Louisville and Lexington, was one of the prettiest "small" cities I have come across. Its three-storied capital building complete with a large central domed section appears as it was lifted from Washington D.C. In front of the capital building is a floral clock whose giant hands in summer pass the time over 20,000 blooms.

Frankfort lies in the heart of "Bluegrass Country" and the drive along Highway 460 overflowed with white-fenced pastures harbouring some of the renowned names in horse racing. "Man O' War Farms," which probably raised the most famous American horse in thoroughbred history. The stallion "Man O' War," born in 1917, won twenty of the twenty-one races he ran and his record of a 2:40 for a mile and 5/8 I believe still stands today. "Calumet Farms," another famous Kentucky name, has produced no fewer than seven Kentucky Derby winners over the years.

As well as horse breeding, Lexington was also the tobacco capital of Kentucky at that time and the miles of leafy tobacco fields I witnessed stressed this fact. Up until just ten or fifteen years ago, tobacco was still the state's top producing cash crop, but with change in public perception toward tobacco products, that industry, like coal, has probably disappeared by now as well.

One hot afternoon somewhere down in Kentucky's eastern highlands ... a region that abounds with pine forests, sparkling blue lakes, fast flowing rivers and steep rock-faced cliffs ... I pulled into a rugged roadside park area consisting of a few picnic tables, washroom facilities and scattered hiking trails. Something in a state brochure had caught my attention about some interesting rock formations around this area. As I pulled up beside a nearly new GMC pickup with Saskatchewan plates, I noticed a pretty brunette, probably in her early thirties, reading a book at a table in front of the pickup.

Through conversation I learned her name was Jill, she and her husband were from the southeastern Saskatchewan town of Weyburn, she taught elementary school and husband Charlie worked for some grain elevator operator. They'd already visited some of the same areas I had in Kentucky, plus a large portion of Tennessee, including the cities of Memphis, Nashville and Chattanooga.

"Is it true you can see seven states from Chattanooga's Lookout Mountain?" I asked.

"Supposedly," Jill answered, "but how would one really know? ... although Charlie claimed he could see them all."

"Where is your husband by the way?"

"Oh, he's hiking some trail down in the canyon below us, searching out new rock creations to photograph."

I told her I was sort of interested in the same thing and was the reason I stopped here. She laughed and added that I should "hook up with Charlie and you two could have a great time doing whatever it is you rock people do!"

"Well, I'm not interested in *just* rocks," I countered, "but in defence of your husband, some rocks can be pretty amazing!"

She merely rolled her eyes.

"I sense you're not as overwhelmed as your husband?"

"Pardon my French," she said, "but I've seen enough goddam rocks these last few days to last a lifetime! I grew up in northern Ontario ... I've seen rocks ... now Charlie, born and raised on the prairies ... for him, even trees are a big deal!"

About this time "Charlie" appeared from around a grove of pine, armed with camera, tripod and a notebook. Charlie was a big husky fellow, probably six foot four with long curly blond hair that cascaded from beneath a "Saskatchewan Wheat Board" baseball cap. After introductions were completed, Charlie launched into a detailed account of what he'd just seen. "You have to go down there, Dave!" pointing back down the trail. "There are waterfalls and some absolutely incredible rock formations! Hundreds ... no probably thousands of years of erosion have stripped away the outer layer of softer rock and left behind this hard rock which has formed vast stone arches that completely span the river down there. It's incredible!"

While Charlie was reciting his geology lesson, Jill glanced at me with an expression that varied somewhere between mild amusement and total disinterest.

"According to your wife it sounds as if we've been moving in the same circles this past day or two," I broke in as Charlie stopped to wipe the perspiration from his brow. "Did you visit Mammoth Cave?"

"Oh yeah!" exclaimed Charlie, "Wasn't that incredible!"

"Speaking of incredible ... was Wendy your guide?" I asked.

"Yes she was! ... you had her too? ... man, she made the tour worthwhile didn't she!" His remark was followed by a hearty laugh.

Jill interrupted at that point. "I'm surprised you noticed her, Charlie ... what with all those "incredible" rock formations surrounding you!" Charlie just smiled and gradually but finally closed out his thesis on the finer aspects of the state's geological history.

"So where are you heading now Dave?" Charlie asked, while stowing his camera and supplies into the back of the truck.

"Well, I still have a bit of Kentucky to explore ... basically the northeast, which is on my way home."

Charlie said they were heading towards Virginia to search out some Civil War battlefields. "I think Jill's a little tired of rocks," nodding towards his wife who was already settled in the front seat. As Charlie slid his large frame into the cab beside her, we wished one another good luck for the duration of our holidays and a safe trip home.

I watched until their pickup disappeared from view then retrieved my own camera from behind the seat and began following the footpath Charlie had recommended. The narrow trail was strewn with loose rocks, and along its borders, wildflowers, Kentucky bluegrass and various species of vegetation flourished. I was probably no more than a quarter mile down this trail when I heard it ... maybe twenty feet ahead of me.

Now I've only heard a rattler's warning on TV westerns, but to this day I've no doubt as to what it was! I came to a dead halt. Again I heard the dry rattling sound, even more intense I thought. If it is a rattlesnake, why is it rattling? I'm not near it ... I then entertained the awful feeling that perhaps the snake was closer than I figured and was now ready to strike!

My heart was pounding like an automatic nail driver as I fought back the frantic urge to run. Carefully and quietly I retraced my steps ... all the while trying to dispel the sensation that an entire herd of diamondbacks was in the process of surrounding me! With almost embarrassing relief I made it back to the clearing where the truck was parked ... threw my camera onto the passenger seat, climbed into the cab and took off ... I'd seen enough "goddam rocks" anyway.

THE PILGRIMAGE

One evening back in the late 1960s, while listening to CKNX, our local radio station, I heard a new song by an artist unknown to me. It was a song about a country funeral, but not the normal "three hanky song" so beloved by country music lovers of that era.

This particular song concerned a less than enthusiastic grave digger whose biggest worry was that the beer he brought along wasn't going to stay cool while he dug away in the hot sun. While waiting for the service to end, he wryly notes the shiny chrome on the hearse and how good the widow looks in black. The last verse finds him sitting in his pickup truck as the mourners leave the cemetery, where he cynically hopes the recently departed is "resting peaceful as he owes me forty bucks."

The singer and writer I learned was a guy by the name of Tom T. Hall. From that moment I was hooked, purchasing every album he recorded. I found his style refreshing as his songs were simply about average people doing average things and the often satirical message was obtained without syrupy rhyme and righteous morals.

There was no doubt then while touring Kentucky in the summer of 1976, I would make a stop at Tom. T. Hall's hometown of Olive Hill, which according to my map was in the northeastern section of the state, about forty miles from the West Virginia border.

From what I'd read, the folks of Olive Hill in recognition of the notoriety of their famous son, had erected a monument in his honour and Tom had reciprocated by staging a free concert each July 4 for the hometown fans. It had been my original intent to be in Olive Hill for this grand occasion, but conflicting schedules had ruled that idea unworkable. However, just to visit Olive Hill and talk to a few townspeople about my hero would be more than enough.

As I zigzagged my way north, it was evident this hilly and rocky area of the state was on the lower rung of the prosperity ladder. Mile upon mile of depressed economy was apparent. Unpainted, run-down houses with a washing machine and a couple of galvanized tubs on the front porch; uncut lawns strewn with old tires, blocks of wood and other debris. Most properties possessed at least one old car in varying degrees of decay. Barns, if they could be seen at all, were falling down, many nothing more than foundation shells. Occasionally a few cows would be visible wandering aimlessly. Fences ... at least fences that could contain livestock, seemed not to exist.

I wondered how a person could ever begin to make a living in agriculture in this area of Kentucky. I'm certain moonshine was still being manufactured in the hills through which I was travelling. It used to be said there were but three choices of occupation in this part of the state; "moonshine ... coal mine ... or move on down the line."

Faith seems to be the sustaining factor as billboards quoting scripture and other verses of inspiration and enlightenment abounded, many printed in large block letters on the roofs of buildings. These signs often had to compete with more commercial endeavours such as "Mail Pouch Tobacco" and "Alka Seltzer."

Every few miles the unchanging scenery would be broken by a small town that looked exactly like the previous town ... a general store incorporating a post office, a gas station selling "regular" only, and because this was the "Bible Belt", a church ... usually Baptist. Frequently at a river crossing somebody ... usually kids or old men, would be fishing. Tom T. Hall could easily have been thinking of this region when he penned these lines.

Past the hound dogs and some domineckered chickens,
temporary looking houses with their lean and bashful kids.
Every hundred yards a sign proclaimed that Christ was
coming soon and I thought, well ... he'd sure be disap-
pointed if he did.

It was late afternoon when I entered Carter County, following the faded sign that directed me to my destination. Around a shallow bend a sign read: Olive Hill, Population 2500. I had to admit I thought there would have been some statement of recognition on this sign. In fact, I figured that's where the monument would be located.

My first impression of Olive Hill was a little disappointing ... brown grass, a few boarded-up stores. Dust and gravel layered the asphalt, creating a minor dust cloud with the passing of each vehicle. But I'd driven through towns like this all day so there was no reason Olive Hill should be any different. I drove slowly down the main street, perplexed that I hadn't seen this big monument. The focal point of the main thoroughfare appeared to be the high school, sitting atop a hill overlooking the town.

I pulled into a gas station and at the sound of the bell a kid about sixteen slowly extracted himself from under the frame of a '62 Chrysler. While the tank was being filled, the lad retrieved a large blue handkerchief from his coveralls and wiped the sweat from his face. I mentioned that things looked kind of dry. "No rain to speak of in five weeks," he drawled.

Following a bit more small talk, I asked what was foremost on my mind. "I understand there's some sort of monument concerning Tom T. Hall around here." He looked at me with sort of an empty expression.

"Nope ... don't know anything about that."

I thought to myself ... how can he not know? He lives or at least works here doesn't he? To keep my faith intact, I justified his ignorance to youth.

Changing the subject, I asked if there were a motel nearby. "There's Wades, 'bout a mile from town." I thanked him and followed his directions eastward. I drove slowly past the town limit sign on the chance the monument was at this end. No luck. No monument. On a slight grade on the left side of the road appeared a fairly new twenty-unit motel on one level. I could see no sign of life, however, not a person or a car. A small cardboard notice on the door of the office revealed a phone number for assistance. A man's voice promised to be "right there."

I regarded my surroundings as I waited. Directly across the road, a dozen Hereford cattle foraged on the brown slopes. Just barely visible above the trees of a wooded hollow jutted the rusty roof of a barn, and somewhere from where I couldn't see, the drone of a tractor could be heard. Two black work horses standing side by side stared off in the direction of the barn ... or was it the tractor they were watching? Perhaps recalling days when they were king ...

This reflective mood was broken by the crunching of rubber tires on gravel. A black '66 Pontiac sedan pulled alongside me. The lone occupant, a heavy-set man probably in his late fifties, exited. He was a friendly fellow like most everyone I had met on this trip and asked general questions about the part of Ontario I was from. We talked about the crops and weather both in Southern Ontario and Northeastern Kentucky. We also talked about my truck. What engine was in it, what kind of gas mileage I was getting, how far I had travelled on my vacation ... ?

It was easy to see this guy enjoyed talking and was in no hurry, so I figured he was the logical candidate to clear up this Tom T. Hall issue. As though it had just occurred to me, I asked. "Isn't there some sort of monument in town dedicated to Tom T. Hall?"

His face turned thoughtful ... "No ... not that I know of."

What? ... was this some sort of conspiracy to demonstrate I was crazy? Had I simply dreamt this? No, of course not ... I had a picture of it on the cover of one of Tom's albums. Yet, here in this stupid town no one had an inkling of its whereabouts!

He continued to ponder and puzzle over my question. "No ... I don't know of any monument. He comes and does a show every year and they put a banner across the main street, but that's it ... it's not like he's real famous or anything ... perhaps if he died or something they might erect some sort of memorial ... I don't know."

At that juncture I wished I could have been a kid again and just stood there and bawled. It would have made me feel so much better!

I checked into my room, had a shower and proceeded to get something to eat. I'd noticed a restaurant next to the gas station. Maybe after a good meal things would appear brighter. I'm a slow learner I guess, for I asked the waitress the same question I'd been asking everyone it seemed. Same answer. My spirit, buoyed with excitement just a couple of hours earlier, was now at low ebb. Back in my motel room I drowned my disillusionment in a couple of Schlitz beers, inserted a Tom T. Hall eight-track tape into the player, turned off the lamp and crawled into bed. As I lay there in the Kentucky darkness listening to that familiar voice, I wondered if he realized nobody in his hometown cared.

A warm dry breeze and cloudless sky greeted my departure the next morning. "Are you staying around awhile?" the motel owner asked.

"No, I guess I'll be leaving right after breakfast." What was to stay around for? I ordered a "No. 2" from the restaurant menu. Grits, ham, fried potatoes, fried eggs, two pieces of homemade toast, juice and coffee. At least the food was good. As it was a different waitress this morning, I briefly entertained asking "the question" but changed my mind. No sense twisting the knife.

From my corner table I had a wide perspective of the main intersection and a half dozen stores. A couple of teenagers were washing windows at the bank directly across from where I was seated. Right outside my window a man was struggling to install a new muffler on an old Buick.

The old rusty unit was lying on the sidewalk beside the car, causing passers-by to step over it.

Most of the action, if one could call it that, seemed centred around the butcher shop, situated kitty-corner to the restaurant. A mid-'60s Chevrolet truck sporting a closed wooden box had pulled up in front of the store. The driver had gone inside for a few minutes before emerging with someone I presumed to be the proprietor. The two peered into the back of the truck, which I could see was piled high with quarters of what I guessed as beef. The two men talked at length while the load sat in the already warm morning sun. The butcher would gesture occasionally to make a point, while the truck driver merely nodded or shook his head in accordance with the conversation.

Onto the scene at this point lumbered a hound dog. He stopped as his nose picked up the scent and walked over to the rear of the truck. The driver shouted something to the dog, which simply moved around to the front of the truck. When the driver disappeared into the store with an armful of meat, the dog returned for a closer inspection and noting all was clear, hopped into the back, his tail wagging back and forth, advertising his feelings. Sipping my coffee, I couldn't help but smile at this comical scene. I wondered what would have crossed some government inspector's mind if he or she had happened by and noticed this load of meat exposed to the hot sun and a dog having a picnic in the back.

I was definitely cheering for the dog, hoping he'd get at least a little time to enjoy the feast. I'd only known this old hound for a few minutes but had already experienced a sort of bonding.

Suddenly the scenario turned dramatic as the driver reappeared. "Move, Hound!" I warned my new-found friend under my breath. As the man spied the dog's rear end he let out a yell ... at least I figured he did. Hound turned and jumped in one motion onto the ground, hightailing it across the street with the driver helping him along with the toe of his boot.

I watched as if in slow motion ... the dog starting across the street ... the arc of the boot contacting the dog's backside ... the van travelling too fast for a quiet street, striking the dog squarely with the front bumper ... I went sick inside as the poor animal disappeared beneath the van and came spinning out under the rear bumper. The van's brake lights flashed momentarily then accelerated away, while the dog came to rest in the middle of the road.

I wondered how much time would pass before someone picked up the dog's lifeless body. But wait! Hound wasn't dead ... whether nerve or shock, but something compelled him to get up and dive beneath a parked pickup. For a moment I felt elation ... but then imagined the pain and suffering Hound was no doubt experiencing and the sickly sensation returned. It wasn't enough this town had disappointed me over the "monument" thing ... now this! All I wanted was to get the hell out of there ... but I just couldn't leave Hound lying beneath that truck. Nobody but me knew he was there, with the exception of the guy who'd kicked him across the street and he was obviously unconcerned. He'd simply turned and walked back into the butcher shop.

A stranger trying to coax an injured dog from his hiding place, then taking him to a veterinarian if there indeed was one ... sounded very complicated. The easy solution would be to simply leave, but realized such a decision would haunt me all the way home.

While I grappled with my conscience, a couple of young lads sporting fishing poles wandered by the butcher shop. One spotted the dog lying beneath the vehicle. Lowering himself to his knees, he slapped his thighs in an inviting gesture. To my utmost relief out came Hound! Both boys patted his head, he responded with a wag of his long tail and all three walked up the street together. Hound seemed to have no ill effects with his brush with death ... not even a limp.

I interpreted this bright moment as a signal to get out of town before negative forces once again assumed control. Across the street from the school I'd noticed a grocery store, so before leaving, stocked up on pop and snacks for the trip home. A friendly check-out girl chatted away as she rang up my order and just as I was paying, I noticed some records in a rack beside the counter. On top was a Tom T. Hall album ... the one with the elusive monument! On impulse I enquired of the young lady, "Where is this?"

Her eyes followed where my finger was pointing. "Oh, right there," pointing across the street. I stared in disbelief ... I'd driven past this spot three or four times but my eyes had always been drawn to the imposing school building atop the hill.

It might not have been as large as shown on the album cover and more resembled a plaque than a monument ... but at that moment I couldn't have felt more excitement and emotion than Alex Haley when he discovered the African village in which his ancestor Kunta Kinte was born!

The cashier was incredulous that so many of the people I asked had no clue of the plaque. "I thought everyone knew that!" We chatted for a few minutes about his music and our favourite albums and I told her she had made my day in a way she could never know. After all the disappointment I had finally discovered a true Tom T. Hall admirer, a person genuinely excited and proud of her town's famous resident. I had an impulse to take her in my arms, give her a big hug and kiss and suggest we get married and spend the remainder of our lives on some tropical island listening to Tom T. Hall recordings.

I walked across the street where a four-foot-high cement retaining wall featuring the literary work of Olive Hill's graffiti artists provided a backdrop for the sidewalk. Behind the wall, a steeply sloping grassy incline led up to the reddish-brown secondary education centre. At eye level, embossed on granite stone, I read this tribute:

OLIVE HILL IS THE BIRTHPLACE OF TOM T. HALL, BORN TO VIRGIL L. AND DELLA LENA HALL. HE USED HIS GOD-GIVEN TALENTS TO BECOME FAMED AS ONE OF AMERICA'S BALLADEERS, TELLING IN MUSIC FORM THE STORY OF THE COMMON FOLK AND THE DAILY HAPPENINGS WHICH COLOR THEIR LIVES. A RECORDING ARTIST OF INTERNA-TIONAL STATURE, A MEMBER OF THE GRAND OLE OPRY AND A COUNTRY MUSIC SONG-WRITER/PERFORMER OF NOTE, HE NEVER FORGOT THAT HE CAME FROM THE SOIL AND ALWAYS TREATED HIS FELLOWMAN AS FRIEND AND NEIGHBOR ... ERECTED JULY 4, 1972.

As I departed the parking lot I noticed the Buick still didn't have its new muffler, and turning east onto Main Street the gas station attendant was still working on the old Chrysler. Although the rear doors had been closed, the meat truck still sat in the mid-morning sun in front of the butcher shop. Just beyond the edge of town a small creek trickled beneath the road, and on the bank sat the two young fishermen and Hound. I blew the horn and waved and the pair kind of looked at me but responded with an equally enthusiastic wave. I'm not certain ... but I'm pretty sure Hound wagged his tail.

Thirty minutes later I merged east onto Interstate-64, stuck a tape into the player beneath the dash, turned up the volume and settled myself comfortably into the foam seat ... "Okay Tom ... take me home!"

ACKNOWLEDGEMENTS

I want to acknowledge the writings of the following for providing data, facts and other pertinent information that contributed to the completion of this book.

SPLIT RAIL COUNTRY (Mildred Hubbert), published by Stan Brown Printers Ltd.

HURRICANE HAZEL (Betty Kennedy), published by Macmillan of Canada

TWO DIVISIONS TO BLUEWATER (Peter Bowers), published by Boston Mills Press

WORLD BOOK ENCYCLOPEDIA, CANADIAN ENCYLOPEDIA and "GOOGLE"

Special thanks to Sean, Linda and Emily at Inkwater Press for their support and encouragement from the outset. Being a member of their "family" has made the preparation of this book a warm and wonderful experience.

A most heartfelt debt of gratitude to my wife Mary for her extreme patience (most of the time) over the last twenty-five years, while I pursued my favourite past time and hobby. Monumental thanks also, for her computer expertise in helping prepare these stories for publication, in particular scanning of photos.

After years of writing endless essays of family history and countless contributions to magazines, it was her suggestion I pursue the "short story" venue, adding "the great thing about a short story ... if a person doesn't like it they haven't wasted much time."

CPSIA information can be obtained at www.ICGtesting.com
Printed in the USA
LVOW08s2017230716

497059LV00001B/2/P